"Other" Voices

Historical Essays on Saskatchewan Women

"Other" Voices

Historical Essays on Saskatchewan Women

Edited by David De Brou and Aileen Moffatt

Canadian Plains Research Center
University of Regina
1995

Copyright © Canadian Plains Research Center

Canadian Plains Research Center
University of Regina
Regina, Saskatchewan S4S 0A2
Canada

100173346⁴

Canadian Cataloguing in Publication Data

Main entry under title:
"Other" voices: historical essays on Saskatchewan women

(Canadian plains studies; 32)

Includes bibliographical references and index.

ISBN 0-88977-088-3

1. Women – Saskatchewan – History. 2. Women – Saskatchewan – Social conditions. I. De Brou, David, 1950- II. Moffatt, Aileen, 1957- III. University of Regina. Canadian Plains Research Center. IV. Series.

HQ1459.S2085 1995   305.4'097124   C95-920134-3

Cover Design: Agnes Bray/Brian Mlazgar
Cover photographs (clockwise from left): Marie (Labelle) Pilon with her child, courtesy of Brian Mlazgar; Anna (Salamon) Mlazgar, courtesy of Patricia Salamon; Native woman with children, courtesy of Saskatchewan Archives Board (R-B1449); Farm wife feeding chickens, courtesy of Saskatchewan Archives Board (R-A18516)

Printed and bound in Canada by
Hignell Printing Limited, Winnipeg, Manitoba

Printed on acid-free paper

For

Denise De Brou
Josephine Little Spruce
Aneta Wicks

And in memory of Margaret Moffatt

Saskatchewan women who shaped our lives

CONTENTS

PREFACE

Two and a half years ago when we agreed to work together on this project, we shared the single goal of filling an obvious gap in the field of Canadian women's history: a collection of historical essays dedicated exclusively to Saskatchewan women. As we went through the process of recruitment and selection, a second objective emerged. We wanted to engage our readers in one of the most significant debates in Canadian women's history today: the role of gender in shaping women's lives. We asked, is gender the overriding factor in explaining the history of Canadian women? Or does gender sometimes work in conjunction with a series of other factors? We believe that the ten chapters offered in this volume illustrate that while gender-related experiences may be common to some Saskatchewan women, other experiences based on race, ethnicity, class, religion and language divide Saskatchewan women. This is why it is essential that we recognize that a single voice does not do justice to the many and varied experiences of Saskatchewan women. "Other" voices need to be heard.

Two editors working with eight intelligent, dynamic individuals is not an easy task, but somehow goodwill and common sense prevailed. Patient and enthusiastic are two words that frequent many prefaces, but we find them appropriate in describing those involved in the project who helped us to complete this collection of essays.

At the top of our list of those we want to thank are the eight persons who contributed chapters to this book. Anna, Jo-Anne, Julie, Lesley, Mathilde, Miriam, Nadine and Theresa, we thank you for your diligence and eagerness. Without your commitment and your written contributions, this book would not exist.

Next on our list are those who responded to our requests for editorial comment and advice. From the University of Saskatchewan, history professors Bill Waiser and Jim Miller, and Dave De Brou's fourth-year honour students who participated in his course on Canadian women's history in 1993-94 and 1994-95; from the University of Manitoba, Gerald Friesen whose optimism buoyed at least one of the editors on numerous occasions; from the College of William and Mary, Chandos Brown, Director of the Commonwealth Center for the Study of American Culture, who generously provided the opportunity for this work to continue when one editor moved to Virginia, and also from William and Mary, Robert J. Scholnick, Graduate Dean of Arts and Sciences whose financial support and friendship were invaluable. A special thanks to the anonymous external reviewer who helped us to clarify our thinking regarding the issue of gender in women's lives.

We also owe thanks to the University of Saskatchewan History Department for providing secretarial help, supplied specifically by Joni Mazer who faxed, laser printed and photocopied the many different drafts of this book. We also acknowledge with gratitude members of the University of Saskatchewan Publication Fund Committee who provided funding for manuscript preparation. Part of that money went to paying Merle McGowan, a Masters of Arts candidate in history at the University of Saskatchwan who helped to produce the index.

We also recognize the essential role played by Brian Mlazgar, Coordinator of Publications of the Canadian Plains Research Center (CPRC), his assistant, Agnes Bray, and the members of the CPRC Publications Board who responded positively to our initial proposal and remained supportive and patient throughout. Finally, to the internet and email ... well, it just couldn't have happened any other way.

On a personal note, we thank our friends and family who by now know more about this project than they ever wanted to. Dave thanks his loving partner Denise, three children Norma, Bruce and Audrey who always remind him of what is important in life. To his big brother Jim, goes a special heart-felt thanks. Aileen would like to thank Nan Frame and Margaret Buckner, two remarkable Saskatchewan women whose voices have always been filled with encouragement and pride; the SNPGA, the most "other" group of Saskatchewan women's voices; and Marland, the greatest cheer-leader an historian could ask for.

INTRODUCTION:
"OTHER" VOICES AND THE CHALLENGE FROM WITHIN

Dave De Brou and Aileen C. Moffatt

"Other" Voices: Historical Essays on Saskatchewan Women brings together for the first time in a single collection of essays, individuals and groups of Saskatchewan women frequently overlooked or neglected by writers of Saskatchewan history. The book examines Saskatchewan women, as diverse in their experiences as they are in their identities. This approach — focussing on "polyphonic" or "multi vocality"[1] — is not new to women's history or other feminist disciplines, but it is new to Saskatchewan women's history. By highlighting the province's diversity in race, ethnicity, class, religion and language, this collection of essays brings Saskatchewan women's history to the forefront of an important and current historical debate over the role that gender plays in the lives of Canadian women.

Writers of Canadian women's history agree that gender influences the course of women's lives; they do not agree as to the extent to which other factors also have an impact on women's lives. On one side, there are those who stress the commonality of women's experiences, contending that ultimately women's lives are defined by "patriarchical custom and male authority."[2] On the other side, there are those who, while acknowledging women may have some similar experiences based on their place within a male-dominated society, insist that other factors such as class, race, ethnicity, age and sexual preference may also shape women's lives.[3] Accordingly, they

---

1   bell hooks, "An Interview with bell hooks," in *Yearning; race, gender and cultural politics* (Boston: South End Press, 1990), 228.

2   Veronica Strong-Boag, *"Janey Canuck": Women in Canada 1919-1939*, Historical Booklet No. 53 (Ottawa: Canadian Historical Association, 1994), 2. Having "tried to understand women's different as well as similar experiences," Strong-Boag concludes that "ultimately, however, women were defined and delimited not so much by any lesser capacity for work or determination or thought, but by patriarchical custom and male authority. Men's sisters, however situated relative to other women, encountered more confined horizons than their brothers of the same class, race or colour. From birth, Canadian women daily worked through the consequences of a gender identity that informed every part of their experience" (ibid.). Also see: Gillian Creese and Veronica Strong-Boag, "Introduction: Taking Gender into Account in British Columbia," in Creese and Strong-Boag, eds., *British Columbia Reconsidered: Essays on Women* (Vancouver: Press Gang Publishers in association with The Centre for Research in Women's Studies and Gender Relations at the University of British Columbia, 1992), 2-3; Ruth Roach Pierson, "Experience, Difference, Dominance, and Voice in the Writing of Canadian Women's History," in Karen Offen, Ruth Roach Pierson and Jane Rendall, eds., *Writing Women's History: International Perspective* (Bloomington: Indiana University Press, 1991), 94; Alison Prentice, Paula Bourne, Gail Cuthbert Brandt, Beth Light, Wendy Mitchinson and Naomi Black, *Canadian Women: A History* (Toronto: Harcourt, Brace, Jovanovich, 1988), 12-13; and Veronica Strong-Boag and Anita Clair Fellman, "Introduction," in Strong-Boag and Fellman, eds., *Rethinking Canada: The Promise of Women's History*, 2nd. ed. (Toronto: Copp Clark Pitman Ltd., 1991), 2.

3   For example, in their introduction to *Gender Conflicts: New Essays in Women's History*, the contributors point to gender conflicts: "By this we mean not only the conflicts and tensions that characterized relations between men and women, but also conflicts among women of different racial, class, and cultural backgrounds." These tensions historically have resulted in various groups of women having different and, at times, conflicting gender experiences; see Karen Dubinsky et al., "Introduction," in Franca Iacovetta and Marianna Valverde, eds., *Gender Conflicts: New Essays in Women's History* (Toronto: University of Toronto Press, 1992), xii.

argue for difference rather than commonality.[4] As the title of our book suggests, we believe that in the end a single voice does not capture the diversity and intricacies of women's experiences.

The writing of women's history in Canada in 1995 is not an easy task. The main difficulty today is not one of lack of scholarly recognition from a profession still dominated by white, middle-class, Euro-Canadian males. Rather, the difficulty in writing women's history today is that it has become so complicated and complex. However, we do not perceive complexity negatively. Instead, the complexity is a positive development that suggests the possibility of inclusion rather than exclusion, considering all women instead of only selected groups of women. As a result of the work of a new generation of scholars, the historical study of women in Canada is beginning to reach a level of sophistication that makes it one of the most innovative, invigorating fields in Canadian historical scholarship.

The present complex state of women's history is best understood as an intersection of two paths. One path leads back to the early 1970s where a group of young, white, middle-class female scholars sought to gain acceptance for a feminist perspective in the writing of history. The second path has a more recent beginning, the last five years, which saw the emergence of a challenge from within, calling into question the primacy of gender itself.

The first path has its origins in the late 1960s and early 1970s when the Canadian historical establishment was reluctant to accept women's history as a legitimate field of study. Gradually scholars of women's history succeeded in having gender included among modes of historical explanation. This was not easy and to some extent the bias against gender still continues today; however, few social historians would not acknowledge the need to consider gender as one of the primary factors in any historical explanation.

Part of the resistance to women's history in the 1970s and the early 1980s was rooted in the androcentrism of the Canadian historical profession. Regardless, there was also a legitimate intellectual concern that those writing the history of women were oversimplifying history by focussing on a monocausal explanation.[5] This type of criticism was also levelled at writers of working-class history, many of whom assumed the primacy of a single factor in historical explanation.[6]

---

4   Gerda Lerner explains: "if one ignores 'differences,' one distorts reality"; see Gerda Lerner, "Dialogue: Reconceptualizing Differences Among Women," *Journal of Women's History* 1, no. 3 (Spring 1990): 108. Françoise Lionnet agrees: "we women are so diverse and live in such varied cultural, racial, and economic circumstances that we cannot possibly pretend to speak in a single voice"; see Françoise Lionnet, *Autobiographical Voices: Race, Gender, Self-Portraiture* (Ithaca: Cornell University Press, 1989), xi.

5   A few scholars did "complicate" matters in the 1970s by exploring the lives of Canadian women within the context of class. See, for example: Alice Klein and Wayne Roberts, "Beseiged Innocence: The 'Problem' and Problems of the Working Woman — Toronto, 1896-1914," in Janice Acton, Penny Goldsmith and Bonnie Shepard, eds., *Women at Work: Ontario, 1850-1930* (Toronto: Women's Press, 1974): 211-59; Wayne Roberts, *Honest Womanhood: Feminism, Feminity, and Class Consciousness among Toronto Working Women, 1893-1914* (Toronto: New Hogtown Press, 1976); and Joan Sangster, "The 1907 Bell Telephone Strike: Organizing Women Workers," *Labour/Le Travailleur* 3 (1978): 109-30.

6   David Bercuson, for one, suggested in 1981 that the working-class cultural analysis of the new generation of "working-class" historians (Greg Kealey and Bryan Palmer, for example) was faulty and limited because it highlighted class and downplayed other factors such as ethnicity, religion, gender and regionalism; see David J. Bercuson, "Through the Looking Glass of Culture: An Essay on the New Labour History and Working-Class Culture in Recent Canadian Historical Writing," *Labour/Le Travailleur* 7 (Spring 1981): 95-112. Bercuson contended that "historians must prove that Canadian

The writing of Canadian women's history parallelled working-class history and other histories in another important way. An examination of the literature on Canadian women's history[7] suggests three historiographical stages: celebration, where scholars celebrate the success of individual women; exploitation, where scholars underline the exploitation of women as a group; and active agency, where scholars affirm the resistance, strategies, influence and accomplishments of women within their various cultural communities.[8] In the case of Canadian women's historiography, elements of all three stages are discernable in histories written in the last quarter of a century. Nevertheless, as a means of understanding developments in the field of Canadian women's history, it is useful to delineate three, albeit overlapping, chronological phases where a single element dominated: celebration in the pre-1970 period; exploitation throughout the 1970s and early 1980s; and active agency which appears in the late 1970s but really does not not come into full bloom until the mid-1980s.

Women's history written prior to 1970 tended to celebrate the contribution of individual women who had "made it in a man's world." This earlier history celebrated Canada's first female parliamentarians, doctors, lawyers and educators, for example.[9]

---

workers, men and women, skilled and unskilled, were bound by a common culture that was primarily the product of their class experience before they can use culture to explain anything. Historians must show that the workers themselves experienced a common bond of culture, or of class, and that they were conscious of that bond. In examining the historical record which Canadian labour historians have so far pieced together, and it is admittedly a very incomplete one, the evidence shows that working-class culture bonded workers together and provided resources on some occasions but not on others. Workers seem to have responded as much from consciousness of job, place, church, ethnic group, and other factors as from a culture of class" (ibid., 108). Greg Kealey disputed Bercuson's conclusions in "Labour and Working-Class History in Canada: Prospects in the 1980s," *Labour/Le Travailleur* 7 (Spring 1981): 67-94.

7   For a review of recent developments in Canadian women's history, see: Gail Cuthbert Brandt, "Postmodern Patchwork: Some Recent Trends in the Writing of Women's History in Canada," *Canadian Historical Review* 72, no. 4 (December 1991): 441-70; Wendy Mitchinson, "Women's History," in Douglas Owram, ed., *Canadian History: A Reader's Guide*, vol. 2, *Confederation to the Present* (Toronto: University of Toronto Press, 1994): 202-27; and Roach Pierson, "Experience, Difference, Dominance," 79-106; Veronica Strong-Boag, "Writing About Women," in John Schultz, ed., *Writing About Canada: A Handbook for Modern Canadian History* (Scarborough, ON: Prentice-Hall Canada, 1990): 175-200.

8   We are not the first to categorize Canadian women's historiography in terms of celebration, exploitation and active agency. Consider the comments of the contributors to *Gender Conflicts*, as they explain the purpose of their book: "Nor do we want to supplant the old model of middle-class heroines and working-class victims with a heroic model of working-class women. Without creating romanticized pictures of immigrant and working-class women, we want to suggest some of the ways in which those with limited power could nevertheless find ways of exercising a measure of control over their own and others' lives" (Dubinsky et al., "Introduction," *Gender Conflicts*, xvii). Similarly Strong-Boag and Fellman write: "Although our selections cover a wide range in time and space, they reflect a shared view of Canadian women as actors rather than as that acted upon. The authors do not ignore the structures or ideas that affect women's well-being and limit the expression of females' talents and autonomy. Nonetheless they acknowledge, whether explicitly or implicitly, female resilience, energy, and ingenuity in situations where women might have wished the ground rules to be more equitable. While recognizing women's subordinate status in Canadian life, the contributors to this volume continue to move away from the 'women as victim' motif that so often preoccupied investigators in the 1960s and 1970s. Their stance argues for the significance, the variability, and the richness of female experience (Strong-Boag and Fellman, "Introduction," in *Rethinking Canada*, 9).

9   See, for example: Jean Bannerman, *Leading Ladies: Canada, 1639-1967* (Belleville: Mika Publishing, 1977); and Mary Quayle Innis, ed., *The Clear Spirit: Twenty Canadian Women and Their Times* (Toronto: University of Toronto Press, 1966).

In the 1970s the celebratory trend continued but it was joined and eventually surpassed by a history that, rather than celebrate the accomplishments of extraordinary individual women, focussed on women as a group. This history pointed to the apparent political, social, economic and sexual discrimination that supposedly joined all women in a common experience. Economic, social, ethnic, racial, regional or sexual differences were seen as secondary to the common bond of discrimination and exploitation. Like all historical writing, this type of history reflected the worldview held by those doing the writing — in this case, the scholarly pioneers who had made a place for themselves in a profession and a society with androcentric structures and values. Thus, in the 1970s and through the first half of the 1980s, the common theme in women's history, as it was in other historical fields, was exploitation. As a result, the work done by the first post-1960s generation of writers explores how women were exploited in various ways.[10]

Yet the theme of exploitation, no matter how instructive, is restrictive in the sense that the focus continues to be on the dominant group. In this scenario, women remain powerless victims or manipulated pawns. Admittedly some people consider it a theoretical advance in women's history to recognize women as a group and some may even find scholarly satisfaction in the label of victim, but the historiographical stage of exploitation has its limits. Particularly, exploitation adds little to the knowledge of the active role that women played in shaping developments in Canada. In the end the exploited group, while no longer ignored by history, remains a group upon which events act, rather than a group that shapes events.

Women as active agents were always implicit, though submerged, in the stages of celebration and exploitation. Nonetheless, it took the social history revolution of the 1970s and the eventual realization that "women as heroines/victims" was limiting as an historical paradigm, before a few writers of Canadian women's history began to accept active agency as a useful historical model in the late 1970s. This third historiographical stage focusses directly on "those going through the gate rather than the gatekeepers" and explores their actions and reactions within a society they did not dominate. Thus, in active-agency history women become: "*femmes favorisées,*" business women in the economy of New France; "women-in-between," key players in the fur trade; "Sainte-Anne widows," with strategies for survival in late nineteenth-century Montreal; "women of the veil," finding an education and career satisfaction within the Roman Catholic church; the "girl of the new day," endeavouring to continue the battle of equality in postsuffrage Canada; and women "who rolled up their sleeves for victory," discovering during World War II that men were not the only ones capable of making sophisticated military weapons.[11] In the historiographical stage of active agency there is a recognition that women were more than heroines

---

10   See, for example: Clio Collective, *Quebec Women: A History* (Toronto: Women's Press, 1987 [originally in French, 1982]); Prentice et al., *Canadian Women: A History.*

11   Jan Noel, "New France: Les femmes favorisées," *Atlantis. A Women's Studies Journal/Journal d'études sur la femme* 6, no. 2 (Spring/printemps 1981): 80-98; Sylvia Van Kirk, *"Many Tender Ties": Women in Fur-Trade Society, 1670-1870* (Winnipeg: Watson and Dwyer, 1980); Bettina Bradbury, *Working Families: Age, Gender, and Daily Survival in Industrializing Montreal* (Toronto: McClelland and Stewart, 1993); Marta Danylewycz, *Taking the Veil: An Alternative to Marriage, Motherhood, and Spinsterhood in Quebec, 1840-1920* (Toronto: McClelland and Stewart, 1987); Veronica Strong-Boag, *The New Day Recalled: Lives of Girls and Women in English Canada, 1919-1939* (Toronto: Copp Clark Pitman: 1988); and Ruth Roach Pierson, *"They're Still Women After All": The Second World War and Canadian Womanhood* (Toronto: McClelland and Stewart, 1986).

and victims. Women resisted, devised strategies and accomplished much on their own terms.

Concomitant with this notion of women as active agents was an evolving view of what constitutes historical importance. As a result of the social history revolution of the 1970s, what is worthy of historical investigation is no longer only measured in terms of political or economic success. This new approach to history was necessary if women and other groups were to move away from the periphery of historical scholarship. Active agency also meant that women have become, or at least are becoming, part of the historical mainstream.

Developments in the last five years have also meant that it is not only white Anglo-Saxon/French middle-class women who have become part of mainstream scholarship. Challenges to the first generation of female historians as interpreters of all women's experiences have come from a new generation of historical scholars.

In her recent assessment of the literature, historian Bettina Bradbury describes the generational differences:

> Writing about women in Canada's past seems poised at the point of a major shift. Most of the book-length studies that have appeared between 1986 and 1993 were written by what could be viewed as the first cohort, or perhaps even generation, of women's historians practising and publishing in Canada. Their goals have largely paralleled those of second-wave historians elsewhere: to recuperate women's past, to show they too had a history; to explain their oppression; to describe their work and their involvement in suffrage campaigns and reform movements. Theoretical inspiration, to the extent that historians have been consciously theoretical, has derived from liberal, radical and especially socialist feminism. Among the most recent publications are the works of a new generation of scholars who have begun asking new questions and seeking new sources and theoretical approaches. Influenced by post-structuralist theoreticians and by the challenge of integrating considerations of differences of race, class and sexual preference more explicitly into their writing, these scholars challenge earlier women's history as well as the profession as a whole.[12]

This new generation examines women's history as a multiplicity of voices, rather than in stark contrast of one voice for women and one for men. Further, these scholars recognize that historical voices are complicated by issues of race, ethnicity, class and sexuality as well as gender.[13] In this sense, this new generation of historical writers has complicated the writing of women's history in Canada by questioning the primacy of gender as an explanatory factor. This is not a rejection of gender but a recognition that gender is inextricably linked to other factors which are fundamental to the historical equation.[14]

---

12   Bettina Bradbury, "Women and the History of Work in Canada: Some Recent Books," *Journal of Canadian Studies/Revue d'études canadiennes* 28, no. 3 (Fall/automne 1993): 160-61.

13   For example, see: Peggy Bristow, coordinator, Dionne Brand, Linda Carty, Afua P. Cooper, Sylvia Hamilton and Adrienne Shadd, *"We're Rooted Here and They Can't Pull Us Up": Essays in African Canadian Women's History* (Toronto: University of Toronto Press, 1994); Ruth A. Frager, *Sweatshop Strife: Class, Ethnicity, and Gender in the Jewish Labour Movement of Toronto, 1900-1939* (Toronto: University of Toronto Press, 1992); and Franca Iacovetta, *"Such Hardworking People": Italian Immigrants in Postwar Toronto* (Montreal and Kingston: McGill-Queen's University Press, 1992).

14   For a discussion of historians' treatment of the relationship between gender, race, ethnicity and class, see: Peggy Bristow et al., "Introduction," in *"We're Rooted Here,"* 3-12; Dubinsky et al., "Introduction," in

For those writing the history of Saskatchewan women, the challenge from within is also a reality. Yes, gender is an important determinant of the lives of women (and men), both past and present, but other explanatory factors including race, ethnicity and class must also be accounted for. The lives of all women did not follow the same path. For example, Native women witnessed their traditional lives challenged by the incoming hordes of Euro-Canadians who had an insatiable thirst for Aboriginal land. Non-Anglo-Saxon immigrant women who travelled thousands of miles with expectations that their lives would be better in Canada found an imperfect world where the adoption of the English language and British ways was just as important as hard work. And in times when work was not to be found, women on relief faced obstacles of class and ethnicity as well as gender.

"Other" Voices, while continuing to underline the importance of gender as a factor in historical explanation, points to the complexities of Saskatchewan women's lives. It emphasizes the important contributions that women have made to the development of this province in their public and private lives. The book also endeavours to give voice to "other" women, not just members of the political, social and economic elite. Furthermore, the book also hopes to demonstrate that capturing this myriad of other voices sometimes requires going beyond the traditional sources (diaries, newspapers, minutes of meetings, for example) because these kinds of documents do not always lend themselves to analyses of non-white, non-middle-class, non-English-speaking women. As some of the writers in this collection show, oral interviews and other techniques and models from other disciplines (anthropology and sociology, for example) are effective in uncovering the many voices of Saskatchewan women.

Voice as a theoretical tool is extremely useful in the recovery of Saskatchewan women's history. Yet, the premise of letting women speak for themselves, or as the cliché implies, doing history "by, for and about women,"[15] is not as simple as it sounds. Considerations of who is writing about what and for which audience must be taken into account. Voice is never unfettered; it is always filtered through contexts, and personal and social agendas. The question of who speaks for whom is not only a simple matter of ordering; it can also be construed as an overt political act. Accordingly, in considering women's historical voices, readers must also account for the hidden voices of their interpreters, those who record the stories. Lest this sound like a "buyer beware" disclaimer, we insist that voice remains a viable and valuable component of women's history. Because the day-to-day life of Saskatchewan women has not generally been documented, historians have few recorded sources to consult. In this respect, as five of the nine essayists in this collection discovered, oral history was the only way to locate the data they sought.

The book begins with Aileen Moffatt's "Great Women, Separate Spheres, and Diversity: Comments on Saskatchewan Women's Historiography." Moffatt's essay

---

Iacovetta and Valverde, eds., *Gender Conflicts*, xi-xxvii; Patricia A. Monture-Okanee, "The Violence We Women Do: A First Nations View," in Constance Backhouse and David H. Flaherty, eds., *Challenging Times: The Women's Movement in Canada and the United States* (Montreal and Kingston: McGill-Queen's University Press, 1992), 193-204; Glenda Simms, "Beyond the White Veil," in *Challenging Times*, 75-81; Marianna Valverde, "Racism and Anti-Racism in Feminist Teaching and Research," in *Challenging Times*, 160-64.

15 Sherna Berger Gluck and Daphne Patai, "Introduction," in Sherna Berger Gluck and Daphne Patai, eds., *Women's Words: The Feminist Practice of Oral History* (New York: Routledge, 1991), 2.

traces the development of Saskatchewan women's history through three stages — great women, separate spheres/women's culture, and diversity. Beginning in the 1930s, stage one Saskatchewan women's history focussed on "notable" women of great or exceptional achievement, particularly those active in the suffrage or social reform campaigns. Stage two emerged in the 1970s with the support of the burgeoning women's movement. Spurred on by notions of sisterhood and women's shared experiences, scholars argued for a commonality that united women. However, only white, English-speaking women were the focus of most historical inquiries, creating a paradigm of exclusion of "other" women, those who did not "fit in." Stage three Saskatchewan women's history, in evidence since approximately 1990, explodes the "sameness" myth and appropriates diversity, multiculturalism and lived experience as the basis for scholarship. Moffatt concludes that historians need to examine the plurality of Saskatchewan women's cultures in order to more fully understand the diversity of Saskatchewan's history.

In "The Interplay of Ethnicity and Gender: Swedish Women in Southeastern Saskatchewan," Lesley Erickson discovers that "Swedish women's ethnicity and their gender determined their role in the family, the church and the community" (40). In adapting to their new Saskatchewan home, Swedish women were able to assume new roles that allowed them to become "active participants in the religious, social and economic development of their communities" (27). Erickson argues that as Swedish men were forced to seek employment away from home, Swedish women "gained a degree of independence that would have been uncommon in their homeland" (29). This independence afforded Swedish women a significant influence in the family decision-making process as well as in religious affairs. Yet, there was another side to this independence. As Swedish women became more active in the "outside world," their lives became more "complex and cosmopolitan" (40). Erickson concludes, these new roles, drawn from the intersection of their own experience and the dominant culture, eventually may have become "more constricting than what rural Swedish women had experienced on their isolated farmsteads" (40).

Mathilde Jutras's "*La Grande Nostalgie*': French-Speaking Women and Home-sickness in Early Twentieth-Century Saskatchewan" analyzes a large pool of taped interviews of French-speaking pioneering women. In concluding that "despair and loneliness were frequent visitors" (59), Jutras calls into question the traditional image of the stout-hearted, French-Catholic female colonist who gladly came to western Canada in the name of God and *la nation*. Like other non-English-speaking immigrant women, these women were linguistically, culturally and geographically isolated; however, unlike other immigrant women, for French-speaking Quebec women this isolation occurred within the boundaries of their own country.

Anna Feldman's "'A Woman of Valour Who Can Find?': Jewish-Saskatchewan Women in Two Rural Settings, 1882-1939" looks at how these women met the challenges of isolation, loneliness and anti-Semitism in the half century prior to World War II. Basing her analysis on written secondary and primary sources as well as a series of oral interviews with pioneering Jewish settlers, Feldman distinguishes between those Jewish women living in small rural communities and those farming on their homesteads. The former, she suggests, were less isolated than their farming sisters, but in general both groups were successful in using "their religion, culture, language and social ties with others of a similar background to help cope with [the] isolation and the anti-Semitism" (61) that they had to endure.

Nadine Small considers the relationship between Saskatchewan women and imperialism during World War I in "The 'Lady Imperialists' and the Great War: The

Imperial Order Daughters of the Empire in Saskatchewan, 1914-1918." Small argues that the Imperial Order Daughters of the Empire's (IODE) imperialism "consisted of two major components: patriotism and militarism" (92), and because the IODE was "waiting and prepared for another imperial war" (92) in 1914, it was able to make a "significant contribution" to the war effort. Small maintains that the Order "engendered a patronizing, elitist attitude" (93). As she explains: "consistent with their middle- to upper-class compositions, prairie chapters of the Order had a paternalistic, condescending attitude toward immigrants and the lower ranks of society" (80). Small also demonstrates how the Saskatchewan chapters were intimately connected to chapters across Canada and concludes that "the singleness of purpose and the centralized organization of the national women's society contributed to the continuity of IODE aims throughout the Dominion" (92).

In "Engendering Resistance: Women Respond to Relief in Saskatoon, 1930-1932," Theresa Healy considers how the state attempted to impose its "expectations of behaviour for the working class — both male and female" (109) on recipients of relief in Saskatoon at that time. The sit-down strike by forty-eight women and their children in November 1932 provides the entrée into the complex and politically charged issue of relief and "women's strategies of resistance to the control of the state inherent in its relief policy" (95). Healy shows that women resisted the state's attempt at control over their lives in three ways: they "tried to manage the household so as to keep the family off relief"; "they tried to improve the conditions and quantity of relief and instill more dignity into relief services, which directly challenged the class and gender assumptions of the policy"; and, they "worked towards changing the political and economic system which they believed was responsible" (110). Healy argues that in rejecting state relief policies, women "challenged other boundaries, writing their ideas into a new and emerging national script on the place of the state and relief in Canadian society" (110).

In "'You Just Did What Had To Be Done': Life Histories of Four Saskatchewan 'Farmers' Wives'," Julie Dorsch calls into question traditional views concerning Saskatchewan farm women. Drawing from interviews she conducted with four Saskatchewan women in their sixties and seventies, she argues that in terms of work Saskatchewan farm women were not homogeneous, but diverse in the "great variety and scope in the work that they performed" (117). Also, contrary to the traditional view which minimizes the contribution of women inside and outside the home, Dorsch suggests that "the oral evidence contradicts the usual division of labour that describes the farm wife as responsible solely for the nurture, maintenance and reproduction of farm labour" (123). The four women that Dorsch interviewed "did all the tasks that farm men did. These women were clearly involved in activities usually defined as 'farming'" (123). After discussing work, financial status, social and legal constraints, female friendship, and women's role in rural communities, Dorsch concludes that "for long enough historians have ignored rural women's contribution outside as well as inside the home and left the impression that men alone built Saskatchewan's agricultural society" (130).

In "From the Bush to the Village to the City: Pinehouse Lake Aboriginal Women Adapt to Change," Miriam McNab calls upon her training in anthropology and her links to the Native community to analyze the strategies used by a group of northern Saskatchewan First Nations women to cope with the social and economic changes which the northern part of the province has gone through in the last thirty years. Using oral interviews as her evidence, McNab contends that, in contrast to an earlier generation of already urbanized southern Native women who lament the cultural changes that have occurred, recent arrivals from the bush and the village see the city as an opportunity "to pursue meaningful, productive lives" (143). This strategy of adaption, McNab argues, has historical roots, representing a continuation of the "adaptive strategies and flexibility which characterized the northern Metis in the last century" (131).

In our final offering, Jo-Anne Lee's "'Living in Dreams': Oral Narratives of Three Recent Immigrant Women," three newly arrived Saskatchewan immigrant women share parts of their own life histories. The stories that they tell reveal how difficult it is for non-white, non-European, non-middle-class women to build "a day-to-day life in a new country while still living the memory of the old" (145). Drawing from her own discipline of sociology, Lee goes beyond race, class and gender, and discusses oracy, the ability to speak, reminding us that the lack of fluency in one of Canada's two official languages is a huge obstacle to participation in public life.

"Other" Voices does not represent the last word on Saskatchewan women's history. The province was and continues to be the home of numerous and varied groups of women. Many of their voices still remain silent. It is our hope that in presenting these essays, more Saskatchewan women will be inspired to speak.

GREAT WOMEN, SEPARATE SPHERES, AND DIVERSITY: COMMENTS ON SASKATCHEWAN WOMEN'S HISTORIOGRAPHY

Aileen C. Moffatt

In reflecting on Saskatchewan women's recorded histories, it is clear that until recently scholars did not keep pace with national and international developments in women's history.[1] Most of Saskatchewan women's history was compensatory and contributory, simply writing "great" women and events into existing historical interpretations.[2] Often studies consisted of a narrative with no critical analysis or articulate theoretical foundation. Further, historians of Saskatchewan women frequently viewed their subjects through the artificial lens of static separate male and female spheres in the process of emphasizing a distinct women's culture. Historians also commonly considered only Saskatchewan's white, English-speaking women who were active in the public sphere, and disregarded the province's diverse multicultural population and heritage. The result was history limited in focus and narrow in interpretation.

The purpose of this essay is to provide a guide to the predominant stages in Saskatchewan women's history. It is not intended as a comprehensive literature review; rather, it is designed to provide a map of the shifting historiographical impulses in Saskatchewan women's history. Accordingly, not every work mentioning Saskatchewan women is discussed. Instead, examples are provided to illustrate characteristics of each historiographical stage.

Women's history as an academic endeavour developed slowly and sporadically in Saskatchewan. Until the mid-1980s, no sustained effort at scholarship existed in this field. Three general, although not rigid, stages in Saskatchewan women's history are discernable. The first introductory/celebratory stage began in the 1930s and continued into the mid-1970s, although provincial and prairie history texts published as late as 1984 still demonstrated characteristics of this first phase. Studies introduced women as historical actors in one of two ways: as helpmates to men, or as "great" or "noteworthy" individual women. Authors celebrated "great" events, especially female suffrage and the early twentieth-century reform movement. Perhaps historians of Saskatchewan women have focussed on extraordinary or "great" women in the public sphere because it is often easier to study the public record or follow the lives of public

---

1   I would like to thank Gerald Friesen, Dave De Brou, Michael McCulloch and Marland Buckner for their thoughtful comments on earlier drafts of this essay.

2   Gerda Lerner defines "compensatory history as the history of notable women," and "contribution history as describing women's contributions to and subjection in a male-defined world"; see Gerda Lerner, "Placing Women in History: Definitions and Challenges," in Lerner, *The Majority Finds its Past* (New York: Oxford University Press, 1981), 145-53. In 1986 Lerner elaborated on her meaning of compensatory history explaining that women trained as historians in the past fifty years were "well trained by their male mentors. So they too found what men were doing on the whole more significant and, in their desire to upgrade the part of women in the past, they looked hard for women who had done what men did. Thus, compensatory history was born"; see Lerner, *The Creation of Patriarchy* (New York: Oxford University Press, 1986), 13.

figures. Whatever the reason, the result was compensatory or contributory history —
an attempt at writing women into the existing historical record. The second, or
separate spheres/women's culture stage, included the period between the mid-1970s
and approximately 1990. With the growth of women's history as an accepted
academic field, feminist historians examined women as a group (usually prominent,
white, English-speaking women only) and often located women within the separate
spheres paradigm.[3] Frequently researchers focussed on women's organizations. The
element uniting most work in this second stage is exploitation — women as victims
of injustice and oppression. Stage three, work done primarily during the 1990s,
emphasizes diversity. Influenced by theoretical developments in literary criticism,
anthropology, cultural and ethnic studies, historians of Saskatchewan women began
to adopt and adapt new methodological strategies to study Saskatchewan women in
their various cultural communities.

Authors all but neglected women as historical actors prior to the first stage of
Saskatchewan women's history. As Ann Leger Anderson noted in 1980, general
provincial history texts published early in the province's history (written exclusively
by male scholars) "rarely mention women."[4] Included are works by Norman Fergus
Black in 1913, Adam Shortt and Arthur G. Doughty in 1914, and John Hawkes in
1924.[5] The first stage of Saskatchewan women's history was ushered in with the

---

3   Influenced by the women's movement of the 1960s and 1970s, students of women's history in Britain
     and the United States first adopted separate spheres as a methodological framework. Linda Kerber's
     analysis in 1988 is the most cogent reading of the development of separate spheres scholarship; see
     Kerber, "Separate Spheres, Female Worlds, Woman's Place: The Rhetoric of Women's History," *Journal
     of American History* 75, no. 1 (June 1988): 9-39. Kerber notes separate spheres has been judged to be both
     positive and negative for women. In examining American scholarship on separate spheres, Kerber
     identifies three stages of development in the separate spheres paradigm. The first stage, introduced in
     1966 by Barbara Welter, submits that separate spheres made women subordinate; see Welter, "The Cult
     of True Womanhood: 1820-1860," *American Quarterly* 18 (Summer 1966): 151-74. Within three years
     both Aileen Kraditor and Gerda Lerner added class as a variable to Welter's equation, linking the
     Industrial Revolution to the development of the separate spheres ideology; see Aileen S. Kraditor, ed.,
     Up From the Pedestal: Selected Writings in the History of American Feminism (Chicago: Quadrangle Books,
     1968); and Gerda Lerner, "The Lady and the Mill Girl: Changes in the Status of Women in the Age of
     Jackson," *Midcontinent American Studies Journal* 10 (Spring 1969): 5-15. During the 1970s, the second
     stage attempted to develop the separate spheres theme and introduced the idea of a woman's culture.
     For example, in 1975 Carroll Smith-Rosenberg reinterpreted separate spheres as positive because it
     encouraged sustaining relationships between women, or in other words, a distinct woman's culture; see
     Smith-Rosenberg, "The Female World of Love and Ritual: Relations Between Women in Nineteenth
     Century America," *Signs* 1 (Autumn 1975): 1-29. The third stage Kerber identifies began in 1980 in
     response to this dual interpretation of separate spheres. As Kerber states, historians set out to show how
     woman's sphere "was socially constructed both for and by women," rather than one or the other; see
     Kerber, "Separate Spheres," 18. Kerber suggests there are three major characteristics to the third stage:
     first, separate spheres can be applied to all eras of history, not just the nineteenth century. Second,
     separate spheres is relational and therefore assumes varying postures with changing circumstances. It
     could both serve women's interests and restrict their actions. Third, historians are now examining the
     literal interpretation of woman's sphere, or the physical space assigned to women. In short, the separate
     spheres paradigm need not be static or rigid.

4   Ann Leger Anderson, "Saskatchewan Women, 1880-1920, A Field For Study," in H. Palmer and D.
     Smith, eds., *The New Provinces: Alberta and Saskatchewan 1905-1980* (Vancouver: Tantalus Research,
     1980), 66.

5   Leger Anderson refers to: Norman Fergus Black, *History of Saskatchewan and the North-West Territories*, 2
     vols. (Regina: Saskatchewan Historical Co., 1913); Adam Shortt and Arthur G. Doughty, eds., *Canada
     and Its Provinces: A History of the Canadian People and Their Institutions by One Hundred Associates*, vols. 9 and
     10, *The Prairie Provinces* (Toronto: Brook and Company, 1914); and John Hawkes, *The Story of Saskatchewan
     and Its People*, 3 vols. (Chicago: S.J. Clarke Pub. Co., 1924).

Canadian Frontiers of Settlement series, nine volumes published between 1934 and 1940 discussing the social, economic and geographic systems and characteristics of the Canadian Prairies. The authors of this series assumed men were farmers and women helpmates. A reading of the volume by A.S. Morton, *History of Prairie Settlement*, for example, leaves the erroneous impression that men alone settled the Canadian Prairies. Morton makes only three references to women. In the first instance he writes that Doukhobor women at Blaine Lake "used to spin and weave."[6] The second reference is to travelling dairy schools "sent out to educate the farmer's wives on the farms."[7] Morton mentions women a third time in a discussion of the University of Saskatchewan's Extension Department. He notes that responsibility for education about farming practices often fell to the Extension Department's Agricultural Societies for farmers and Homemakers' Clubs for farmer's wives.[8] In short, for Morton women had little or no role in the history of prairie settlement.

Another example of the men as farmers, women as helpmates perspective from the Canadian Frontiers of Settlement series is *Pioneering in the Prairie Provinces: The Social Side of the Settlement Process* by C.A. Dawson and Eva R. Younge. Here, although the authors pay closer attention to women than does Morton, the images of women they project are highly romanticized:

> As for the pioneer woman, what shall we say? When her man was at home she stood shoulder to shoulder with him in the conduct of the day's affairs. When he was absent ...she cared for the family, she looked after the stock, she took upon her lone shoulders burdens which were none too light for husband and wife to bear.[9]

Despite Dawson and Young's idealistic portrayal of pioneers, the volume is still useful to historians of Saskatchewan women because of the prairie demographic data included. Especially important are discussions of sex ratios, average ages of farmers and homemakers, marital status of farmers, number of children, and level of education of farmers and homemakers. The information is easily understood and provides a valuable starting point for rural studies of this period.

Three subsequent provincial histories were written to coincide with particular anniversaries — in 1955 J.F.C. Wright's *Saskatchewan: The History of a Province* commemorated the province's fiftieth anniversary; in 1980 John Archer's *Saskatchewan: A History* marked Saskatchewan's seventy-fifth anniversary; and in 1982 Don Kerr and Stan Hanson's *Saskatoon: The First Half-Century* was published as a Saskatoon centennial project. These volumes are celebrations of progress, tenacity and development. All three fit into the first or introductory/celebratory stage, giving just a slight nod to Saskatchewan women, but again only to "great" public women.

Wright's book depicts the province's history as a step-by-step advancement of a progressive, vibrant society. Wright's "people" are survivors, citizens with vision. G.W. Simpson, Wright's colleague at the University of Saskatchewan, highlights this vision in his introduction to the book, writing: "to an exceptional degree the people of

---

6   A.S. Morton, *History of Prairie Settlement* (Toronto: The MacMillan Company of Canada Limited, 1938), 113.

7   Ibid., 136.

8   Ibid., 157.

9   C.A. Dawson and Eva R. Younge, *Pioneering in the Prairie Provinces: The Social Side of the Settlement Process* (Toronto: The MacMillan Company, 1940), 19.

Saskatchewan have shown buoyancy, courage and a readiness to respond to an imaginative or generous idea."[10] In keeping with the characteristics of the introductory/celebratory first stage of Saskatchewan women's history, Wright celebrates women active in suffrage and social reform campaigns prior to 1920.

Saskatchewan: A History marked Saskatchewan's seventy-fifth anniversary.[11] Written by John H. Archer, this extremely detailed provincial history emphasizes political life. As such, it is not surprising Archer's analysis does not extend beyond the contributions made by women in the suffrage and temperance movements. The result, however, is another history which valorizes "great" women and overlooks all other women and their everyday lives.

Saskatoon: The First Half-Century by Don Kerr and Stan Hanson, was a centennial project endorsed by Century Saskatoon and Saskatoon City Council. This book shares stage one introductory/celebratory characteristics with other general provincial histories — only "noteworthy" and "great" women are included. Kerr and Hanson mention women just four times: one, in giving examples of women's club work in the province's early years; two, in referring to wage rates for women, 1910-14; three, in discussing the suffrage movement and women's war work during "the Great War"; and four, in adding four paragraphs about Ethel Catherwood, the Saskatoon Lily, who achieved fame as an Olympic high jumper in 1928. Names of some public women are included with reference to particular civic or provincial events but their contributions appear minimalized. Kerr and Hanson, like Morton, Dawson and Younge, Archer, and Wright, favour the history of "great" men and women in the public sphere and consequently reveal little about the vast majority of Saskatoon's other citizens.

The two general histories of the western Canadian region published in the early 1980s, one by J. Arthur Lower, the other by Gerald Friesen, follow the familiar pattern of generally overlooking women as historical actors. It is interesting to note that Lower and Friesen mention most of the same "great" women as do the authors of the Saskatchewan histories and demonstrate the same indifference to women's contributions out of the public sphere and in their day-to-day lives of home and family responsibility. J. Arthur Lower's *Western Canada: An Outline History* is a chronicle of western settlement.[12] There is little substance or analysis in this text. Lower mentions few women; those he does cite are most often listed as the wife of a public man (with no contributions of her own) or as the stereotypical "great" woman political activist. Lower devotes one section to discussing what he calls "Women as Persons," where in only two partial pages he covers the very complex issues of suffrage, reform and the 1929 Persons Case.[13] There is no other discussion of women's contributions or roles in the historical development of western Canada.

---

10   J.F.C. Wright, *Saskatchewan: The History of a Province* (Toronto: McClelland and Stewart, 1955), xi.

11   John H. Archer, *Saskatchewan: A History* (Saskatoon: Saskatchewan Archives Board and Western Producer Prairie Books, 1980). The companion volume is: Douglas H. Bocking, *Saskatchewan: A Pictorial History* (Saskatoon: Saskatchewan Archives Board and Western Producer Prairie Books, 1979).

12   J. Arthur Lower, *Western Canada: An Outline History* (Vancouver: Douglas and McIntyre, 1983).

13   The Persons Case is the legal action brought by Emily Murphy, Nellie McClung, Irene Parlby, Henrietta Muir Edwards and Louise McKinney to petition the Supreme Court of Canada to rule on the constitutional question of whether women were persons or not. The action was started by Judge Emily Murphy in 1919 in an attempt to secure women's right to Senate appointments. Hitherto women were excluded from the Senate because the federal government claimed women were not considered persons under the

One year later, in 1984, Gerald Friesen published *The Canadian Prairies: A History.*[14] Friesen's work is an analytic and eloquent synthesis of Canadian prairie scholarship. However, because of Friesen's emphasis on western socioeconomic development, women do not appear as significant actors. When Friesen was writing *Canadian Prairies,* scholars were only beginning to consider rural women as economic contributors. It was not until the publication of Marjorie Cohen's 1988 book *Women's Work, Markets and Economic Development in Nineteenth-Century Ontario* that scholars seriously analyzed women's activity in the market sphere.[15]

The scholarship of this first stage of Saskatchewan women's history in many respects mirrored the work being done by scholars in the wider Canadian context until the explosion of the "new" social history in the early 1970s.[16] Nationalism, regionalism, economic development and international affairs had previously occupied generations of Canadian historians, those in Saskatchewan included. Consequently, the resulting histories featured "great" men and women and their public activities. Saskatchewan history was no exception. But even after social history began to make an entrée into academic circles in other regions of Canada, historians of Saskatchewan women continued for some time to write stage one "great" persons history. Perhaps it was because examining public records and the public activities of men and women was much easier than reconstructing the lives of those whose lives were more obscure. Analysis of published writings of notable women, for example, was less complicated and complex than piecing together fragments of day-to-day living.

Consider, for example, Michael Hayden's study of his colleague, Hilda Neatby, in *So Much to Do, So Little Time: The Writings of Hilda Neatby.*[17] A respected historian at the University of Saskatchewan, Neatby was also known for her controversial challenge of the public educational system in 1953. Neatby criticized the new "progressivism" in the classroom which she believed "encouraged the idea of a uniform low standard easily obtainable by almost all."[18] She proposed an educational system that challenged students to develop their intellect and encouraged them to understand "the inheritance of western civilization."[19] Hayden's book presents not only Neatby's

---

terms of the British North America Act. When the Supreme Court ruled women were not persons in that sense, the petitioners appealed to the British Judicial Committee of the Privy Council in England. The decision came in October 1929 with the Privy Council unanimously agreeing the word persons included women; see Alison Prentice, Paula Bourne, Gail Cuthbert Brandt, Beth Light, Wendy Mitchinson and Naomi Black, *Canadian Women: A History* (Toronto: Harcourt Brace Jovanovich Canada Inc., 1988), 282.

14   Gerald Friesen, *The Canadian Prairies: A History* (Toronto: University of Toronto Press, 1984).

15   Marjorie Griffin Cohen, *Women's Work, Markets and Economic Development in Nineteenth-Century Ontario* (Toronto: University of Toronto Press, 1988). Cohen argues that "economic growth brought women's productive efforts increasingly into the market sphere" (10).

16   Carl Berger, *The Writing of Canadian History: Aspects of English-Canadian Historical Writing since 1900* (Toronto: University of Toronto Press, 1986).

17   Michael Hayden, *So Much to Do, So Little Time: The Writings of Hilda Neatby* (Vancouver: University of British Columbia Press, 1983).

18   Hilda Neatby, *So Little for the Mind* (Toronto: Clarke, Irwin and Company Limited, 1953), 15. Neatby states that progressivism "seems to be about as easy to define as the shape of an amoeba." Thus in her book she makes "no attempt to define it" (8). She does, however, characterize it as "anti-intellectual" (15), "anti-cultural" (16), and "amoral" (17). She concludes, "the present preoccupations with body building and character moulding are useless and may even be dangerous so long as we neglect and starve the mind" (335).

19   Ibid., 16.

sometimes volatile views on education, but also her historical writings and commentary on the world around her. It is an interesting though impersonal book providing little information about Neatby's life outside of the academy. Neatby, however, could never be called ordinary. Hers was definitely a public life of teaching and public service. She was an exceptional woman with a well-known public persona.

In only a few studies written during this first stage are women portrayed as primary agents or key players in Saskatchewan's history. There are, however, two topics that popular and academic historians have repeatedly reconsidered in which women are given a central role — the story of the Barr Colonists who emigrated from England in 1903 totally unprepared for their lives as homesteaders, and the female suffrage campaign which culminated in the franchise for Saskatchewan women in 1916. These two subjects have been examined in both the first and second stages of Saskatchewan women's history and thus serve as a bridge between the two stages.

Stories of the Barr Colonists and the difficulties they encountered in transit and in settlement are popular in Saskatchewan folklore. It appears, however, that academic historians have largely left discussions of the Barr Colony to popular and amateur historians as there is not yet a critical treatment or analysis of the Colony. But because of the popular interest in this notorious chapter of Saskatchewan's history, various first-person accounts have been published over the years. *Gully Farm*, for example, by Mary Pinder Hiemstra, is a poignant account by a young British girl of her family's ordeals as Barr Colonists. Alice Rendell's letters home, published in *Alberta History* in 1963, provide a glimpse of the adult Colonist's experiences. And, Lynne Bowen has written a vivid narrative of the Colonists' ordeal in *Muddling Through: The Remarkable Story of the Barr Colonists*, published in 1992. Both Heimstra's memoir and Rendell's published letters fall within the first introductory/celebratory stage of Saskatchewan women's history even though they are not about "great" public women. They do, however, celebrate individual vision and triumph over the elements, in a similar vein to J.F.C. Wright's *Saskatchewan: The History of a Province*. Bowen's book, although it is not primarily about women, does exhibit characteristics of the second stage as Bowen carefully outlines how the Colonists were exploited.

Though Mary Pinder Hiemstra wrote *Gully Farm* from a child's viewpoint, it is neither childish nor trivial. Heimstra's observations are especially moving when she writes about things her mother would not likely have recorded had she been the author:

> Mother often said she wished she was a bigger and stronger woman. But she never wished she liked Canada, there were too many hardships, though sometimes it almost seemed as if she was glad of the difficulties and the irritations.[20]

Perhaps because Mary Pinder Hiemstra was not a "great" woman, historians have largely overlooked her memoir. This is unfortunate because this type of personalized account is invaluable to historians. Ordinary women and men are central characters in Saskatchewan's history. Historians need both to fully utilize these sources and to consider new ways of examining everyday life in order to more completely explicate the Saskatchewan experience.

In a series of circular letters to friends and relatives, "as I am quite unable to write each individually,"[21] Alice Rendell discusses the Barr Colonists' journey: living in a

---

20   Mary Pinder Hiemstra, *Gully Farm* (Toronto: McClelland and Stewart, 1955), 173.

21   Alice Rendell, "Letters From A Barr Colonist," *Alberta History* 11, no. 1 (Winter 1963): 12.

tent while men built houses, the high cost of supplies, and the many inconveniences Colonists endured. The tone of Rendell's letters is optimistic, making it difficult to determine whether this enthusiasm was for the benefit of her British relatives (who may have been worried about her), or whether she was genuinely pleased with her new home. The final letter, dated January 1904, repeats the familiar warning to potential immigrants: "I would never advise anyone to come out here who is the least afraid of work. They are better off at home," she wrote.[22]

In *Muddling Through*, Bowen, whose family were Colonists, vividly describes the many hardships, scams and schemes, starvation and isolation many Colonists experienced.[23] Although the book is primarily a narrative of the ordeal, it provides an interesting contrast to women's "liberating experiences" described by historian Susan Jackel in *A Flannel Shirt and Liberty: British Emigrant Gentlewomen in the Canadian West, 1880-1914*.[24] Unlike Jackel, Bowen leaves readers considering that perhaps many Colonists regretted leaving Britain for the Canadian West, a position Bowen supports with substantial evidence.

Examinations of the female suffrage movement also bridge the first and second stages of Saskatchewan women's history. Scholars have approached female suffrage both as a celebration of a "great" event in the first stage, and later in the second stage by adding class as a variable. Historians have been particularly interested in campaigns waged in the West, perhaps because the prairie provinces were the first to grant female suffrage. First stage studies of female suffrage in Saskatchewan include those by Christine MacDonald and Catherine Cleverdon. MacDonald's 1948 analysis of how Saskatchewan women obtained the vote briefly outlines the provincial women's suffrage movement as a campaign led by farm and small-town women.[25] Catherine Cleverdon's 1950 study of the Canadian suffrage movement groups together Manitoba, Saskatchewan and Alberta in one chapter, drawing parallels between the three movements.[26] Cleverdon credits the Saskatchewan Grain Growers' Association as the primary motivator behind the provincial suffrage movement. She also contends that farm men insisted on equality for their wives and for this reason men supported female suffragists. This is a simplistic interpretation. Male central farm associations backed the female suffrage movement for practical reasons, not the least of which was to increase the farm vote.

June Menzies's 1968 study of Saskatchewan female suffrage links the first introductory/celebratory stage of Saskatchewan women's history and the second separate spheres/women's culture stage. Menzies celebrates suffrage much as MacDonald and Cleverdon did, but her analysis goes further as she reevaluates the campaign as a "battle of the sexes," where women had to prove they wanted the vote.[27]

---

22   Ibid., 24.

23   Lynne Bowen, *Muddling Through: The Remarkable Story of the Barr Colonists* (Vancouver: Douglas and McIntyre, 1992).

24   Susan Jackel, ed., *A Flannel Shirt and Liberty: British Emigrant Gentlewomen in the Canadian West, 1880-1914* (Vancou.   University of British Columbia Press, 1982).

25   Christine MacDonald, "How Saskatchewan Women Got the Vote," *Saskatchewan History* 1, no. 3 (1948): 1-8.

26   Catherine Cleverdon, *The Woman Suffrage Movement in Canada* (1950; Toronto: University of Toronto Press, 1974).

27   June Menzies, "Votes for Saskatchewan's Women," in Norman Ward and Duff Spafford, eds., *Politics in Saskatchewan* (Toronto: Longmans Canada Limited, 1968), 79. For a more recent examination of

Menzies also demonstrates the connections between suffrage and prohibition in Saskatchewan. Carol Lee Bacchi's 1979 study builds on Menzies's work in an analysis of farm women's involvement in suffrage and social reform. Bacchi explains the differences between farm women and urban middle-class suffragists:

> The organized farm women wanted the vote for several reasons: to rectify certain injustices against women, to strengthen the Protestant, Anglo-Saxon clique to which they belonged and to increase the political awareness and representation of the agrarian sector. The urban middle class suffragists could readily sympathize with the first two goals but the last made it difficult for the women to work together.[28]

At least two historians of prairie women criticize Bacchi's work. Susan Jackel considers Bacchi's study "seriously oversimplified and distorted,"[29] while Eliane Leslau Silverman calls it "reductionist."[30] Perhaps Jackel and Silverman do not agree with Bacchi as they seem to prefer a women's culture interpretation of history, an interpretation Bacchi shuns.

The second stage of Saskatchewan women's history, that which examines separate spheres/women's culture, moves from general history texts mentioning only "great" individual women, to studies focussing on women as a group. In examining this stage, it is evident that scholars of Saskatchewan women's history, like their British, American and other Canadian colleagues studying women's history, consciously or unconsciously compartmentalized Saskatchewan women's lives into the separate spheres paradigm of private (male) and public (female) domains. Accordingly, scholars incorporated the separate spheres framework into the early literature and research in Canadian women's history. The tendency of Canadian historians working within the separate spheres model was to examine the subordination of women — presenting women as victims of an unjust system or society — or to celebrate women of extraordinary talent and determination who triumphed over exploitation. Saskatchewan scholars followed suit.

The notion of a separate women's culture, a feature of second stage Saskatchewan women's history, derives from the separate spheres paradigm. Women's culture has been, and continues to be, a popular subcategory of Canadian women's history.[31]

women's suffrage in Saskatchewan, see: Carole Bryant, "'To the Fairmindedness of Men': Female Suffrage in Saskatchewan, 1912-1916" (MSW thesis, University of Regina, 1988); and Elizabeth Kalmakoff, "Women Suffrage in Saskatchewan" (MA thesis, University of Regina, 1993).

28   Carol Lee Bacchi, "Divided Allegiances: The Response of Farm and Labour Women to Suffrage," in Linda Kealey, ed., *A Not Unreasonable Claim, Women and Reform in Canada 1800s-1920s* (Toronto: The Women's Educational Press, 1979), 100. An edited version of this article appears in Bacchi's book, *Liberation Deferred? The Ideas of the English-Canadian Suffragists, 1877-1918* (Toronto: University of Toronto Press, 1983).

29   Susan Jackel, "Prairie Women's History in Canada: A Bibliographic Survey," *The CRIAW Papers* 14 (Ottawa: CRIAW, April 1987): 18.

30   Eliane Leslau Silverman, "Writing Canadian Women's History, 1970-1982: An Historiographical Analysis," *Canadian Historical Review* 63, no. 4 (December 1982): 525.

31   Prentice et al., *Canadian Women*. This book, the first survey text on Canadian women's history, specifically proposes the idea of a distinct women's culture in Canada. The authors suggest this culture was most prominent in the early twentieth century during the era of reform movements and the growth of women's separate organizations. They also state that this women's culture, although it may have waned at some junctures, continues to be a factor for women. This book fits into the category "history of women's oppression" because, as Peter Ward succinctly notes, "the underlying assumption of the book is that the history of women is principally the history of their inequality, of their attempts to overcome it, and of

Women's culture developed as a model during the second stage but continues to flourish today because of recent theoretical, philosophical and political developments adopted by some feminist scholars. In particular, theoreticians of women's culture are interested in discussions of the similarities women share and how women differ from men.[32] Proponents of a unique women's culture suggest there are experiences, attitudes, practices and periodization common to all women regardless of social or geographic location.[33] This interpretation suggests women can be viewed as a group by virtue of the commonalities they share, and that the possibility of a "universal woman" exists as a result of these commonalities. The greatest difficulty with this interpretation is that individual identity is ranked secondary to group identification. Identity is presumed to be socially constructed and imposed rather than self-created. Opponents of the women's culture framework argue that grouping women together simply because they are women is reductionist because of the disregard for the primacy of key variables such as class, race, religion, sexuality, (dis)ability and location, among others. Further, they argue that the idea of a "universal woman" is also completely ahistorical as it does not recognize that definitions of woman and womanhood are historical creations situated in particular places and times.[34]

their quest for expressions of feminine community"; see Peter Ward, "Review of Prentice et al., *Canadian Women: A History,*" *Canadian Historical Review* 70 (September 1989): 382. The book is another example of how historians have attempted to unite women in a women's culture based on oppression and identity-in-difference.

32   There are four basic approaches to questions of difference and/or similarity between women and men. One, radical or cultural feminists assert all women have certain feminine or female characteristics in common that have been denied or devalued by patriarchy. The most influential studies in this area include: Mary Daly, *Gyn/Ecology: The Metaethics of Radical Feminism* (Boston: Beacon Press, 1978); and, Carol Gilligan, *In a Different Voice, Psychological Theory and Women's Development* (Cambridge: Harvard University Press, 1982). Two, Marxist standpoint theorists argue the sexual division of labour affords women a unique vantage point from which to view capitalist patriarchy. For examples, see: Nancy M. Hartsock, "The Feminist Standpoint: Developing the Ground for a Specifically Feminist Historical Materialism," in Sandra Harding, ed., *Feminism and Methodology* (Bloomington: Indiana University Press, 1987), 157-80; and, Sandra Harding, "Rethinking Standpoint Epistemology: 'What is Strong Objectivity'?" in Linda Alcoff and Elizabeth Potter, eds., *Feminist Epistemologies* (New York: Routledge, 1993), 49-82. Three, poststructuralists focus on difference, plurality, power and multiplicity. See: Chris Weedon, *Feminist Practice and Poststructuralist Theory* (Oxford: Basil Blackwell, 1987); and Gisela Bock and Susan James, eds., *Beyond Equality and Difference* (London: Routledge, 1992). Four, liberal scholars promote a vision of strict equality between men and women. Betty Friedan is perhaps the best known proponent of liberal feminism; see Betty Friedan, *The Feminine Mystique* (1963; New York: Dell Publishing, 1984).

33   For example, Gillian Creese and Veronica Strong-Boag in 1992 wrote: "Women's experiences of life within patriarchal structures, whether overtly brutal or outwardly benevolent, like their particular responsibilities for childbirth, has set them apart from male relatives, however much they might wish it otherwise." See: Creese and Strong-Boag, "Introduction: Taking Gender into Account in British Columbia," in Creese and Strong-Boag, eds., *British Columbia Reconsidered: Essays on Women* (Vancouver: Press Gang Publishers, 1992), 2.

34   Integral to studies of women's culture is an analysis of gender — socially constructed delineations by sex. In the view of some scholars, gender has become the primary category in women's history. In 1988, Joan Scott, in a significant study of gender and history, defined gender as "a constitutive element of social relationships based on perceived differences between the sexes, and gender is a primary way of signifying relationships of power"; see Joan Wallach Scott, *Gender and the Politics of History* (New York: Columbia University Press, 1988), 42. Scott states that gender is an historical phenomenon that changes over time. Denise Riley takes this one step further by suggesting the term "woman" is ambiguous and historically constructed. It is, she says, "a volatile collectivity in which female persons can be very differently positioned"; see Denise Riley, *"Am I That Name?": Feminism and the Category of "Women" in History* (Minneapolis: University of Minnesota Press, 1988), 2. Scholars have concluded

Yet, women's culture remains popular with historians of Canadian women. Many leading scholars have applied a women's culture paradigm to their work. One of the earliest examinations of a Canadian women's culture is found in Eliane Leslau Silverman's 1982 historiographical essay in the *Canadian Historical Review* where she calls for historians to confront "the issue of a woman's culture."[35] Silverman challenges historians to question if women had their own culture apart from that of the male culture. She asks, "did [women] live two kinds of lives, one in the male culture where they were controlled by tradition, fear, loyalty, and love, and the other in a parallel society of women where their actions could range from intimacy to power?"[36] The problem with Silverman's query is her determination to find what she calls "heterogeneous feminists" who "shared in the culture of marginality."[37] Silverman posits a women's culture which assumes all women similarly experience marginality. This does not take into account the influence of variable social, economic, political or geographic locations. However, Silverman's analysis and challenge was very influential and Canadian women's historians, including those examining prairie women, followed her lead in adopting this limited-perspective women's culture model.[38]

Early in the second, or separate spheres/women's culture stage, Saskatchewan women's history finally achieved a modicum of recognition as a serious scholarly pursuit. Historians began researching women and so-called women's topics largely in an effort to demonstrate women were active historical actors in their own right. In this second stage, women are the focus; the province is secondary. Works by Grant MacEwan and Candace Savage, for example, are on the cusp of the first and second stages and thus exhibit characteristics of both stages. Both authors definitely celebrate "great" public women, but they also append the historical record which hitherto examined only women's suffrage and reform activities.

In 1975, Grant MacEwan published ... *and mighty women too: stories of notable western canadian women*, the companion volume to his *Fifty Mighty Men*.[39] As MacEwan's title suggests, he does not tell stories only of Saskatchewan women. The style is chatty and even gossipy as MacEwan sketches biographical accounts of "notable western Canadian women." The subjects are famous public figures — exceptional women: farm activist and journalist Violet McNaughton and history professor Hilda Neatby,

---

that gender is culturally determined and is based on power and relationships of power that shift and change, overlap and extend, combine and connect.

35   Silverman, "Writing Canadian Women's History," 521. There were other earlier historiographical essays on Canadian women's history, but none which addressed women's culture as a central issue. For example, see: Margaret W. Andrews, "Review Article: Attitudes in Canadian Women's History 1945-1975," *Journal of Canadian Studies* (Summer 1977): 69-78; Veronica Strong-Boag, "Raising Clio's Consciousness: Women's History and Archives in Canada," *Archivaria* 6 (Summer 1978): 70-82; and Leger Anderson, "Saskatchewan Women." Leger Anderson states, "most of what we have neglects complex matters of class and ethnicity, the latter of special importance in polyglot Saskatchewan" (76).

36   Silverman, "Writing Canadian Women's History," 521.

37   Ibid., 527.

38   Also see Eliane Leslau Silverman, *The Last Best West: Women on the Alberta Frontier 1880-1930* (Montreal: Eden Press, 1984) where Silverman writes, "the life cycle of each woman, and not the events of the public realm, tended to determine her perception of her experience" (iv). In this book, a compilation of Alberta farm women's experiences, Silverman actively seeks out similarities among women.

39   Grant MacEwan, ...*and mighty women too: stories of notable western canadian women* (Saskatoon: Western Producer Prairie Books, 1975).

for example. Yet as MacEwan suggests in his foreword, "[women's role] was in no way less important [than men's]."[40] MacEwan's book is thus a first step towards a recognition of women's many roles in Saskatchewan's history.

Candace Savage's *Foremothers: Personalities and Issues from the History of Women in Saskatchewan* also was published in 1975. Savage's purposes were "on the one hand, [to] celebrate the accomplishments of a few distinguished prairie women; and on the other hand [to] explore a number of themes in the history of Saskatchewan women as a class."[41] Savage compiled the stories from a weekly newspaper column; the style is journalistic and the sketches lack analysis. Certainly the subjects fit into the category of "great" women, as all are well-known public figures. Yet as she acknowledges, Savage considers women to be a class. Accordingly the approach she takes in her sketches demonstrates characteristics from the first stage, in examining "great" women, but she also clearly moves into the second stage, women's culture, by approaching women as a class.

Savage's next project was an examination of prairie women's history undertaken with Linda Rasmussen, Lorna Rasmussen and Anne Wheeler. In 1976 this group published *A Harvest Yet to Reap: A History of Prairie Women*, a collection of letters, clippings and speeches with many excellent photographs. Although the authors have included material about public figures, the book is particularly valuable for its documentation of the lives of ordinary women, and for recording women's voices previously muted by historians examining only the public record. Rasmussen et al. did many interviews, sought out personal recollections, and searched archives. The result is English-speaking prairie women candidly writing about their own lives. Numerous photographs provide visual representations to accompany the written text. Although there is little analytic substance to this book, it continues to be an invaluable store of memorabilia. As the authors point out in the preface, "it is an overview of the history of white women on the Canadian prairie in the early years of agricultural settlement; it is a place to begin."[42]

Memorabilia, clippings and biographical sketches were all part of the first wave of the separate spheres/women's culture stage as historians began to collect women's artifacts. Authors also began writing biographies and autobiographies, both popular and academic, celebrating women in Saskatchewan and the other prairie provinces.[43] As scholars delved further into the archives and recovered works by prairie women, publication of collections of letters and writings followed. For example, in 1982 Susan Jackel reprinted a collection of articles written by middle-class British women living in western Canada. The title, *A Flannel Shirt and Liberty: British Emigrant Gentlewomen in the Canadian West, 1880-1914*, is a quote from Moira O'Neil, one of the book's contributors. Jackel argues "that the story of prairie settlement still has a few chapters

---

40   Ibid., foreword.

41   Candace Savage, *Foremothers: Personalities and Issues from the History of Women in Saskatchewan* (n.p., 1975).

42   Linda Rasmussen, Lorna Rasmussen, Candace Savage and Anne Wheeler, *A Harvest Yet to Reap: A History of Prairie Women* (Toronto: The Women's Press, 1976), 8.

43   For example, see: J.F.C. Wright, *The Louise Lucas Story* (Ottawa: The Runge Press, 1965); Fredelle Bruser Maynard, *Raisins and Almonds* (Toronto: Paperjacks, 1973); Ruth Matheson Buck, *The Doctor Rode Side-Saddle* (Toronto: McClelland and Stewart, 1974); and Edna Jacques, *Uphill All the Way: The Autobiography of Edna Jacques* (Saskatoon: Western Producer Prairie Books, 1977).

missing" and "there is a need for some rethinking of the period."[44] She intends to show that the history of the Canadian West is incomplete unless historians consider female as well as male emigrants. Her focus is, however, limited to a specific class-defined group, a narrow selection enabling her to conclude, "emigration to the Prairies was a liberating experience for a significant number of British gentlewomen."[45] Based on these selections, readers might be tempted to agree with Jackel, but it must be noted that the writers she has chosen for her collection are privileged women. Most were professional writers, women whose work was often commissioned and published by their sponsors. Ella Sykes, for example, was supported by the Colonial Intelligence League for Educated Women, a British female emigration society for the "right sort of woman." Although it is an interesting collection of articles and essays, when compared to other studies of the same period, readers are left wondering how many British homesteaders or beleaguered Barr Colonists, for example, would agree with Jackel and call their experiences "liberating"?

Many characteristics of the second stage of prairie women's history, separate spheres/women's culture, are evident in Susan Jackel's reprint of Georgina Binnie-Clark's *Wheat and Women*. This book provides an example of the injustice/ oppression genre of women's history, in particular how women were disadvantaged by legal constraints. Originally published in 1914, Binnie-Clark's book received little attention as growing interest in World War I overshadowed many less pressing issues — including homesteading in the Canadian West. In 1979 Jackel reprinted *Wheat and Women* with the addition of her well-documented introduction which helps to place Binnie-Clark's experiences into historical context. Jackel suggests, "perhaps the strongest claim to re-examination lies in the light it sheds on sexual politics in this country during the century's early years."[46]

Wheat and Women is the second of two volumes written by Binnie-Clark about her life on the Saskatchewan Prairies. The first, *A Summer on the Canadian Prairie*, recounts how Binnie-Clark and her sister Hilaria first came to Canada on vacation to visit their brother who was homesteading, not very successfully, in the Qu'Appelle Valley. Binnie-Clark wrote the first volume in the style of the popular travelogue books of the time. *Wheat and Women* begins where the first volume ends, covering the harvest of 1905 through the harvest of 1908. Her purpose in writing this second book was to demonstrate "what men had done for themselves in agricultural pursuits on the prairie, women could also do for themselves."[47] Unlike *A Summer on the Canadian Prairie*, *Wheat and Women* is written in a less literary style using language reflecting Binnie-Clark's no-nonsense approach to farming. Jackel's introduction provides a valuable historical framework supported by Binnie-Clark's personalized account of general farming problems and difficulties particular to woman farmers.

Veronica Strong-Boag is another of the leading scholars in the examination of a Canadian women's culture. Her 1986 study of feminism on the Canadian Prairies points to "the sense of same sex identification"[48] Canadian women experienced. She

---

44   Jackel, *A Flannel Shirt and Liberty*, xiii.

45   Ibid., xxvi.

46   Georgina Binnie-Clark, *Wheat and Women* (1914; Toronto: University of Toronto Press, 1979), vii.

47   Ibid., 305.

48   Veronica Strong-Boag, "Pulling in Double Harness or Hauling a Double Load: Women, Work and Feminism on the Canadian Prairie," *Journal of Canadian Studies* 21, no. 3 (Fall 1986): 34.

states, "prairie activists were highly sensitive to the particular situation of their sex."[49] Strong-Boag agrees that women demonstrated class and regional loyalties, but she also argues that 1920s prairie feminism was a working feminism concentrating on women-helping-women in the private sphere. Like many other women's culture proponents, Strong-Boag applies the women's oppression model. She writes that this 1920s feminism "was not for the most part an organized movement as the campaign for enfranchisement had been, but it flowed from a similar awareness of women's oppression and a desire to end it."[50]

In the introduction to their 1986 collection *Rethinking Canada: The Promise of Women's History*, editors Veronica Strong-Boag and Anita Clair Fellman argue that women share a culture of rituals, traditions and customs "that cannot be presumed to mirror the position of male reality."[51] They also note that "while [women's] experiences have differed from group to group and time to time, in some ways women's lives resemble each other's as much or more than they resemble those of the men with whom they are closely associated."[52] However, Sara Brooks Sundberg, in one of the collection's essays, takes issue with this position and demands recognition of the diversity of women's lives. Sundberg admonishes those who assume all women's experiences were the same; her study proved that not all prairie women had similar experiences or responsibilities. Accordingly, Sundberg objects to simplistic categorizations that assume all prairie women were helpmates. Such an interpretation, she argues, denies the diversity of pioneer women's lives.[53]

An important feature of second stage or women's culture/separate spheres studies is the examination of women's clubs and organizations. Until recently, most Saskatchewan women's organizations studied were those whose members were white and English-speaking. Among the urban organizations examined by historians are the Women's Christian Temperance Union, Imperial Order Daughters of the Empire, the Young Women's Christian Association, the Regina Council of Women, and the Saskatchewan Registered Nurses Association.[54] Historians of Saskatchewan

---

49   Ibid., 35.

50   Ibid., 34.

51   Veronica Strong-Boag and Anita Clair Fellman, eds., *Rethinking Canada: The Promise of Women's History* (Toronto: Copp Clark Pitman Ltd., 1986), 3

52   Ibid., 2. Strong-Boag further develops her ideas about a distinct women's culture in her book *The New Day Recalled: Lives of Girls and Women in English Canada 1919-1939* (Markham: Penguin Books Canada Ltd., 1988). Here she concludes gender informed every aspect of a woman's life and that a female culture was sustained through "a predisposition to intimacy, rooted in patterns of socialization" (218). Strong-Boag notes that although class loyalties were shared with male relatives, "class stratification did not supersede sex stratification" (3). She suggests class is "a fundamentally imperfect method of indicating a woman's relationship to a capitalist male hierarchy" because it only gauges the relationship of the family to the capitalist society (3). It does not account for the gender hierarchy in that society that ultimately lumps together all women as inferior to all men.

53   Sara Brooks Sundberg, "Farm Women on the Canadian Prairie Frontier: The Helpmate Image," in Strong-Boag and Fellman, eds., *Rethinking Canada*, 95-106

54   Nancy M. Sheehan, "The WCTU on the Prairies 1886-1930," *Prairie Forum* 6, no. 1 (1981): 17-33; Marcia A. McGovern, "The Women's Christian Temperance Union Movement in Saskatchewan 1886-1930: A Regional Perspective of the International White Ribbon Movement" (MA thesis, University of Regina, 1977); Nadine Small, "'Stand By the Union Jack': The Imperial Order Daughters of the Empire in the Prairie Provinces During the Great War, 1914-1918" (MA thesis, University of Saskatchewan, 1989); Catherine Tomlinson Wylie, "'God's Own Cornerstones: Our Daughters': The Saskatoon YWCA 1910-1939" (MA thesis, University of Saskatchewan, 1989); Janet Harvey, "The

women have also shown increasing interest in rural women's associations. In the first or introductory/celebratory stage of Saskatchewan women's history, authors focussed on the largely male central provincial farmer organizations, only mentioning the formation of women's sections as auxiliaries to the central.[55] Historians writing during the second stage feature analyses of the separate women's farm organizations. In these studies, authors recognize farm and rural women as active participants in rural communities. They no longer assume the women's sections were mere auxiliaries of male-dominated farmer associations.

L.J. Wilson's examination in 1978 of the Saskatchewan Grain Grower's Association's educational work did not specifically address women's topics.[56] However, Wilson demonstrates that the Women's Sections were actively involved in adult and extension education for rural women and men. In 1985, the Saskatchewan Women's Grain Grower's Association (WGGA) became the focus of R.G. Marchildon's path-breaking study. This was the first scholarly examination of the Saskatchewan organized farm women's association. Marchildon argues that the "WGGA concentrated mainly upon social, cultural and economic issues that influenced the quality of rural life."[57] He provides examples of these issues including the campaign for labour-saving devices in the home, cooperative marketing practices and the establishment of rest rooms and libraries in towns. Marchildon's study is interesting because he only mentions the WGGA's involvement in the suffrage movement, while studies of suffrage in Saskatchewan focus on female suffrage as the apex of women's associations.

Veronica Strong-Boag's examination in 1986 of postsuffrage prairie feminism argues that feminism did not disappear but rather shifted from public campaigns to women's issues in the private sphere.[58] Strong-Boag's analysis focusses on the popular organized farm women's associations. Farm and rural women's organizations were also studied by Georgina Taylor, who examined women in the Homemakers' Clubs, the WGGA and the Co-operative Commonwealth Federation, and by Aileen Moffatt, who analyzed the Women's Section of the Canadian Council of Agriculture.[59] Both

Regina Council of Women 1895-1925" (MA thesis, University of Regina, 1991); Marguerite E. Robinson, *The First Fifty Years* (Regina: Saskatchewan Registered Nurses Association, 1967).

55   Louis Aubrey Wood, *A History of the Farmers' Movements in Canada, the Origins and Development of Agrarian Protest 1872-1924* (1924; Toronto: University of Toronto Press, 1975); Harald S. Patton, *Grain Growers' Cooperation in Western Canada* (Cambridge: Harvard University Press, 1928); Paul F. Sharp, *The Agrarian Revolt in Western Canada: A Survey Showing American Parallels* (Minneapolis: University of Minnesota Press, 1921); W.L. Morton, *The Progressive Party in Canada* (Toronto: University of Toronto Press, 1950).

56   L.J. Wilson, "Educating the Saskatchewan Farmer: The Educational Work of the Saskatchewan Grain Growers' Association," *Saskatchewan History* 31, no. 1 (Winter 1978): 20-33.

57   R.G. Marchildon, "Improving the Quality of Life in Rural Saskatchewan: Some Activities of the Women's Section of the Saskatchewan Grain Growers, 1913-1920," in D.C. Jones and Ian MacPherson, eds., *Building Beyond the Homestead* (Calgary: University of Calgary Press, 1985), 97.

58   Strong-Boag, "Pulling in Double Harness," 32-52.

59   Georgina Taylor, "'Should I Drown Myself Now or Later?': The Isolation of Rural Women in Saskatchewan and their Participation in the Homemakers' Clubs, the Farm Movement and the Co-operative Commonwealth Federation, 1910-1967," in Kathleen Storrie, ed., *Women: Isolation and Bonding — The Ecology of Gender* (Toronto: Methuen Publications, 1987), 79-100; Georgina Taylor, "Equals and Partners: An Examination of How Saskatchewan Women Reconciled Their Political Activities For the CCF With Traditional Roles For Women" (MA thesis, University of Saskatchewan, 1983); and Aileen C. Moffatt, "'where the emphasis on sex was less': The Women's Section of the

Taylor and Moffatt found that in the interwar period rural women did not shy away from accepting public responsibilities. On the contrary, rural and farm women agitated for political, social and economic reforms that would benefit their various communities.

During the second or separate spheres/women's culture stage, historians of Saskatchewan women's lives began publishing analytic studies instead of narratives of "great" women or events, stage one history. Further, the every day life of ordinary women became a central issue in scholarly debates.[60] Historians have also turned to Saskatchewan labour history and the history of education in recent years in order to further interpret Saskatchewan women's experiences.[61] These types of studies overlap the third stage of Saskatchewan women's history where women's diversity is featured. Some scholars are now testing more sophisticated methodological approaches and the field of study has widened to include more than just white English-speaking women. Yet, historians have not generally incorporated cultural studies, gender studies or postmodern methods into historical scholarship of Saskatchewan women. Largely influenced by the work of cultural historians and informed by discourse theory borrowed from literary criticism, feminist historians in other regions now examine hierarchies of power and the social construction of gender.[62] Instead of writing women's history as part of a distinct separate sphere, feminist historians utilize techniques which examine, for example, the shifting boundaries of so-called masculine and feminine spheres. In Canadian scholarship, the best example of this approach is Joy Parr's 1990 study, *The Gender of Breadwinners.*[63] This is history with a wide vision — a cultural history — examining varying dimensions

Canadian Council of Agriculture" (MA thesis, University of Saskatchewan, 1990). On the Homemakers' Clubs, also see: Saskatchewan Women's Institutes, *Legacy; A History of Saskatchewan Homemakers' Clubs and Women's Institutes 1911-1988* (Regina: Focus Publishing, 1988);

60   Mary Kinnear, "'Do you want your daughter to marry a farmer?': Women's Work on the Farm 1922," in Donald Akenson, ed., *Canadian Papers in Rural History* 6 (Gananoque, ON: Langdale Press, 1986), 137-53; Theresa Healy, "Prayers, Pamphlets and Protest: Women and Relief in Saskatoon 1929-1939" (MA thesis, University of Saskatchewan, 1989); Jacqueline Bliss, "Seamless Lives: Pioneer Women of Saskatoon 1883-1903," *Saskatchewan History* 43, no. 3 (Autumn 1991): 84-100; Angela E. Davis, "'Country Homemakers': The Daily Lives of Prairie Women as Seen Through the Women's Page of the *Grain Growers' Guide* 1908-1928," in Donald H. Akenson, ed., *Canadian Papers in Rural History* 8 (Gananoque, ON: Langdale Press, 1992), 163-74; Angela E. Davis, "'Valiant Servants': Women and Technology on the Canadian Prairies 1910-1940," *Manitoba History* 25 (Spring 1993): 33-42.

61   Christine Smillie, "The Invisible Workforce: Women Workers in Saskatchewan From 1905 to World War II," *Saskatchewan History* 39, no. 2 (Spring 1986): 62-78; Apolonja Maria Kojder, "The Saskatoon Women Teacher's Association: A Demand for Recognition," *Saskatchewan History* 30, no. 2 (Spring 1977): 63-74; Sheilah Steer, "The Beliefs of Violet McNaughton: Adult Educator 1909-1929," (MCE thesis, University of Saskatchewan, 1979); Michael Hayden, "Women and the University of Saskatchewan: Patterns of a Problem," *Saskatchewan History* 40, no. 2 (Spring 1987): 72-82; Kerrie Strathy, "Saskatchewan Women's Institutes: The Rural Woman's University 1911-1987," (MCE thesis, University of Saskatchewan, 1987); Irene Poelzer, *Saskatchewan Women Teachers 1905-1920; Their Contributions* (Saskatoon: Lindenblatt and Hamonic Publishing Ltd., 1990).

62   Two excellent examples of how new methodological approaches are being applied in Canadian women's history are: Franca Iacovetta and Mariana Valverde, eds., *Gender Conflicts: New Essays in Women's History* (Toronto: University of Toronto Press, 1992); and Karen Dubinsky, *Improper Advances: Rape and Heterosexual Conflict in Ontario, 1880-1929* (Chicago: University of Chicago Press, 1993).

63   Joy Parr, *The Gender of Breadwinners: Women, Men and Change in Two Industrial Towns 1880-1950* (Toronto: University of Toronto Press, 1990). In this study of two Ontario towns, Parr examines gender and class relationships as historical processes. She suggests social position is determined through a "multiplicity of elements" which "are changeable rather than fixed" (9).

and definitions of public and private. Parr's analysis provides a valuable model previously lacking in historical scholarship of Saskatchewan women.

The difficulty in writing third or diversity stage history is how to recognize differences among women yet still find similarities that unite them. In order to "do" women's history there must be unifying features that connect individual subjects. Yet, it is impossible to write a single history for all women because women's experiences, situations and interpretations are various and complex. Women are not all alike. Saskatchewan's large population of women immigrants, for example, often feel "doubly disadvantaged" because of gender and race.[64] Women's diversity thus becomes problematic to those searching for commonality and homogeneity. The solution may be to account for cultures rather than culture, to recognize that women belong to a series of cultures and communities that are interconnected in the creation of individual and group identity.

If historians are to recover the varied experiences of Saskatchewan's women, they can no longer rely only on traditional archival materials as historical evidence. For example, Saskatchewan has a rich material culture that opens the doors to new historical interpretations. Unfortunately, historians have in the past been quick to assume historical artifacts such as household technology, farm implements or various modes of transportation, are the property of museumologists, anthropologists or archaeologists. In fact, they are as much, if not more, the historian's tools. Instead of sequestering themselves in archives, historians need to develop and promote links among the various communities of scholars so they might have the benefit of one another's experience and expertise.

Historians of Saskatchewan women must also begin to collect their own evidence and artifacts. Scholars should talk to people, collect oral histories, read family and community histories, and look at how and where people lived. Some enterprising Saskatchewan women and their families have published their own historical narratives. Included are Rose Seaman McLaughlin's *Grainbuyer's Wife*, and Edith Hewson's *We Swept the Cornflakes Out the Door*.[65] These volumes provide a unique perspective on Saskatchewan women's lives. Historians can learn much from these books based on actual lived experience. They provide excellent primary material for more academic, analytic and historical studies of Saskatchewan women.

Opportunities for original scholarship in Saskatchewan women's history are legion. Saskatchewan has a diverse ethnic heritage which remains largely unexamined. Although ethnic history has recently become more popular in Saskatchewan, it is still in its preliminary stages. In particular, very little is known about how ethnicity and gender interact in Saskatchewan. There is also an appalling lack of Native women's history published. Popular culture — especially creative in rural situations — too awaits investigation. Many avenues of research are open for discovery here: sports, music, folk art, travelling theatre and chautauqua, to name only a few. Historical studies of sexuality in Saskatchewan are nonexistent. There are

---

64   Immigrant Women of Saskatchewan, *Doubly Disadvantaged: The Women Who Immigrate to Canada* (Saskatoon: Immigrant Women of Saskatchewan, 1985); Angela W. Djao and Roxana Ng, "Structured Isolation: Immigrant Women in Saskatchewan," in Storrie, *Women: Isolation and Bonding*, 141-58.

65   Rose Seaman McLaughlin, *Grainbuyer's Wife* (Regina: Focus Publishing, 1989); Edith Hewson, *We Swept the Cornflakes Out the Door* (Saskatoon: Modern Press, 1980).

no gay or lesbian histories. Studies of family relationships should also be undertaken. In short, most of Saskatchewan women's history is yet to be explored.

Perhaps the most important contribution historians of Saskatchewan women can make is to draw parallels and make connections to regional, national and international developments. History cannot be written or understood in an intellectual vacuum. It is necessary to trace the influence of wider social, cultural, economic and political movements on local situations. Then, Saskatchewan women's history will be valuable not only for its own sake, but for what it can offer to women's history in an international context.

THE INTERPLAY OF ETHNICITY AND GENDER: SWEDISH WOMEN IN SOUTHEASTERN SASKATCHEWAN

Lesley Erickson

In 1893 Karen Olson, with her husband and children, arrived in Stockholm, Saskatchewan. While her husband worked as a tailor in Whitewood, Saskatchewan, she and her eleven children farmed their homestead — bringing in extra money by making butter, packing it into thirty-five pound tubs, and selling it in Whitewood for ten cents a pound.[1] Like many Swedish women who farmed in Saskatchewan between 1880 and 1940, Olson experienced the loneliness of being separated from her husband. She farmed alone with her children, and she engaged in market-based activities to earn extra cash. Contrary to what she had known in Sweden, Olson now had a unique opportunity to make decisions in the family and to expand her role in the Swedish-Canadian community. Unlike the case for other ethnic groups, the Swedish clergy and males in the community made few attempts to use the church as a form of social control over the endeavours of Swedish women like Olson. Consequently, Swedish women became active participants in the religious, social and economic development of their communities in Saskatchewan, contributing to the formation of a distinct prairie society. Swedish women's experiences in Saskatchewan demonstrate the extent to which ethnic women's gender and ethnicity intertwine to define their role in the family, community and Saskatchewan society.

In 1891, Swedes represented only 3.1 percent of the population of southern Saskatchewan. Swedish women remained a minority throughout the period of investigation: in 1931 there were only 2,570 women as compared to 5,010 men in Saskatchewan.[2] It is interesting, therefore, that women played such an influential role in the development of their communities. This essay focusses on Swedish women who settled in the Stockholm, Percival, and to a lesser extent, the Dubuc districts in south-eastern Saskatchewan. These Swedish communities were homogeneous and easily identifiable. To assess the interplay of gender and ethnicity in the lives of the women of these communities, Carol K. Coburn's method has been adopted.[3] Coburn studies the lives of ethnic women by departmentalizing their lives into the "networks" of church, school, family and the outside world. As Coburn argues, this method makes it possible for historians to determine how these networks transmitted education and culture throughout a woman's life cycle and across generations. Furthermore, her theoretical framework "does not assume a dichotomy between public (male) and

---

1   Gladys M. Halliwell and Zetta Persson, *Three Score and Ten: A Story of the Swedish Settlement of Stockholm and District* (Yorkton: Redeemer's Voice Press, 1959), 8.

2   Helge Nelson, *The Swedes and the Swedish Settlements in North America* (New York: Arno Press, 1979), 356, 409.

3   Coburn, an American historian, uses an adaptation of Barbara Finkelstein's theory of "networks of association" to study the role of German Lutheran-Missouri Synod women in Block, Kansas. Although Coburn contends that dividing women's activities into the areas of church, school, family and the outside world is ideally suited for women within a patriarchal structure, the four networks serve to define the parameters of most rural women's lives.

private (female) spheres … because for many women a clear separation does not and never has existed."[4] Discussing Swedish women's lives in terms of their relationship with their church, school, family and their contacts with the world outside the ethnic enclave reveals formal as well as informal ways Swedish women functioned in and adapted to the Saskatchewan environment.[5]

The majority of Swedish women who settled in southeastern Saskatchewan came directly from Sweden rather than via the United States. The first Swedish immigrants settled at Stockholm, north of the Qu'Appelle River, in 1886. In time, the Stockholm settlement expanded to include three townships and fifty-four sections. In the early 1890s Swedes from Stockholm moved to Percival and established a new Swedish community alongside the Canadian Pacific Railway (CPR) between Whitewood and Broadview. Dubuc, approximately ten miles west of Stockholm, was also an outgrowth of the Stockholm colony. Most Swedish women did not accompany their husbands, but followed a few years after their husbands had filed on homesteads. This practice enabled husbands to gain employment in Canada, to save money for their family's passage, and to build a shelter on the land before sending for their families. For instance, Mrs. P.O. Eckstrand and her children arrived in Dubuc in 1911, two years after her husband.[6] Likewise, Martin Nelson immigrated from Sweden to Percival in 1911, where he worked on an elevator construction gang until he raised enough money to support his family's passage to Canada in 1913.[7]

To reach Stockholm, Dubuc and Percival, Swedish women and their children followed various migration routes determined by the district in which their husbands had set up the family farm. The route by which most Swedish women travelled to reach Stockholm was long and tedious. Departing from Ostersand, Sweden, women sailed to Hull, England, and then caught the train heading for Liverpool, the common point of departure for immigrants heading to North America. More often than not, Swedes, like many immigrants, crossed the Atlantic Ocean in converted cattle boats. Arriving finally in New York, they travelled by river boat to Duluth, Minnesota, and from there took the train to Winnipeg. If the Swedish woman was travelling alone, a Swedish immigrant agent directed her to her husband's homestead.[8] The migration pattern to Percival was somewhat different, perhaps because the district lacked an immigrant agent. In an article "Percival Hamlet," Meda Johnson recalled that settlers came to Percival by various modes of transportation: first by ship, then by train and wagon. To reach Percival, women generally followed a straight line route from Halifax to Montreal, and then to Winnipeg.[9] In "Percival School District no. 2101," a Percival School student in 1955 claimed that Swedish

---

4   Carol K. Coburn, "Ethnicity, Religion, and Gender: The Women of Block, Kansas, 1868-1940," *Great Plains Quarterly* 8 (Fall 1988): 222.

5   Ibid., 223. This study retains Coburn's four original networks — family, church, school and outside world — because these networks closely reflect Swedish women's (and most rural women's) interactions with the wider ethnic community.

6   Dubuc and Community 75th-Anniversary History Committee, co-ordinated by Linda Unger, *Dubuc: From Here to Yesterday: Dubuc 1905-1980* (Yorkton: Dowie Quick Print Ltd., [1980]), 10.

7   Broadview History Society, *Oakshela, Broadview, Percival, 1882-1982: Centennial Tribute* (Broadview: Broadview History Society, 1982), 380.

8   Halliwell and Persson, *Three Score and Ten*, 8.

9   Meda Johnson, "Percival Hamlet," in Cliff Ashfield, ed., *Whitewood and Area: 1882-1992*, vol. 1, (Regina: Brigdens Printers and Publishers, 1992), 86.

women and their families, upon arriving in Whitewood, stayed in an immigrant house until their husbands came to meet them.[10]

Once Swedish women were settled on the family farm, and prior to the establishment of the local church and school, the family was their only sphere of activity. Danielle Juteau-Lee and Barbara Roberts argue, it is "in the family [that] the double bind of 'ethnicity' and femininity may be keenly experienced."[11] The following examples will illustrate, however, that Swedish women did not experience a "bind," but rather an expansion of their role in the family and in the Saskatchewan community. As Roberto Perin argues in "Writing About Ethnicity," immigrants do not carry their ancestral culture with them and transplant it in the new land so that it survives unaltered through successive generations. Rather, ethnic intellectuals are often dismayed by the discrepancies between their local culture and that of the country of origin.[12] Consequently, studying Swedish women's role in the family reveals how women adapted and how their role changed in the new environment of Saskatchewan.

Upon coming to Saskatchewan, Swedish women of all classes gained a degree of independence that would have been uncommon in their homeland. Because Swedish men tended to be artisans as well as farmers, and since they often lacked the funds required to farm successfully in Saskatchewan, they hired themselves out as labourers or practiced their trade in rural towns. This phenomenon, which made women the temporary head of the household, was not limited to the artisan or farming classes. For instance, Mrs. C.O. Hofstrand, her husband, and a domestic servant arrived in Stockholm in 1888. While her husband, a high school teacher in Sweden, studied, preached, and worked as assistant editor to a Swedish language newspaper in Winnipeg, she farmed in Stockholm. In 1913, her husband again left the farm as vice-consul for Sweden.[13] Likewise, in Percival, Mrs. Magnus Strandlund, who immigrated in 1909, sold goat's milk and farmed while her husband helped to grade the Number One Highway.[14]

In the early years of settlement at Percival, the absence of husbands from the homestead was more prevalent than in Stockholm because of the economic nature of the community. Unlike Stockholm or Dubuc, the CPR ran through the Percival district and the grain elevator became the economic centre of the community. When the railway was relocated in 1897 Swedish men worked on Co-operative Elevator Company construction gangs and on the CPR construction crews, leaving their wives and children on the farm to fulfill the requirements of the Dominion Lands Act (1872).[15] As they had no children, both Mr. and Mrs. Lars Polson worked: Lars worked on bridge-building gangs for the CPR; and Christina cooked for the crew.[16] Considering

10   Saskatchewan Archives Board (SAB), Anonymous, "Percival School District no. 2101," handwritten, microfilm, 1955, 2.

11   Danielle Juteau-Lee and Barbara Roberts, "Ethnicity and Femininity: d'après nos experiences," *Canadian Ethnic Studies* 13 (1981): 4.

12   Roberto Perin, "Writing About Ethnicity," in John Schultz, ed., *Writing About Canada: A Handbook for Modern Canadian History* (Scarborough: Prentice-Hall Canada Inc., 1990), 203.

13   Halliwell and Persson, *Three Score and Ten*, 41.

14   Broadview History Society, *Oakshela, Broadview, Percival*, 418.

15   Johnson, "Percival Hamlet," 88.

16   Broadview History Society, *Oakshela, Broadview, Percival*, 396.

that most husbands of Swedish women were artisans and labourers who worked at odd jobs to earn money, the influence of these women over their families, and their ability to influence the decision-making process in the family were significant.

Frances Swyripa in *Wedded to the Cause: Ukrainian-Canadian Women and Ethnic Identity, 1891-1991* agrees that periodic male absence from the homestead may have "challenged traditional gender roles and relationships in Canada," although substantial evidence is not available in the case of Ukrainian women.[17] That male absenteeism from the farm did challenge traditional gender roles among the Swedes in Saskatchewan is without doubt, for the situation was the reverse from that experienced by many Swedish women in the homeland. In Sweden, rural farm women and their daughters traditionally spent summers in the hills, caring for cattle and goats and all other aspects of dairy production. While the females were in the hills, the males remained on the farmstead and were responsible for grain production.[18] Accustomed to the isolation and loneliness of living in the hills, Swedish women, when they came to Saskatchewan, had to adapt to a new scenario which increased their control over their children's development and the power structure in the family.

In *Such Hard Working People: Italian Immigrants in Postwar Toronto*, Franca Iacovetta notes the importance of power relationships in the family and the central role that women often played in influencing the decision-making process in the home. Iacovetta argues that although Italian women assumed a submissive role in the public sphere, in the private sphere they could wield influence over their families through informal means of persuasion. Likewise, Italian men, who might boast of their authority in public, would share decision making in the family as a matter of course.[19] Thelma Hofstrand Foster's novel *Wild Daisies* provides evidence that the ability of Swedish women to make decisions within the family was not confined to the homestead years. In fact, the decision-making process was complex in nature, depending on a woman's age and marital status. In *Wild Daisies*, Foster, through the character of Anna Sandell, relates her experiences growing up Swedish and female in Saskatchewan in the 1920s and 1930s. Told from a female perspective, the novel is an invaluable source for determining power relationships in the Swedish family, a topic not commonly found in primary sources or dealt with as extensively as does Foster. For instance, upon the death of Anna's father in 1925, Foster writes:

> Daniel's death brought many changes into the lives of Anna and her mother. They were to come and live at the manse: this was Grandma's decision. Esther [Anna's mother], who rose from her sick-bed weak and irresolute, had no say in the matter at all.[20]

Once Esther Sandell was widowed she no longer filled the role of mother to Anna, but again became the daughter who could be ruled by her mother's iron will. When Esther remarried she resumed a position of power in the family — she, and not her

17   Frances Swyripa, *Wedded to the Cause: Ukrainian-Canadian Women and Ethnic Identity, 1891-1991* (Toronto: University of Toronto Press, 1993), 252.

18   Halliwell and Persson, *Three Score and Ten*, 10. Living in the hills of Sweden gave many women a keen knowledge of the medicinal value of herbs, barks and roots, which they used to good effect in Saskatchewan.

19   Franca Iacovetta, *Such Hardworking People: Italian Immigrants in Postwar Toronto* (Montreal and Kingston: McGill-Queen's University Press, 1992), 82-83.

20   Thelma Hofstrand Foster, *A Novel: Wild Daisies* (Saskatoon: Modern Press, 1977), 9.

new husband, made the decision to sell the land she inherited upon her former husband's death.

Acknowledging that ethnic women were not always passive forces in the family makes their contributions to maintaining ethnic identity in the family more significant. For instance, Juteau-Lee and Roberts pinpoint the essential connection between ethnicity, gender and the importance of women's activities in the family. They argue that much of what we perceive as being "ethnic" is based on activities traditionally done by women: language spoken in the home, food eaten, type of clothing worn, character of family life, costumes, festivals, education or training activities outside the normal school hours to teach the practices of the group.[21] And indeed, ethnic groups often embrace symbols of their ethnicity that acknowledge this fact. In the Ukrainian community, for instance, Swyripa argues that the peasant immigrant pioneer as *baba*, the old woman or grandmother, came to symbolize customs and cultural artifacts identified with Ukrainianness, especially food preparation and handicrafts — activities traditionally associated with women.[22]

In the Swedish settlements in southeastern Saskatchewan women strove to maintain the ethnic traditions of the homeland in the family and the community. Weddings and holiday celebrations became more elaborate as ties with the homeland became more tenuous.[23] The congregation of New Stockholm Mission Covenant Church, for instance, celebrated the first wedding in the colony on 1 February 1899. Sarah Johanson wore a white lace-trimmed cashmere dress with a high collar, lily-point sleeves, and a veil decorated with orange blossoms. Following the wedding ceremony the women of the congregation organized a reception — the highlight of which was a Swedish high tea.[24] In Percival, Olaf Pearson married Lena Strandlund in the Lutheran church on 7 June 1909. Prepared by the ladies of the church, the wedding celebration lasted for two days: the first day for the adults and the second day for the children.[25]

Women were also responsible for the dishes and feasts that were so much a part of the celebration of Christmas. Christmas Eve began with a thorough housecleaning and ended with a supper of rice porridge, *lutefisk*, and pudding made with fruit juice and flour. As the Swedish communities in Saskatchewan became more entrenched, Christmas Eve dinners became more elaborate and Swedes adopted unfamiliar traditions such as gift giving. On Christmas morning women prepared an early breakfast of porridge, thin bread, and *Mes Ost* (a dark cheese). The family then went to the six o'clock church service. After the service, the family returned home to enjoy another, more elaborate, breakfast. The community again convened in the local church to celebrate the eleven o'clock church service.[26] Obviously, what might have been an enjoyable experience for men and children, was mostly hard work for Swedish women.

Swedish women maintained ethnic traditions in the home and occasionally

---

21 Juteau-Lee and Roberts, "Ethnicity and Femininity," 5.

22 Swyripa, *Wedded to the Cause*, 248.

23 Juteau-Lee and Roberts, "Ethnicity and Femininity," 5.

24 Halliwell and Persson, *Three Score and Ten*, 25.

25 Broadview History Society, *Oakshela, Broadview, Percival*, 391.

26 Halliwell and Persson, *Three Score and Ten*, 71.

capitalized on their skills to make an economic contribution to the community. For instance, in 1936, women of the Scandia school district in the Stockholm region entered a CPR contest that was organized to promote interest in the handicrafts of the Old World. The Scandia school district women won second place for their display of handicrafts and foods and they used the money to buy a purebred Hereford bull for the community.[27]

Prior to the creation of schools at Stockholm, Dubuc and Percival, many Swedish women taught their children at home. Attending public schools in Sweden had given Swedes a high level of education that they hoped to maintain in the new country. Alma Wickberg, who, unlike her husband, had completed her public school education, strove to educate her children. She taught Swedish in her home as a supplement to the Swedish learned in the church and Sunday School and she was instrumental in establishing East Mount School in 1907.[28] Foster reiterates this point in *Wild Daisies*, implying that Swedish women, more so than men, had an interest in their children's education. In the novel, Anna's mother used the money she earned from selling her chickens to buy papers that would keep the family informed: *The Country Guide, Western Producer, Family Herald, Free Press*, and *Saskatchewan Farmer.*[29] Surprisingly, Foster includes neither Swedish newspapers nor women's journals in this list. Although speculative at most, this exclusion could indicate that Swedish women were concerned with easing their husband's and their children's transition into Canadian society.

In the Swedish family in Saskatchewan mothers also demonstrated a marked interest in teaching their children the religion of the homeland. Olaf Olson claims that his mother combined education with religion: she taught the children and her husband how to read Swedish by using the Bible as a textbook.[30] The portrait that Foster paints of religious education in the Swedish home in Saskatchewan is compatible with Olson's. For instance, in the Sandell family Anna's mother, not her father, taught her the evening prayer in Swedish: "These words and her mother's kiss signalled a peaceful night and complete trust in Someone all-powerful."[31]

Sociologists often offer statistics concerning language maintenance in the home as an indication of the degree to which ethnic groups have been assimilated into Canadian society. In "Assimilation in the Bloc Settlements of North Central Saskatchewan," for instance, Alan Anderson notes the swiftness by which Swedes adopted English as the language spoken in the home. While only 8 percent of first-generation immigrants spoke English, 44 percent of second-generation Swedes did, while almost all third-generation Swedes, 97 percent, could speak English.[32] Although statistics are useful for generalizing the experiences of ethnic groups, their usefulness for understanding the realities of ethnic women's lives is limited. Statistics cannot tell the reader, for instance, that rural immigrant women, isolated on farms, did not have the

---

27   Ibid., 170.

28   SAB, Olaf Olson, "And So It Happened: The Olson History," 1987, unpublished typescript, 4, 32, 25.

29   Foster, *Wild Daisies*, 92.

30   SAB, Olson, "And So It Happened," 31.

31   Foster, *Wild Daisies*, 21.

32   Alan Anderson, "Assimilation in the Bloc Settlements of North Central Saskatchewan: A Comparative Study of Identity Change among Seven Ethnic Religious Groups in a Canadian Prairie Region" (PhD dissertation, University of Saskatchewan, 1972), 230, 232.

same access as did men to the "informal educational networks" necessary to learn English.

In the Swedish immigrant family in Saskatchewan a lag existed between the rates by which men and women learned English. My father, Gary Erickson, whose grandfather immigrated to Percival in the late nineteenth century, indicated that when he was a child in the 1950s the women in the household, including his sister, always spoke Swedish, whereas the men tended to speak English. In a letter to his sister Maria in Sweden, Neils Persson Dahl writes: "John [his son] has been away working for two months partly for to learn to work here and to learning something of the language."[33] Because women remained on the farm and were responsible for the care of children it is, therefore, not unusual that children could speak little or no English upon entering the public school system. When Glen Olson started at Broadview School in 1948 he could not speak one word of English, although his mother had immigrated to Canada in 1927.[34] But when children entered school, it often gave Swedish women the opportunity to learn the language. Mrs. Nels Peter Jacobson, who came to Stockholm in 1888, studied English at home with her children when they began to attend Svea School in 1891.[35] Swedish men and women adapted to the dominant society in Saskatchewan at different rates; it is one of the many instances in which their gender and their ethnicity determined their role in the family and the larger Swedish community.

First-generation Swedish women, like most immigrant women in Saskatchewan, performed both indoor and outdoor labour in the homesteading years. Mrs. H. Closson, who settled with her husband in Dubuc in 1909, remembers: "There were many hardships but I preferred Canada to the Old Country. We had nothing to start with. I used to work in the fields helping my husband with oxen and horses. We also used a small seeder."[36] The "we" in this statement is telling for it shows that Closson recognized the value of her labour and viewed the homesteading experience as a joint economic venture. As Roberto Perin notes in "Writing About Ethnicity," immigrant families were often coherent economic units in which wives and children played an integral and valued part.[37] Analysis of Foster's Wild Daisies suggests that even when a family was well established, women still did outdoor work traditionally associated with men if the situation was warranted. In the novel, Anna cares for the livestock and helps her stepfather with the stooking and planting. Her stepfather requires her labour because her siblings were, as yet, too young to work outdoors. A husband's illness or death would also necessitate women working and running the farm. For example, in the 1930s, when Hans Hanson's health began to fail, his wife Esther did most of the outdoor work because her sons were too small. When Hans died in 1947, Esther, with the aid of her sons, continued to farm.[38]

---

33   SAB, Neils Persson Dahl to Maria, Ohlen, Nov. 6, 189? [date illegible]. In *Wedded to the Cause* (21), Swyripa notes a similar situation in the rural Ukrainian community. Because women had fewer contacts with the "English world," the Ukrainian elite perceived them to be more backward than men, in need of greater "modernization" and emancipation.

34   Broadview History Society, *Oakshela, Broadview, Percival*, 344.

35   Halliwell and Persson, *Three Score and Ten*, 25.

36   SAB, Mrs. H. Closson, Reminiscence for the Dubuc History Committee, handwritten, photocopy, 2.

37   Perin, "Writing About Ethnicity," 212.

38   Broadview History Society, *Oakshela, Broadview, Percival*, 344.

Women's indoor labour included cooking, spinning wool and sewing clothing. In some instances Swedish families brought only women's household utensils from the homeland. Mr. and Mrs. Mikael Strandlund's son recalls:

> We just had to have with us the copper coffee grinder, the big copper kettle that mom used for making cheese and *Mes Ost*, the spinning wheel and wool carders, and the sewing machine. Dad snuck in a few tools such as a hand saw, a plane, a hammer and an axe. These things are a must in the new land where our money was scarce as hens' teeth.[39]

While men and women made shoes, women alone were responsible for making cheese, thinbread and butter. Mrs. Isakson, who arrived in Stockholm in 1902, in one year made 1,200 pounds of butter that she sold at thirty-five to forty cents a pound.[40] In the first decades of Stockholm's development, the Swedes were determined to create a replica of the homeland through economic self-sufficiency. In this scenario Swedish women's earnings from the sale of butter and livestock helped to make the community's ideal a reality.

Another equally important aspect of Swedish women's work in the family setting was their "reproductive" and nurturing labour: childbearing, midwifery and treating ailments. A careful analysis of local histories reveals that Swedish women had anywhere from four to fourteen children. In *Wild Daisies*, Esther delivers all of her children except her last (in 1929 a physician in Estevan delivered the newborn) with the aid of midwives. Most Swedish women at some point in their lives acted as midwives to their relatives and neighbours although some women in the communities specialized in midwifery. Alexandra Svea Stenberg remembers: "Mother was an amateur nurse, [who] was called up when anyone [was] sick. She acted as Maternity nurse to over 600 babies, often and mostly without Doctors present."[41] Home remedies included chokecherry syrup made from the strained liquid of boiled bark, and linseed and bread poultices for boils and swells. Women frequently extended their healing knowledge to their communities' livestock. Mrs. Eric Wickberg, for instance, delivered many calves and was known to have set the leg of a colt.[42]

The quantity and quality of the work that Swedish girls performed reflected the girls' ages and the "rights of passage" through which they had passed. Carol K. Coburn refers to this same phenomenon among German Lutheran women. In the life cycle of the German Lutheran-Missouri Synod woman, Confirmation was the point in a girl's life after which she could participate in Holy Communion, leave school to do labour as a domestic servant, or take on a larger workload in the home.[43] In *Wild Daisies*, Foster makes frequent references to the work required of Swedish girls at a certain age. At the age of ten, Anna's mother taught her to hemstich, knit mittens and embroider lazy daisies; Anna was then expected to do her share of the work for the Ladies Aid. At the age of twelve, Anna became responsible for helping her mother with indoor tasks. During the summer, and following her completion of school, she hired herself out as a domestic servant to other families in the

---

39   Ibid., 419.

40   Halliwell and Persson, *Three Score and Ten*, 75.

41   SAB, Alexandra Svea Stenberg, Reminiscence for the Dubuc History Committee, handwritten, photocopy, 3.

42   Halliwell and Persson, *Three Score and Ten*, 70.

43   Coburn, "Ethnicity, Religion, and Gender," 226.

community.[44] In the Percival district girls tended to seek employment in Broadview, Percival, or on a neighbour's farm after the completion of grade eight or ten.[45]

Outside of the family, Swedish women displayed a marked interest in the establishment and development of the local church. In "Writing About Ethnicity," Perin notes that many immigrants built their local community church as a symbol of their "arrival." But he also acknowledges that it is not always clear what the church symbolized. Did immigrants hasten to establish churches, for instance, because of their "innate religiosity"?[46] In the case of the Swedish women at Dubuc, Stockholm and Percival the church fulfilled their immediate need for a sense of belonging. Involvement in church organizations also gave Swedish women access to informal educational networks that broke down rural isolation. As Alan Anderson suggests, the church may have symbolized or meant more for Swedish women than it did for Swedish men who, unlike women, had wider access to activities and organizations outside of the local community. In "Assimilation in the Bloc Settlements," Anderson notes the activity of Swedish women in the church as compared to the inactivity of men. He claims that unlike French, Ukrainian, Polish and Doukhobor immigrants, Swedish women attended church more often then men. Furthermore, 88.1 percent of Scandinavian women participated in ethnic-orientated voluntary associations as opposed to no men, which is, again, opposite to other ethnic communities.[47] Because Swedish men showed a relatively casual attitude towards the church, they did not use the church as an instrument of social control over women to the extent that men in other ethnic groups did. Consequently, Swedish women display a marked ability to influence the decision-making process in religious affairs to an extent uncommon in other rural ethnic communities.

When it came to establishing a local church at Stockholm, Swedish women made their voices heard. On 30 June 1888 Swedish immigrants at Stockholm met with the intention to establish a church called the Scandinavian Christian Brotherhood. The women present at the meeting objected because they felt that the men were taking the creation of the community's church too lightly. The women were interested in establishing a Scandinavian Mission Church on the Winnipeg model. Reaching a stalemate, the potential congregation called another meeting for 20 October 1888. In October, the women approved the adoption of the following doctrines and tenets:

1. The Bible is the only authentic authority for moral behaviour.

2. The congregation to labour for God's Kingdom and to live according to God's Word.

3. Each person to experience conversion and to be baptized before becoming a member of the church.

4. New members to be accepted at regular meetings and open confession of faith.

5. Members' names to be inscribed in the church membership book, and members thereafter to make annual contributions for the support of church work.

---

44   Foster, *Wild Daisies*, 11, 49.

45   Broadview History Society, *Oakshela, Broadview, Percival*, 177.

46   Perin, "Writing About Ethnicity," 213.

47   Anderson, "Assimilation in the Bloc Settlements," 234.

6. Stewards to be elected for the term of one year, and a minister to be elected by a two-thirds' majority vote.[48]

The Swedish Mission Covenant Church was established in 1888 with C.O. Hofstrand acting as the first minister. With less controversy, Swedish Lutherans at Stockholm built their own church in 1889.[49] The Swedish population at Percival was less divided; immigrants organized only one church, Immanuel Evangelical Lutheran Church, on 8 June 1897. Because the Percival congregation consisted of Swedish migrants from Stockholm, the New Stockholm Lutheran Church was quick to give the Percival group letters of transfer.[50]

The congregation to which a Swedish woman belonged affected the extent to which the church acted as an agent of social control over her behaviour. In *Wild Daisies*, Foster illustrates some of the differences between the Swedish Mission Covenant and Lutheran churches and the implications that these differences had on Swedish women's lives. One dialogue in the novel suggests that the relationship between the two congregations was anything but amicable:

> "Yes, Carl is a good worker," Pell was saying. "It is too bad he is just a heathen." "He goes to the big church," Mama defended. The big church was the Lutheran church to the West [probably New Stockholm Lutheran Church]. The Sandells had attended it on special occasions. Anna loved its beautiful stained-glass windows and deep-toned bell. The Mission Friends looked upon it as too rich, its congregation too worldly. "I am afraid the women go there to show off their immodest clothes and painted faces," murmured Mrs. Pell.[51]

As Mrs. Pell's exclamation suggests, it is evident that the Swedish community saw the appearance and behaviour of their female members as a reflection of the differing moral codes of their particular congregation. Perhaps more significant, however, is that members of the Swedish Mission Church, unlike Swedish Lutherans, strongly bound their ethnicity to their religion. Swedish women of the Mission Church were therefore instrumental in establishing a church that would act as a safety valve against assimilation. The majority of Swedish women in southeastern Saskatchewan, however, belonged to the Lutheran faith which provided them with a variety of outlets for their energies as well as access to informal networks of education.

Swedish Lutheran women interacted with and were involved in the activities of their local church in a variety of ways. The Percival Church School, for instance, was established in 1911. This school, designed for adults, gave Swedish farm women the opportunity to study Swedish, English, Math, History, Christianity and Music.[52] A list of the organists at the Immanuel Evangelical Lutheran Church in Percival also indicates that throughout the congregation's history all of its organists were women.[53] Because Swedish society highly valued music, this was often a position of prestige. More importantly, playing the organ increased second- and third-generation Swedish girls' contacts with the world outside of their ethnic enclaves. The first organist at the

---

48   Halliwell and Persson, *Three Score and Ten*, 43, 80.

49   Ibid., 80, 83.

50   Broadview History Society, *Oakshela, Broadview, Percival*, 122.

51   Foster, *Wild Daisies*, 23.

52   Meda Johnson, "The Immanuel Evangelical Lutheran Church," in Ashfield, *Whitewood and Area*, 96.

53   Ibid., 97.

New Stockholm Lutheran Church took music lessons in Whitewood, at that time the most cosmopolitan centre in southeastern Saskatchewan: "It came to be a saying that one should know eleven languages to do business in Whitewood."[54] Swedish women also volunteered their time to teach Sunday School and lead the church choir.

Swedish females, like their counterparts in other ethnic communities, were active in various church organizations. Each of the congregations in Percival, Dubuc and Stockholm had an affiliated Ladies Aid. On 7 January 1895, at the annual congregational meeting at New Stockholm Evangelical Lutheran Church, members passed a resolution urging the women of the congregation to organize a Ladies Aid Society. In 1895 alone, the Ladies Aid met thirty-six times. For the first thirty-five years the Ladies Aid donated the money it raised to building funds that contributed to the church's and community's development. Its first project, however, was to buy an organ for the church which it presented to the congregation on 27 June 1897.[55] In Percival the activities of the Ladies Aid are less well known. The 1936 records for the Immanuel Lutheran Church indicate that fifteen women belonged to the "Mary Marthas," a Ladies Aid, but a list of its activities is not provided. The records also indicate that there were fourteen members in the Girls' Auxiliary.[56] Anderson found similar organizations among Scandinavian Lutherans in north-central Saskatchewan. These organizations were similar to youth groups in Sweden, such as the "Little Children of the Reformation" and the "Lutheran Daughters of the Reformation."[57] The records do not mention a Boys' Auxiliary, suggesting, perhaps, that Swedish females experienced a more intimate relationship with their church.

Until recently, many historians have not acknowledged the importance of women's involvement in organizations such as Ladies Aids. As Coburn argues, membership in Ladies Aids and youth organizations gave Lutheran females access to an expanding, though informal, educational network of the kind not previously viewed as educational by sociologists and historians.[58] Swedish females who joined Ladies Aids and youth societies learned financial management, leadership skills and group interaction: they broke the isolation so prevalent on rural farms by interacting with other women. In doing so, they contributed to the development of social institutions in their communities.

Because Swedish immigrants settled in bloc settlements where they could more readily retain the traditions of the group, first-generation Swedish women, isolated in the home and in the ethnic church, may have been unaware of their "ethnicity." In "Constituting Ethnic Phenomenon," Roxanna Ng makes a distinction between the immigrant's perception of herself and the dominant society's perception of her. Ng argues that ethnicity arises for people only when they come to Canada and are confronted by the dominant culture and people from differing ethnic backgrounds.[59]

---

54 John Hawkes, *The Story of Saskatchewan and its People*, vol. 2 (Chicago: The S. J. Clarke Publishing Co., 1924), 691.

55 Anonymous, *90th Anniversary, New Stockholm Evangelical Lutheran Church: 1889-1979* (Stockholm: n.p., 1979), 8-9.

56 Cited in Broadview History Society, *Oakshela, Broadview, Percival*, 123.

57 Anderson, "Assimilation in the Bloc Settlements," 309.

58 Coburn, "Ethnicity, Religion, and Gender," 225.

59 Roxanna Ng, "Constituting Ethnic Phenomenon: An Account from the Perspective of Immigrant Women," *Canadian Ethnic Studies* 11 (1981): 97.

Juteau-Lee and Roberts likewise distinguish between "Ethnicity" and "ethnicity." "Ethnicity" comprises those attributes of an ethnocultural group which are observable to those outside of the group. These attributes include: language, traditions, country of origin, religion, attitudes, food, and social patterns. In contrast, "ethnicity" is the social meaning assigned to the items on this list — minority status and subordination or, conversely, majority status and domination.[60] When second-generation Swedish girls attended public schools they met children and teachers from other ethnic backgrounds: this interaction did much to affect Swedish girls' perceptions of their status in society.

When the North-West Territories began to be populated by immigrants from eastern Europe, Clifford Sifton, federal Minister of the Interior (1896-1905), saw the public school system as a potential agent of assimilation. In the Swedish settlements of Saskatchewan, schools served this purpose by providing Swedish girls with female role models from different ethnic backgrounds. At Percival School, for instance, Esther Hanson, who began teaching in 1958, was the only teacher of Swedish background who taught at the school between 1908 and 1965.[61] That the other teachers at Percival hoped to Canadianize their students is evident. In 1911 the teacher, R. Hawkes, complained bitterly of the continued use of Swedish on the school ground and in the classroom.[62] In *Wild Daisies*, Foster describes, probably from experience, the assimilationist tendencies of Anglo-Celtic teachers who taught in Swedish ethnic enclaves. Miss Brown, a teacher of British-Canadian descent, taught Anna when she was nine:

> Miss Brown's self-imposed task seemed to be to foster in her pupils love for their country and pride in the British empire. A large map of the world hung on the wall. On it, marked in red, were all the nations that claimed England as their mother country. The pupils were proud to belong to the family of nations on which the sun never set. They all thought of themselves as English.[63]

In the 1930s, when Anna was in her teens, her teacher, Miss Bramble, introduced the world of fashion to her Swedish students. As Foster writes: "Miss Bramble was changing them all. ... Anna came home from school with the latest sheet music. She began to long for the stylish dresses in Eaton's catalogue."[64] The values taught in the school were often at odds with the values of the ethnic church and family. The Anglo-Celtic teacher taught Swedish girls values that were not only ethnic, but generational. Consequently, the teacher's influence over her female students may have undermined the authority of the mother in the family. Despite Anna's mother's admonitions that the wearing of makeup, rayon stockings and jeans would lead to her moral downfall, Anna insisted on wearing them.[65]

In Percival, photographs of students and lists of their names indicate that all or most of the students were from Swedish backgrounds. In contrast, the Stockholm and Dubuc districts, beginning in the early 1900s, began to be populated by

---

60   Juteau-Lee and Roberts, "Ethnicity and Femininity," 1.

61   Broadview History Society, *Oakshela, Percival, Broadview*, 180.

62   Meda Johnson, "Percival School," in Ashfield, *Whitewood and Area*, 93.

63   Foster, *Wild Daisies*, 17.

64   Ibid., 59.

65   Ibid.

Hungarians. When Swedish girls attended school they interacted with children of Hungarian background. In *Wild Daisies*, Foster creates a parallel between Swedish interactions with Hungarians and the fostering of ethnocentrism among Swedes. To her credit, Foster does not attempt to hide the prevalence of discrimination in the Swedish community:

> "Did you know there's a new girl starting school today? She's Hungarian, I think." Oh! Anna was disappointed. A foreigner with limited English, bare feet, and likely smelling of garlic.[66]

However, as more Hungarians attended the public school system, intermarriage occurred between the two groups. Because young Swedish men postponed marriage until they were well established on their own farms, women found the option of marrying men from differing ethnic backgrounds appealing. Anderson analyzes intergenerational attitudes towards ethnic intermarriage among Scandinavians in north-central Saskatchewan, and the results backup what Foster portrays in *Wild Daisies*. While 95 percent of first-generation Scandinavians opposed intermarriage, only 90 percent did in the second generation. Third-generation Scandinavians, like Anna, showed a marked drop in disapproval: 62 percent.[67]

As western-Canadian society became more developed economically and socially, Swedish women were increasingly confronted by the outside world: their activities became more cosmopolitan, their organizations more secular. The CPR, built through Percival in the 1890s, became the lifeblood of the community. It was rather common for girls, upon completing school (or coming to Canada), to work in Broadview or Percival until they were married. For instance, Emma Maria Larson immigrated with her family to Percival in 1905. She then worked in the Broadview Hotel and at the CPR dining hall until she married in 1909. Lena Strandlund, born in Percival, worked at the Broadview Hotel until she married Olaf Pearson in 1909. Similarly, Katrina Anderson worked in the CPR dining hall before marrying Carl Strandlund from Stockholm in 1918.[68]

While first-generation Swedish farm wives in Stockholm viewed brief trips into town as a relief from the monotony of farm life, the Swedish women who relocated to rural hamlets, villages and towns learned new skills and met women of all backgrounds. For young Swedish girls, rural centres were a place to gain employment outside the ethnic enclave and a place, perhaps, to meet potential husbands. In 1905 Sven Erickson Svedberg purchased the Temperance Hotel in the village of Stockholm. He employed local Swedish girls and provided them with a sitting room upstairs where they could entertain men (carefully chaperoned of course).[69] Likewise, Sarah Erickson and her husband moved to Stockholm in 1906. In 1912 they bought a corner store which they turned into a confectionary. While Sarah managed the shop, her daughter, Elinda, served as a clerk.[70]

Swedish farm women also became involved in agricultural societies and organizations that promoted an expanded role for women in the community. In 1895

---

66 Ibid., 32.
67 Anderson, "Assimilation in the Bloc Settlements," 230-32.
68 Broadview History Society, *Oakshela, Broadview, Percival,* 361, 391, 416.
69 SAB, Carl Ian Walker, "Sven Erickson Svedberg: A Swedish Pioneer," 8.
70 Halliwell and Persson, *Three Score and Ten,* 138.

farmers in the Stockholm area organized and named themselves the Stockholm Little Cut Arm and Qu'Appelle Society. The society included members of both sexes, from Ohlen, Esterhazy and Stockholm. In this organization, Swedish women had the opportunity to interact with women from other ethnic communities. They could also hold office in the society: its first secretary-treasurer was a woman. Each year members organized an exhibition in which women could display and sell their produce and handicrafts.[71] Women in the Dubuc Homemakers' Club also began to diversify their activities. The club was established in 1914, and included women from various ethnic backgrounds. Its purpose, by meeting in town, was to give farm women relief from the drudgery of farm life. Following the outbreak of World War I, its members provided war relief in the form of care packages. In the 1920s the women organized a baby clinic with the cooperation of parents and teachers.[72] The Saskatchewan Homemakers' Club, organized in 1911, was modelled after the Ontario Women's Institute. Sponsored by the extension department of the University of Saskatchewan and closely associated with the agriculture department, its *raison d'être* was to solve rural problems by modernizing the skills of the rural housewife. Swedish women's involvement in such an organization marks their entry into the dominant Anglo-Celtic society in Saskatchewan.

The period 1886 to 1940 encompasses three generations of Swedish women who lived in southeastern Saskatchewan. During this time, Swedish women's ethnicity and their gender determined their role in the family, the church and the community. Upon coming to Saskatchewan, Swedish women laboured much as they had in the homeland. However, the nature of the prairie economy and the occupational background of Swedish men required adaptations on the part of the Swedish family. Swedish men were forced to seek employment away from the farm, allowing women to take on a position of authority in the family and to contribute extensively to the economic welfare of the farm. Furthermore, in Saskatchewan, where religious pluralism prevailed, Swedish women had the freedom to establish the church of their choice, an option not available in Sweden. Just as prairie society became more cosmopolitan and complex, so did the lives of Swedish farm women, as their sphere of activity became less defined by their gender and ethnicity and more defined by the dictates of the "outside world." Ironically, as the mandate of the Saskatchewan Homemakers' Society suggests, the dominant culture's ideals of the proper role for women in the family may have been more constricting than what rural Swedish women had experienced on their isolated farmsteads.

---

71   Ibid., 62, 100.

72   SAB, clippings file — women's clubs, "Dubuc Homemakers' Club Looks Back on 37 Years of Community Activity," *Melville Advance*, 2 May 1951.

"*LA GRANDE NOSTALGIE*":
FRENCH-SPEAKING WOMEN AND HOMESICKNESS IN EARLY TWENTIETH-CENTURY SASKATCHEWAN

Mathilde Jutras

> *Il venait du Michigan. C'est une "trompe" qu'on s'est rencontré. J'aurais ben jamais voulu le connaître! J'ai venu dans ce pays-citte que j'ai mauduit depuis la première journée que j'ai rentré dans Saskatchewan! Depuis ce temps-là que j'ai de la misère. J'encourage jamais personne à venir icitte. … Tellement habituée à la misère, j'sé pu comment rire. Ça fait cinquante-sept ans de ça.*

> He came from Michigan. It was a "mistake" that we met. I really wish that I never knew him. I came to this country that I have been cursing since the first day when I arrived in Saskatchewan! Since that time I have been miserable. I never encouraged anyone to come here. … So used to misery, I don't know how to laugh. That makes fifty-seven years of that.[1]

The regret expressed in 1973 by Yvonne Prévost of Mélaval, Saskatchewan[2] who arrived from the United States at the beginning of the century runs counter to the traditional view which extolled the courage, hard work and contribution of French-Canadian men, and by extension their wives, mothers and sisters, to the development of the Prairies and to "*la survivance*" of the French-Catholic populace in Canada. Prévost's lament suggests that not all women who came to the West in the early twentieth century were happy to do so. Indeed, few may have been overjoyed at leaving their homes and relatives for a place where the simple struggle for survival of the family was paramount. It is not surprising, therefore, that "*la nostalgie*," that is, homesickness was a common experience for French-speaking women who found themselves on the Prairies.

The testimony of Prévost and many others like her indicates that French-speaking women, who came to live in a province where English was rapidly becoming the predominant language, were culturally and linguistically isolated. French-speaking immigrant women from Quebec, New England, Belgium and France lacked contact with each other because of work, children and geographic distance. Interaction with their non-Francophone neighbours was also limited because of the language barrier.

---

1   Saskatchewan Archives Board (SAB), R-66, Interview with Mr. and Mrs. Roméo Prévost, 1973 (English translation by D. De Brou). This essay is based on more than 120 taped interviews found in the Saskatchewan Archives with French-speaking (Francophone) Saskatchewan women. The major three sources available in the SAB are: Le Patrimoine Fransaskois, collected by Claudette Gendron in 1980 for the Société historique de la Saskatchewan; Héritage Canadien Français de la Saskatchewan collected by Henri Poulin in 1977-81; and The Francophones collected by Gerald Bériault, Kathleen Dufour, Denis Fournier, Solange Fournier, Constance Martin, Richard Roy, and L.P. Lafrance in 1973. Most of the interviews were conducted in French, but in order to allow an English-speaking audience to hear the voices of these French-speaking women it was necessary to use English translations which, unless otherwise indicated, are by the author. Unfortunately the language nuances which can act as indicators of cultural and social standing are not always transferable from French to English.

2   Unless indicated, geographic locations are found in Saskatchewan.

Other immigrant women faced the same linguistic obstacles. However, the case of French-Canadian women was different: these women were linguistically isolated in their own country.

Based on more than 120 taped interviews with French-speaking pioneer women and on biographies, autobiographies and other written documents, this essay does not deny the important role that French-speaking women played in recent western-Canadian history. Nevertheless, it presents a more complex view of the lives of these women, pointing to their isolation, their homesickness, their desire to return home, and finally, their resignation to their fate.

One such woman was Blanche Vézina-Lefebvre. The photographs of the shack and the homestead had partly prepared her for her life in western Canada. Arriving from Quebec in 1905, she concluded that her fiancé had not attempted to mislead her. He had told her that they were "located near a village. He [had] explained that the land was divided into quarter sections, not following the river like in Quebec." She was less prepared, however, for the conditions found inside her new home: "then I went into the shack. He had done the housekeeping. ... It was ... Well ... adequate."[3] Vézina-Lefebvre was one of the thousands of French-speaking women who followed their fathers, husbands and brothers to western Canada in the early part of the twentieth century. She was part of the wave of settlers that the Canadian government, the Canadian Pacific Railway and the Roman Catholic clergy hoped would fill the uncleared lands of Manitoba, Alberta and Saskatchewan.

Vézina-Lefebvre was fortunate: the majority of women were not so well informed of the kind of life that awaited them in the West. Those from the United States, Belgium and France, and some even from Quebec, did not have a clear idea of what to expect. Biased by personal and financial interests, newspaper reports and agents' descriptions portrayed the West as a farmer's paradise. Certainly the prospective homesteaders knew that the Prairies, "*le pays*," was just opening up to Euro-Canadian settlement. They knew that they would be clearing land; but still it was a shock when they arrived. Béatrice Beaubien-Coots arrived in Wauchope with her family in 1904. She remembers her mother's impressions, which she also shared. Had her mother liked it?: "Well who would have liked that? Arriving from the East, you find yourself on the open prairie; there is no one around, no trees, no water, nothing, nothing!"[4]

The idealism of youth was not enough to overcome the isolation and desolation of Saskatchewan at the beginning of the new century. "I was fourteen years old," recounted Madame Phil Gosselin, who arrived in Willow Bunch in 1917: "I would have gone back [to Quebec], had I been able to. [There were] no buildings ... no church ... [only] a post office [and] a few homes."[5] What a contrast with the numerous villages of Quebec or France, or the industrialized cities of the United States. Justa Denis left France with her father and arrived in Saskatchewan in 1905. In her memoirs, she describes her new home: "[There was] no church, no school. [We were] miles from everything. In Crespin [France] we lived in a big village. On arriving here, there was only prairie. It was like being in a desert."[6]

---

3   SAB, R-9778, Interview with Blanche Vézina-Lefebvre, 1986.

4   SAB, R-10245, R-5175, Interview with Béatrice Beaubien-Coots, 1966, 1980.

5   SAB, R-87, Interview with Mrs. Phil Gosselin, 1973.

6   SAB, R-E1282, Justa Denis, "Mes mémoires," ca. 1964.

The geography isolated families and women. Homesteads were situated far from each other, and if there was a village, it often consisted only of a post office or a general store. "The Coutu family were our closest neighbours. [They were] two-and-one-half miles away," remembered Madame Auguste Lavoie-Allard, who arrived from Saint-Gabriel, Quebec with her husband in 1918. "We didn't visit very often."[7]

Weather was another factor which intensified women's isolation. The cold winters on the Prairies and the frequent and unpredictable snowstorms made it difficult to leave the homestead. The violence of the storms was sometimes fatal; it was safer to stay home. Marie-Thérèse Blanchard, an immigrant from France, was not aware of this when she went to visit friends living about a mile away. Her family reported the results: "By mid-day snow started to fall so she left for home right away but by then it was a blizzard and very cold. She was not dressed for this cold wind and got lost on her way home. She was found frozen to death the next day (about three miles from Duck Lake)."[8]

Massachusetts-born Eliane Saint-Amand survived the winter storms, but she too was shocked by the vagaries of the Saskatchewan weather. She recalled her arrival in Zénon Park in 1912:

> I remember when we came up from Tisdale. There's where we got off the train to come to this land. It was raining, snowing, and hailing, all at the same time. … [This was] not very rosy for a fourteen-year old girl wearing a straw hat, pretty leather button boots, sitting on the back of a "democrat" [carriage] with my four-year old brother in my arms. We had our feet up on the front seat so they would not get wet. There was water in the box, in the "democrat" box. It was running over the edge. My father was in front chopping down trees with an axe to make a path for the horses.[9]

While French-Canadian women[10] were accustomed to harsh weather conditions, they could not, along with their European and Franco-American sisters, escape the isolation resulting from these weather conditions. Outings in the wintertime were cut short not only by blizzards, but also by darkness. With no real landmarks on the prairie, and with the shortness of daylight, it became dangerous to venture out at night. Winter evenings were frequently spent in the sole company of the family.

When the settlers decided to do a *veillée* (an evening of entertainment), it was customary to return home by the light of the next day. The possibility of losing one's way always existed. Madame Auguste Lavoie-Allard of Assiniboia, who came from Quebec in 1918, reported: "in the winter it was very difficult to go out. There was so much snow. We were afraid to lose our way. We did get lost once."[11] French immigrant Madame Pierre Campagne, who arrived in Wauchope with her family in 1904, also revealed that winter travel was not always easy:

> Winter days would go by. Some families would get together to play cards. Neighbours were not very near and in the village there were only three or

---

7   SAB, R-159(a), Interview with Mr. and Mrs. Auguste Allard, 1973.

8   "Blanchard Family," in Duck Lake History Committee, *Their Dreams… Our Memories: A History of Duck Lake and District*, vol. 1 (Altona, MB: Friesen Printers, 1988).

9   SAB, R-1578, Interview with Eliane Saint-Amand, 1977.

10   The term "French Canadian" is used to distinguish French-speaking women born in Canada from those born in Europe or the United States.

11   SAB, R-159(a), Interview with Mr. and Mrs. Auguste Allard, 1973.

four families in the beginning. We travelled by horse. There were no roads. We had to make a new trail every time we went out. It was not as easy as you think. People were not equipped to go out.[12]

For French-speaking women, there was not only physical isolation, there was also social isolation. At the turn of the twentieth century the Catholic clergy of Manitoba was making great efforts to attract Francophone settlers to form a French enclave in western Canada. The clergy thought that French-speaking immigrants should be favoured since they were the first Europeans to reach this area. These efforts were, however, rapidly supplanted by massive non-Francophone immigration, orchestrated by the federal government and the Canadian Pacific Railway Company.[13] Despite the efforts of the clergy in western Canada, the Francophone population in Saskatchewan never amounted to more than 5 or 6 percent of the total population.[14] Non-Francophone immigrants tried to Canadianize themselves as quickly as possible, which more or less meant anglicizing themselves.

The French-speaking settlers found themselves in a province where English became the predominant language. The French were scattered among Metis and Indians, and among the numerous non-French immigrants of Saskatchewan. "We went twelve years without seeing any *canadiens* [French Canadians]!"[15] declared Clara Dupuis who arrived in Esterhazy from Fort Manitoba in 1900.[16] Yvonne Sergent-Casgrain, who settled in Meadow Lake in 1918, also reported that there was no social life: "there seemed to be only Indians and Metis around."[17]

Not only were French communities isolated, they consisted largely of men. This overrepresentation of men was a phenomenon common to the West, where according to the census of 1911, "unmarried men between 20-24 outnumbered eligible women by 2:1 in Manitoba, 4:1 in Saskatchewan and Alberta."[18] Other than their husbands, French-Canadian women were surrounded by bachelors who came to the West to seek their fortune by homesteading or came as *batteux* (those employed

---

12   SAB, R-52(a), Interview with Mrs. Pierre Campagne, 1973.

13   At the turn of the century, fertile land became more rare in Quebec. Thousands of French Canadians moved to the United States, looking for work in the booming textile industries in New England. See: Susan Mann Trofimenkoff, *The Dream of Nation. A Social and Intellectual History of Quebec* (Toronto: Gage Educational Publishing Company, 1983), 132-49. The Quebec clergy saw the mass migration to the United States as a threat because it weakened the numerical strength of French Catholics in Quebec. The clergy was also concerned about the plight of the Franco-Americans (French-speaking Americans). It feared that "*Qui perd sa langue, perd sa foi*" ("Those that lose their language, lose their religion"). From the beginning of the colonization phenomenon, the Francophone clergy of Manitoba endeavoured to convince French Canadians to establish farms in the West. Monseignor Taché of Manitoba hoped to see the creation of blocks of French settlements as well as a French geographic corridor stretching from the East to the West. Despite his efforts, his dream remained unfulfilled as non-French-speaking immigrants flocked westward and overwhelmed the French populace. For a discussion of the clergy's desires, see: Robert Painchaud, *Un rêve français dans le peuplement de la prairie* (Saint-Boniface, MB: Les Editions des Plaines, 1987).

14   Richard Lapointe and Lucille Tessier, *L'Histoire des Franco-Canadiens de la Saskatchewan* (Regina: La Société Historique de la Saskatchewan, 1986), 79.

15   French Canadians commonly used the terms "*canadien*" (male) and "*canadienne*" (female) to describe the French-Canadian population. They called the English Canadians, "*les Anglais.*"

16   SAB, R-5211, Interview with Clara Dupuis, 1980.

17   SAB, R-5210, Interview with Yvonne Sergent-Casgrain, 1980.

18   Moira Armour and Pat Staton, *Canadian Women in History — A Chronology* (Toronto: Green Dragon Press, 1980), 37.

to help in harvesting). Marie Rondeau, a resident of Assiniboia, said that when she arrived from Quebec in 1913, "there were only bachelors around, no one married. … They came by the house to have coffee. My husband had to warn them to watch their language as there was a lady in the house."[19]

French immigrant Madeleine Dumélie-Coupal had a similiar experience when she arrived in Fir Mountain in 1912. She reminisced: "We always had bachelors around. They were like a big family. We had no neighbours for miles and miles. My mother and grandmother were the only two women in the area."[20] The lack of women called for compromise. On rainy days when the *batteux* decided to have a party, Victoria-Joséphine Faubert, who arrived from Ontario in 1904, laughingly recalled that "there was not many girls so the boys would be girls! We would square dance."[21]

In a society numerically dominated by men, the opportunities for woman-to-woman interaction were scarce. Language isolated French-speaking women even more, as they had few occasions to learn the language of the majority society. The husband was more likely to learn English since he was more mobile than other family members were. He was the one who went to the local village on business or sought employment in the lumber camps. This increased his contact with English-speaking Canadians and gave him a chance to learn the language.

Busy with children and the farm, French-Canadian wives were less mobile. Not learning English deprived them of possible contacts with other women and their social circle was limited to the small, isolated French communities, scattered over the province. At times contact with other French women depended on the goodwill of others. Marie-Louise Mullie-Duthoit, who left Ploegsteert, Belgium in 1924 and followed her husband to Arborfield, repeatedly asked Mr. Fournier to bring his wife when he came to the village. The women did not meet often: "When Mr. Fournier went to the village, we always said to him, 'Bring Mrs. Fournier with you when you go to town and then pick her up when you go home.' But he never did."[22] Young Madame Alex Laberge, who arrived in Ferland from Quebec in 1918, also was deprived of interaction with French-speaking women. She recalled: "We experienced two or three very harsh winters, without a furnace, without neighbours. There were only three French-Canadian families in a twenty-mile radius."[23]

The lack of female contact within a society with an English majority had the advantage of enabling French-Catholic women to carry out their role as educators of children and guardians of family and religious traditions. Certainly the clergy underlined the essential role that French-Catholic women played. Monsignor Paquet, a French-Canadian priest, declared that "above all the work of a mother is the religious education of her children. It is she who instills in their souls the germs of faith. Along with the father, she is a sort of collaborator of the priests."[24]

Journalist Marie-Anne Duperreault, who wrote for the French Saskatchewan

---

19   SAB, R-161(a), Interview with Marie-Malvina Rondeau, 1973.

20   SAB, R-5215, Interview with Madeleine Dumélie-Coupal, 1980.

21   SAB, R-126, R-5180, Interview with Victoria-Joséphine Faubert, 1973, 1980.

22   SAB, R-5203, Interview with Marie-Louise Mullie, 1980.

23   SAB, R-54, Interview with Mr. and Mrs. Alex Laberge, 1973.

24   *Le Patriote de l'Ouest*, 28 December 1932.

newspaper *Le Patriote de l'Ouest*[25] under the pen name of "Perrette," agreed with the clergy's view of the role of women.[26] A mother of fourteen children, Duperreault would often remind French-Canadian women of their task: "If men are responsible for the battle to save our precious heritage, we [French-Canadian women] must first save it in our homes where we are the principal protectors. Keeping the family Catholic and French, that is our task."[27]

Associating language with religion, French-Canadian women saw English as a threat to their faith and their family traditions. Some women had little incentive to learn the language of the Protestant majority. "My mother never liked the West," said Eugénie Boivin-Collin who arrived in Wolseley as a child in 1904. "She didn't know English. She never liked learning English."[28] Similarly, Rachel Périgny-Desmarais, whose family arrived in Laflèche in 1912, reported that her mother "could not read English. Even if the Eaton's Catalogue would have been here, she certainly would never have dealt with the English."[29]

The majority of the *Franco-canadiennes* on the Prairies did not learn English. Virginie Bourgeois-Lafrenière was fourteen when she arrived in Willow Bunch from Saint-Gabriel, Quebec in 1909. She regretted never having learned English: without English she remained isolated within a society dominated by English, a society successful in assimilating French Canadians. Her relationship with her grandchildren is a case in point:

> During this time, we didn't have a car, so we didn't go very far. Therefore we were always with the French Canadians. ... Today I regret this. I would give twenty years of my life to know English. [I] can't go anywhere. [I] can't do anything. Even my children, my grandchildren no longer speak French. Particularly the youngest, we have never spoken to each other. I can't speak to her in English, and she does not speak a word of French. She stands and looks at me, and I look at her. I don't even know the sound of her voice.[30]

Another factor added to the French-speaking women's sense of isolation: the lack of church activities. Faith played an important part in the lives of Francophone Catholics. Particularly in Quebec, many of the social events and activities were related to the church or the parish. Such church-centred occasions as baptisms, marriages, funerals, and religious anniversaries constituted the main social interractions of French Canadians because religious observance played a social as well as a spiritual role. For example, after Sunday mass the parishioners exchanged news and took time

---

25   *Le Patriote de l'Ouest* (1910-41) was the first French-language newspaper in Saskatchewan. Begun in Duck Lake, *Le Patriote de l'Ouest* was the principal mouthpiece for the Association Catholique Franco-Canadienne (ACFC). For financial reasons, *Le Patriote de l'Ouest* merged with Winnipeg's *La Liberté* in 1941, becoming *La Liberté et le Patriote*. In 1971, the newspaper reappeared in Saskatchewan under the name of *L'Eau vive*. It continues to be published in Regina.

26   Under the names of "Perrette" and "Crin-Crin," Marie-Anne Duperreault authored many articles for *Le Patriote de l'Ouest* from 1910 to 1941. Duperreault was the first female Francophone journalist in Saskatchewan. Mainly directed to women, her columns discussed a wide range of subjects including education, religion, history, politics, geography and kitchen tips. One of her regular columns was "*Conseil de la ménagère*" (Advice for the Homemaker).

27   *Le Patriote de l'Ouest*, 16-17 August 1916.

28   SAB, R-117(b), Interview with Eugénie Boivin-Collin, 1973.

29   SAB, R-5188, Interview with Rachel Desmarais, 1980.

30   SAB, R-53, Interview with Virginie Bourgeois-Lafrenière, 1973.

to chat on the church steps (*le perron de l'église*). This is still the custom in Quebec churches as well as in Francophone parishes throughout Canada.

It was only years later, as churches were built and parishes became more organized, that the French-speaking population indulged in this cherished custom. Victoria-Joséphine Faubert of Montmartre recalled: "After church on Sunday, everyone would gather on the church steps and we would plan the evening, where we would be having supper. ... We would say: 'Tonight, we are going to do this or that at one's place.' We were like a big family."[31]

At the beginning of the twentieth century, there were few church buildings in Saskatchewan. Often the priest said mass in private houses and on an irregular basis. "Mass was held once a month," said Marie-Yvonne Gallays-Leborgne, who arrived in Saint-Brieux from France in 1909. "Again we were very lucky. Before the construction of the Chapel, mass was said in homes."[32] In some cases, mass was celebrated only once a year. In "Mes mémoires," Justa Denis of Saint-Denis reports that the long intervals between mass celebrations added to her feeling of loneliness:

> We took up residence at Witchekan or Laventure. As for me I never really liked that country; I was very, very lonely during the time I was there. We attended mass only two times, because a priest came to say mass in a private home. The closest train station was twenty-eight miles [away].[33]

The infrequency of mass celebrations limited the number of social interractions between French-Canadian women. Women felt disconnected from their previous lives; the church was a link to their past. Faith was their anchor and not surprisingly French-Canadian wives took charge of preparing the Eucharist, helped the priest call upon "lost" parishioners and offered their houses (in some cases, shacks) as a place for religious celebration. Madame Gilberte Chabot, whose parents arrived in Laflèche in 1918, remembered how mass was organized in that community:

> The priest would arrive there [at her grandmother's house] in the early afternoon. Then, one of my aunts, Armande, would leave on horseback in one direction, and the priest in the other direction, to tell all the Catholic neighbours we knew that mass would be celebrated at a certain time the next day at my grandmother's house.[34]

Social activities varied among the French-speaking women: those originally from Canada would sometimes get together for a *veillée*, play music and dance; their European cousins would rather just visit with the family, over a quiet supper on Sunday evening. "We only visited the family," said French immigrant Marie Bachelu-Ferraton of Wolseley who arrived in 1908. "My husband wasn't very sociable. I had a sister-in-law I always had fun with."[35] Madame Pierre Campagne of Wauchope, who also came from France at the beginning of the century, reported on the cultural differences between the European French and the Canadian French:

> There were very few parties. We [those from France] did not party a lot. People more or less stayed home. They chose to get together on holidays.

---

31   SAB, R-126, R-5180, Interview with Victoria-Joséphine Faubert, 1973 and 1980.

32   SAB, R-5205, Interview with Marie-Yvonne Gallays-Leborgne, 1980.

33   SAB, R-E1282, Denis, "Mes mémoires," ca. 1964.

34   SAB, R-51, Interview with Gilberte Chabot, 1973.

35   SAB, R-116(b), Interview with Marie Bachelu-Ferraton, 1973.

There were a few community suppers, but not very often. We had very few
gatherings. We did not do this [have community gatherings]. We would
rather get together on a Sunday evening. They would go play cards at one
house or another. The women talked amongst themselves, but nothing big.
It just was not the French way.[36]

These cultural differences were most evident at Christmas time. Except for
perhaps the uncontrollable weather, no difficulty was too great for the French
Canadians to overcome. The holiday visits occurred almost daily. Marie-Ange Hamel-
Gaudet, whose parents came to Saint-Isidore-de-Bellevue from Quebec recalled that
"from New Year's Eve to Mardi Gras, we partied every second night. Dancing was
permitted as long as it was square dancing. We danced until midnight, one o'clock."[37]

Irma Carignan-Privé whose family arrived in Ponteix in 1910 also commented on
the Canadian proclivity for partying. "Oh yes there were many parties, 'distractions.'
The French Canadians always loved to party, eh. During the Christmas season ...
every night! One night ... here, the next night at the neighbours. We spent the week
partying."[38] With a less active social life, European women probably suffered more
from isolation and homesickness than their French-Canadian counterparts did. The
cost and the distance of returning to their country of birth added to the loneliness
of the Europeans.

Whether from Europe, Canada or United States, the daily work routine for women
was in many ways a barrier to social activities. At the beginning of the twentieth
century in Saskatchewan, a woman's workload was almost never-ending. Everything
had to be made, done, produced, created or invented, and the woman's role as
housekeeper and farmer was essential to the family enterprise. It was she who was
responsible for such tasks as food preparation, laundry, childcare, husbandry and
gardening. In several cases she also baked bread or did the laundry for the
neighbouring bachelors.

In contrast to their urban sisters, rural prairie women did not enjoy such advantages
of modernization as electricity and manufactured goods. They had to forget about
"modern conveniences" that they had known in eastern Canada or Europe. "Our poor
mother was grossly overworked, with a large family and non-existent modern facilities
at that time," wrote Anne-Marie Lefrançois-Depuis Hawryluk in her autobiography.[39]
Marie Lafrenière-Webber's mother of Prud'homme had a similar experience:

I well remember my dear, patient mother so often speaking of the hardships
that followed [the arrival in Saskatchewan] and how wistfully [she]
compared this primitive lifestyle with the comfortable home they had left
behind ... with its running water and all the other amenities denied her
family after coming to Saskatchewan as pioneers.[40]

In her autobiography, Clémentine Mansière, who arrived from France in 1905,
reported that she had no choice but to do everything: "We had ten dollars left. But

---

36   SAB, R-52(a), Interview with Mrs. Pierre Campagne, 1973.

37   SAB, R-5212, Interview with Marie-Ange Hamel-Gaudet, 1980.

38   SAB, R-5157, Interview with Irma Carignan-Privé, 1980.

39   SAB, R500.75, Anne-Marie Lefrançois-Depuis Hawryluk, "The Story of My Life, 1910-1980."

40   Prud'homme History Committee, *Life As It Was: Prud'homme, Saskatchewan, 1897-1981* (Altona, MB:
Friesen Printers, 1981), 524-25.

we didn't as yet have a stove, beds, etc. So we went to work!"[41] With so much work, and just a few women to do it, there was little time for anything else.[42] When Lucienne Brassard, who grew up in Albertville, was asked about the importance of social life in those times, she answered, surprised: "Excitement? Dumb question! As far as excitement, there really was no excitement. It was nothing but hard, honest-to-goodness work. [We] tried to raise our family to the best of our ability."[43]

The Dupuis family also had little time for social activities. "We had too much work to do," reported Clara Dupuis who also said that they did not go out very often. "Sometimes on Sundays, we would go for a ride, but we had to come back to milk the cows."[44] With long work days, rest was most welcomed in the evening. Julienne Pilon, who left Quebec in 1916 and settled in Gravelbourg, admitted her loneliness: "I never went out. I enjoyed being with people, but still I never went out."[45]

The majority of pioneer women experienced motherhood. Did the child-rearing serve as a means to fight homesickness? Raising children had both negative and positive aspects: it provided the isolated women with human companionship; at the same time, maternal obligations restricted contact with their peers. Adrienne Faubert, who arrived in Montmartre in 1920, said that she had a few neighbours who came once in a while to play cards, "but I was pregnant every year. It was hard for me to get out. When evening came I was tired."[46]

Francophone women who had husbands working in the lumber camps of northern Saskatchewan and Manitoba also suffered a great deal from isolation. With husbands away all winter, they remained at home either alone or with their children. Arriving with her parents in 1905 from Saint-Prospère, Quebec, Madame Jean Bonneau was still a child when her father went to work in the lumber camps in the winter. She recalled one instance when her mother was desperate, trying to find the basic necessities of life for her six children:

> I remember during the winter, we had no more wood. Mom had no wood or coal. My father was gone in the woods to the lumber camps. She [my mother] was waiting for a check from father. I remember very well. All of us kids were in one bed. She dressed us all up. We were all sitting on the bed. We then went to the neighbours with our sad story. My mother said, "my children will all perish. I have no more wood, no more money." Then the neighbours brought us coal. They cut wood right away. They made us a fire with what they had. That afternoon Father Lemieux came to see us. He told mother never to let things get that low again. "Come to the rectory. We will give you what you need. Don't let yourself die." After that, things were better. The neighbours came to visit. Father still had to work in the lumber camps. We were so poor.[47]

Another lumberjack's wife became a prisoner in her own house because of a

---

41   SAB, R500.75, Clémentine Mansière, Autobiographie.

42   Linda Rasmussen, Lorna Rasmussen, Candace Savage and Anne Wheeler, *A Harvest Yet To Reap: A History of Prairie Women* (Toronto: The Women's Press, 1976), 42.

43   SAB, R-2281, Interview with Lucienne M. Brassard, 1980.

44   SAB, R-5211, Interview with Clara Dupuis, 1980.

45   SAB, R-64, Interview with Julienne Pilon, 1973.

46   SAB, R-123(a), Interview with Adrienne Faubert, 1973.

47   SAB, R-55(a), Interview with Mrs. Jean Bonneau, 1973.

blizzard. The snow was piled up over six-feet high against the door. However, she managed to dig a small passage for herself along the wall and get the door opened about one-foot wide by pushing hard against the soft snow. She had to get wood and look after the cow. She and the cow needed water but she was unable to go to the river. With no one likely to find her for some time, her situation was serious. Finally her father's big dog wandered over to her house and came through the narrow passage that she had dug. She then wrote a note to her father, wrapped it up and tied it to a string around the dog's neck and let him out. Shortly afterward, her father was digging her out. One can wonder what would have happened, if the dog had not been there.[48]

For women left alone, having a relative or a neighbour nearby often represented the only remedy to combat their oppressive loneliness. The need to escape this feeling of loneliness was great. Madame Léon Henri of Léoville described how she combatted the isolation:

> I remember when I was alone, my husband being gone to work in Big River. If I felt like it, I'd dress up the children, hitch our oxen on a stone boat and away we'd go visiting relatives or neighbors. Sometimes we'd walk. I often went on foot, with my children to visit and time flew by. If our young people would see pictures of those pioneer times, they would laugh.[49]

Nostalgia or homesickness ("*le mal du pays*") affected most French-speaking women whether they came from eastern Canada or Europe. For Marie-Anne Duperreault ("Perrette") it was the smell of freshly cut hay that brought the memories of her former life: "And during the hard work of July, the smell of fresh cut hay reminded me of our farm in the East and my friends from another time. Ah well, I miss the good old days."[50] Jeanne Bergot-Laporte left France in 1904 with her mother, her brothers and sisters, her three aunts and their "two servants who did not want to leave us" to join her father who had preceded them in Saskatchewan. She and her family left a fourteen-room house in Nantes for a shack in Saint-Brieux. She recalled:

> [We all arrived together,] my three aunts, my mother, the maid and another person who worked for us. The maid spoke only Breton, and very little French. When Marie-Jeanne [the maid] saw that things were getting gloomy [and] forlorn, it was as if we were exiled. We would hear her sobs from the corner of our papa's house (… a log house. We had left a home with so many rooms). We would hear sobbing at night … [We] could hear them all.[51]

When there was no hope of ever going back to family or friends, it did not matter if Saskatchewan's French-speaking women came from Quebec, the United States or Europe: the homesickness was painful. As Mathilda Bruneau, who arrived from Quebec in 1917, declared: "I sure found it hard [not being able to return home]. One does not die from crying, but it's unbelievable how lonely I felt out here."[52] To alleviate their homesickness, mothers described their former lives to their children.

---

48   SAB, Restricted Source.

49   Léoville Historic Committee, *After the Dust. A History of Leoville and Community: Leoville, Laventure, Ranger, Junor, Penn, Chitek Lake, Pelican Reserve, Spruce Creek, Timberland, Timberlost and Capasin* (North Battleford, SK: Turner-Warwick, 1979), 701.

50   Perrette, "Vacances," in *Esquisses Canadiennes* (Willow Bunch, SK: n.p., 1969), 70-72.

51   SAB, R-5216, Interview with Jeanne Bergot-Laporte, 1980.

52   SAB R-86, Interview with Mrs. Mathilda Bruneau, 1973.

The mother of Lucienne Liboiron-Roberge of Ponteix, who arrived in Saskatchewan in 1917, talked constantly of her birthplace, Quebec:

> My mother was always very lonesome. She never did get used to the place. Regardless, she always stayed. She never came right out and said so. She was such a good person, but it was very noticeable to us [her children] because she talked to us everyday of the East. She never ever said it but we knew she would have loved to go back down East.[53]

It was much the same with Denise Bergot-Gillies's mother who settled in North Battleford in 1904: "Mom would often talk about France ... very often. She never talked about going back, for she realized that it was impossible. She spoke often of Mont Saint-Michel. She would tell us about Paris, Portneuf, le Louvre, La Rivière Noire, La Seine."[54]

A way of coping with homesickness was to write home or subscribe to French newspapers and *annales* (parish bulletins). The Montreal papers *La Presse* and *La Voix catholique*, for example, were in circulation in western Canada. *Le Patriote de l'Ouest*, first published in Duck Lake in 1910, was read in many of the province's Francophone households. However, some families did not receive any publications at all, probably because of the family's dire financial situation. This was the case of the Gaucher family of Coderre which came from Quebec in 1914. Madame Emile Gaucher was a teacher prior to her marriage. She reported that she missed reading to the point of rereading her old textbooks:

> The first few years that I was married and no longer teaching, there was nothing to read. I missed being able to read so much that I read old math textbooks. "A farmer buys so much, pays so much etc. ... etc." I needed to read so bad that I read that. I had nothing else to read![55]

Life was also difficult for young women. Few neighbours meant few friends. A large family provided the opportunity of having brothers and sisters as friends, but a large family also meant more work for young women. It was with bitterness that Marie Lafrenière-Webber, who grew up in Prud'homme, remembered the loneliness of her childhood and adolescence, the tasks to be done and the dreams never fulfilled:

> Being born and brought up in the lonely town of Prud'homme was an experience I would not care to relive. I'm afraid that I do not cherish very many fond childhood memories. ... What stands out most in my mind, of the time spent on the farm, are either of hot, scorching winds with no way to cool off but [with] a dip in the stagnant waters of the slough which, inevitably, brought on a rash of welts caused by blood suckers, or bitterly cold blizzardy days that kept you indoors. On the [warmer winter days], I would try my skill at skating on the frozen-over sloughs with my sister's skates that were too big for me. ... I did learn how to milk cows (which wasn't really my bag), and oh those hot summer Sundays when we had to get back on the farm to fetch the bloody cows was something I could never resign myself to. ... But where I felt most deprived was not being able to learn the piano, something, I feel, that would have changed my whole life.[56]

---

53   SAB, R-5160, Interview with Lucienne Liboiron-Roberge, 1980.

54   SAB, R-5217, Interview with Denise Bergot-Gillies, 1980.

55   SAB, R-94(b), Interview with Mr. and Mrs. Emile Gaucher, 1973.

56   Prud'homme History Committee, *Life As It Was: Prud'homme, Saskatchewan, 1897-1981*, 524-25.

Having benefitted from an organized educational system in eastern Canada, the United States or Europe, devoted students could be very disappointed with the one-room school on the Saskatchewan prairie. The small number of students increased the degree of loneliness experienced by young women. Alice Minne was thirteen when her parents decided to leave Marquette, France, and make their fortune in Saskatchewan. They settled in Laflèche in 1922 where ten students constituted the school population. Minne lamented:

> It was so difficult. In France, I went to an all-girls school; we were fifty in the class. Here at our country school [in Laflèche], we were ten boys and girls. It was so difficult and it was cold. There was a stove in the centre of the classroom.[57]

Her school teacher was boarding at her parents, as was often the custom in the West at that time. So Minne and the teacher travelled to school together, even when it was very cold, in the wintertime. She sadly continued:

> Sometimes I was the only one with the school teacher when it was cold. The other children did not come. One day she told me to write to my friends in France telling them of my life out here, how I liked it here etc. I could never complete the letter; it made me weep.[58]

Men also found it hard, but they adapted more easily to the living conditions in western Canada: their circle of social acquaintances was much larger than that of their spouses, often expanding to the English communities. As initiators of the move west, husbands and fathers were more reluctant to admit their disappointment, but some were just as homesick as the women. Having brought his family from Quebec to Willow Bunch in 1914, the father of Maura Boulianne never showed his true feelings. Boulianne described the reaction of her father and her family when they arrived in the West:

> We would have gone back the next day. Dad regretted it [not returning to Quebec], but [he] never showed it. He never let it show. Finally he said it just before dying, how lonely he had been. After that we went on with life the best we could. You have to. You adjust.[59]

For the father of Anne-Marie Lefrançois-Depuis Hawryluk of Prince Albert, the reality of the Prairies did not match his expectations: "Dad was unhappy here. In the morning he would gaze at the birds that were flying east."[60]

Several women wanted to leave but were unable to do so because of the family's poor financial situation. Where could these women have gone? They had sold everything back home, paid for the trip west and for the homestead registration. All that remained was a few dollars. Madame Jean Bonneau, whose family came from Quebec in 1910, said that many settlers, including her parents, believed the priests who had encouraged them to go west had lied about Saskatchewan. Bonneau's mother cried a lot:

> We [the Bonneau family] would have gone back. My father would have gone back, my mother also. We were too poor after that, we could no longer afford to move. We had to stay. I saw my mother cry *many* times. She would think back that if they would have had the money, they would have

---

57   SAB, R-5171, Interview with Alice-Marie Minne, 1980.

58   Ibid.

59   SAB, R-71, Interview, Maura Boulianne, 1973.

60   SAB, R-5204, Interview with Anne-Marie Lefrançois-Depuis Hawryluk, 1980.

returned. We were too poor. We were too poor. We were never able to go back.[61]

French-speaking women on the Prairies did not have the freedom to return home. They were economically dependent on their husbands. They also came from a strong Catholic tradition which preached obedience to the husband. Priests, like Monsignor Camille Roy, reminded them of this from time to time:

> By the design of God, woman is the auxiliary of man, but also, she is similar or equal to him. That is how the hierarchy of actions must be established in the equality of nature. Man, humanity's first-born, the first one to come out from the Creator's hands, is also first in action, in the organization of action, and, at home, the authority who decides on action. The woman is an indispensable helper to him. The principle itself of the hierarchy of authorities is pointed out by God when He makes man head of the family, and when, through St. Paul, he recommends the subordination of the wife to the husband at home. ... Mary herself was submissive to Joseph, and she, herself, was but an assistant, and an auxiliary in the restoration that the Man-God had accomplished. ... What should we conclude from this, in regard to order in women's actions? The woman must remember that she is, by virtue of her creation, an auxiliary to man and that the word, assistant, auxiliary, implies subordination, subordination in the equality of nature.[62]

From childhood, French-Canadian women heard from the pulpit that women must obey men. Women learned to follow their husband and accept his decisions. Mathilda Bruneau first arrived in Verwood with her husband in 1917. She too let her husband decide on their fate. "I always insisted, and I always said 'It's you [her husband] who is the bread winner, if you like it here, we will stay.' But as for myself, I didn't like it."[63] "She came because she had to follow her husband," said Gravelbourg resident Marie-Jeanne Morin-Couture, speaking of her mother. The family left Saint-Bernard, Quebec and arrived in Ferland in 1919. She continued: "But frankly, we [the children] did not really notice that she was suffering."[64]

"I was always very agreeable," revealed Adrienne Faubert. Shortly after her wedding, in 1920, she left Embrun, Ontario and arrived in Montmartre. "[During] the first few years, I would have loved to have gone back because I didn't know anyone [here]. When you're a young newlywed, [everything is] peaches and cream."[65] Once she arrived in Rosetown in 1916, Madame Rose Labrecque changed her mind about staying in Saskatchewan: she wanted to leave the West. Originally from Ham Nord, Quebec, her parents first moved to Maine in the United States when she was six years old. In Maine she later met her husband, and then they moved to Saskatchewan. "I married him, and I intended to change his mind [about leaving] after arriving here [in Saskatchewan]. ... But he did not change his mind. ... So it was me who had to change my mind. [And we stayed because] he loved it [here]."[66] Having worked in

61 SAB, R-55(a), Interview with Mrs. Jean Bonneau, 1973.

62 Camille Roy, "Action féminine ordonnée," *Le Patriote de l'Ouest*, 8 April 1931 [translation by Denyse Smith].

63 SAB, R-86, Interview with Mrs. Mathilda Bruneau, 1973.

64 SAB, R-5168, Interview with Marie-Jeanne Couture, 1980.

65 SAB, R-123(a), Interview with Adrienne Faubert, 1973.

66 SAB, R-118(b), Interview with Rose Brulotte-Labrecque, 1973.

factories all her life, Labrecque did not know much about farm life. She had to learn everything. "I was lucky if I could boil water!" she admitted.[67]

Women stayed at their husband's side because of financial dependency and a strong sense of duty and obedience. But what if they had had the monetary means to leave? "And my mother would have gone back [to France] right then if she would have had the money," remembered French immigrant Alice Minne. For Minne's mother, Saskatchewan was "a lost country." She told Minne: "We will stay in Canada for five years, then we will go back to France." They never did.[68]

Neither did the mother of Marie-Yvonne Gallays-Leborgne who left France to settle on the Prairies. Gallays-Leborgne described her mother's reaction when they reached Saint-Brieux in 1909: "When we arrived here, mother was discouraged. She cried often. She used to say 'If I would have had the money, I would have gone back to France'. "[69]

It was women who wanted to leave the most. The cultural shock was greater for them since their priorities differed from those of their husbands. The welfare of their children and family came first, even if they shared their husband's ambition. They continued to hope that they would return home but gradually the hopes faded. In spite of all their courage, tears were still hard to hide sometimes and husbands did not remain cold to their spouse's sadness. Promises were made, but seldom kept. The father of Rachel Périgny-Desmarais was a carpenter in Quebec before the allure of gold and the promise of farmland drew him westward. He returned to his home province to gather up his family and settled in Laflèche in 1912. Rachel recalled how her father's promises went by the wayside as the profits of a good harvest went into his pockets:

> He promised Mama: "Mama you will cry no more. We are going back down east. We will sell it all and go back." The crop was so good that year that he said, "Well it's not feasible. Look at that beautiful crop! Look at all that money! We can't go back!" He went out and bought another farm.[70]

Promises were also postponed. From harvest to harvest, men's ambitions rose and women's hopes of ever returning home fell. A good crop would have provided the financial resources to return home. However, a good crop confirmed for those needing an excuse to stay that the West was a farmer's paradise. This did not mean that a poor crop meant the family would leave. Surely the family could not return east with empty pockets. It had sold everything back home in order to get to Saskatchewan in the first place. No, the family had to stay. Rachel Desmarais blamed men's ambitions for the fate of women like her mother: "It's ambition that made men like papa. ... But not Mama, because she would have gone back, just like that! For the men it was totally different."[71] Maura Boulianne also blamed her father for their situation: "I could never understand why he wanted to come out West. Mama was lonesome! We were never so lonesome in all our lives! We would have gone back the next day."[72]

---

67   Ibid.

68   SAB, R-5171, Interview with Alice-Marie Minne, 1980.

69   SAB, R-5205, Interview with Marie-Yvonne Gallays-Leborgne, 1980.

70   SAB, R-5188, Interview with Rachel Périgny-Desmarais, 1980.

71   Ibid.

72   SAB, R-71, Interview with Maura Boulianne, 1980.

When the hope of returning disappeared, for most French-speaking women working and raising children became a way of coping with nostalgia. Although work socially isolated women, it also allowed them to put aside their loneliness, if only temporarily. In 1920 unmarried Béatrice Coursol came West to keep house for her brother, a parish priest:

> I found it very hard, very hard. I put myself to work. I was the housekeeper at the rectory. My brother would say: "Don't do too much." Washing the floor ... waxing them was a way to keep myself busy.[73]

It was much the same for Marie Rondeau of Assiniboia, who in addition to housekeeping, worked side by side with her husband in the fields and building their house: "I came with my husband on our honeymoon, I was lonely at the beginning, but I didn't sulk. I rolled up my sleeves and went to work."[74] The husband of Irma Carignan-Privé, who grew up in Ponteix, even attached a homemade platform to the machinery, for her to sit on when he was working in the field:

> The shack was very small, fourteen feet by sixteen feet. There was an old stove that had to be waxed regularly. ... I was lonely because we were far from neighbours. My husband even went as far as to build a platform on his machines, so that I could be with him while he was working. ... I picked up rocks with him. ... You see, I had nothing to do in that little house of nothing![75]

Women without children found life difficult. Those who did not have children were anxious to get pregnant, seeing child rearing as a way of fighting boredom and homesickness. Madame Auguste Lavoie-Allard of Assiniboia, who was childless for the first seven years of her marriage, put it this way: "Yes it was depressing [living in Saskatchewan], especially since we didn't have children for seven years. ... It was very hard, especially on me. He had his work. But me, [I had] no children. ... I found this hard, and very lonely."[76] Gravelbourg resident Julienne Pilon revealed that, "after my first baby, I wasn't lonely any more. We never thought again of returning to Quebec. But before that, oh!"[77] Irène Coupal-Trudeau, for her part, was categorical on the subject when she declared: "But I was never lonely. I had no time to be lonely. I had my children. I had my husband."[78]

If children were not enough, there was always religion. It was from their faith that French-speaking Canadians drew their courage. This was all they really had, since they could not change their circumstances. Journalist Marie-Anne Duperreault ("Perrette" of *Le Patriote de l'Ouest*) put it this way:

> When we [French-Canadian women] are feeling down, what good does it do to say anything? If we feel despair that we are going to overcome it, why involve others? Everyone has their little crosses to bear in this world. These are reminders of the good Lord who loves and wants our sanctification. But if the load seems too hard to bear, we must simply lean on the shoulder of a friend. Who amongst us has not known days of moral weakness more painful than physical pain when, trying not to react, we leave ourselves open

73   SAB, R-5200, Interview with Béatrice Coursol, 1980.

74   SAB, R-161(a), Interview with Marie Rondeau, 1973.

75   SAB, R-5157, Interview with Irma Carignan-Privé, 1980.

76   SAB, R-159(a), Interview with Mrs. Auguste Lavoie-Allard, 1973.

77   SAB, R-64, Interview with Julienne Pilon, 1973.

78   SAB, R-5209, Interview with Irène Coupal-Trudeau, 1980.

to bad thoughts, opening the door to childish fancies, the most disastrous apprehension, as if God was not always there![79]

Duperreault wrote frequently on religion and faith, attempting to encourage and support French-Canadian women. She was echoing the message found in the Oblate-controlled *Le Patriote de l'Ouest.* In one article, Monsignor Bolo, a priest, even declared that women, with their maternal inclination, were better prepared and adapted more easily to suffering than men. According to him, woman was "of all creation, the being best organized for suffering!"[80]

But did these women really feel the suffering less? Or did they merely hide their feelings better than men did? Women were the ones who were taught to console, to be there when their children and husband were discouraged. "The women had ambition," declared Rachel Périgny-Desmarais. In other words, women had courage. "They had to. [They were] the ones who didn't become sick. They had to have ambition for their children, to show them ambition because if mother wasn't there to give ambition, we would have felt it."[81]

Women had to be strong. "My mother, my three aunts and even the maid who would never leave us, never said what they were thinking," reported Jeanne Bergot-Laporte. "They kept it all inside! Mother never said a word. A real trooper! I was proud."[82] Courage and a stout heart were prerequisites for life on the Prairies. The mother of Odélia Henri, of Léoville, kept her sadness to herself: "It would not do to cry in front of the children. Our mother has always had and still has a great faith and accepts events as coming from the hand of God, and never rebels against misfortunes."[83]

Religious faith aided other French-speaking women. "I always prayed," confided Mathilda Bruneau of Willow Bunch.[84] The feeling of accomplishing their duty as well as God's will allowed others to face hardships. "Well, we went through all those years," said Lena Soucy-Crossland of Léoville, "raised fifteen children, and when we stop to think of it, we can say that work doesn't kill. ... I have done my best and God has been good to us all along ... and I am still here waiting to go, when the dear Lord will call me."[85] Faith was also comforting for the mother of Marie Fournay of Ponteix who arrived from Belgium in 1910. Fournay stated: "My mother would say 'It's the good Lord who sent us here'."[86]

Since everyone was in the same difficult situation, it was easier to accept the circumstances of their lives. Some directed their energies toward improving their fate. Madame Emilia Henri of Léoville arrived from Quebec shortly after her wedding in 1916. She had seventeen children and raised twelve of those in the hard times. She explained: "What a life you may say, and rightfully. Yet at the time no one complained

79   Perrette, "Causette," *Esquisses Canadiennes*, 35-67.

80   Monseignor Bolo, "Au Foyer — La femme complète," *Le Patriote de l'Ouest*, 28 May 1930.

81   SAB, R-5188, Interview with Rachel Périgny-Desmarais, 1980.

82   SAB, R-5216, Interview with Jeanne Bergot-Laporte, 1980.

83   "Odélia Henri," in Léoville Historic Committee, *After the Dust. A History of Leoville and Community.*

84   SAB, R-86, Interview with Mrs. Mathilda Bruneau, 1973.

85   "Lena Soucy-Crossland Family," in Léoville Historic Committee, *After the Dust. A History of Léoville and Community.*

86   SAB, R-148, Interview with Marie Fournay, 1973.

since everyone was in the same boat. We took it all in stride, and thought nothing of it. … Besides, we lived on hope, always planning to better our way of living."[87]

Antoinette Lacelle-Longtain of Ponteix, who arrived in Saskatchewan as a child in 1910, said that misery was easier to accept at that time: "We didn't dwell on hard times because in those times we just accepted."[88] Not all French-speaking women in western Canada were so philosophical; some were bitter. The mother of Madame Jean Bonneau refused to keep a journal or even to discuss the past: "I had enough hard times. I do not want to think about the past. I would rather not talk about it."[89] Equally pained was Mathilda Bruneau who had followed her husband to Saskatchewan in 1917. To her despair, someone had given him a newspaper that promoted homesteading in western Canada. Fifty-six years later, the bitterness of her arrival in Saskatchewan was still evident: "it was terrible how I was lonely. Why did he give him that [news]paper? It would not have brought him out West!"[90]

Gravelbourg resident Madame Poirier, who left Sainte-Claire, Quebec and arrived in Laflèche in 1913, also never quite accepted her new home. "I never liked the West," she confessed. "[I] always felt lonely."[91] This was a feeling shared by many and some women did leave. The brother-in-law of Antoinette Longtain of Ponteix was one of the few husbands who kept his promise to return. Longtain reported: "Her husband [her sister-in-law's husband] had told her 'If you don't like it, we'll go back.' After four years, they went back [because] she felt too isolated." Longtain added: "you had to have the right temperament [to stay]."[92] Léoville resident Madame Arthur Poulin made reference to another woman who decided it was time to leave the West:

> [She was] rather an elderly lady in her fifties. She had lived all her life in Montreal. Imagine her dismay upon arriving here in the bush! She did not stay long. She and her husband gave up their homestead and left. They probably returned to Quebec, but we never heard from them since.[93]

Some women categorically refused to accept a fate they had not chosen. Rachel Périgny-Desmarais recounted the story of the neighbour who, with her children, left her husband three times to go back East:

> She and the children left her husband. She said: "You can keep your Saskatchewan, I've had enough!" She was a beautiful woman. She came from around Montreal. She often came over. She ranted and raved about her husband: "Isn't it appalling of him to bring us to [a] country like this! Freeze… did we freeze!" She left. When it [the weather] was nice she came back.[94]

With a scarcity of friends on the Prairies, the departure of one woman affected other women. Irène Coupal-Trudeau of Sedley-Lajord, who arrived with her family in

87   "Emilia Henri Family," in Léoville Historic Committee, *After the Dust. A History of Léoville and Community.*

88   SAB, R-5162, Interview with Antoinette Lacelle-Longtain, 1980.

89   SAB, R-55(a), Interview with Mrs. Jean Bonneau, 1973.

90   SAB, R-86, Interview with Mathilda Bruneau, 1973.

91   SAB, R-70, Interview with Mrs. Poirier, 1973.

92   SAB, R-5162, Interview with Antoinette Lacelle-Longtain, 1980.

93   "Arthur Poulin Family," in Léoville Historic Committee, *After the Dust. A History of Léoville and Community.*

94   SAB, R-5188, Interview with Rachel Périgny-Desmarais, 1980.

1918, never forgave her sister for leaving Sturgeon Valley (where they lived) to head to Sedley in the south of Saskatchewan. The two sisters were married to two brothers, and the two couples were sharing the same house. They also each had a little girl. Irène felt bitter when her sister and brother-in-law made their decision to leave:

> I wasn't at all happy with my sister. They left the next spring. The four of us had lived together. ... When they talked about going back I said nothing. I had my own ideas. She looked so happy to be going. I was mad! It made me mad to see her in such good spirits that she was going, that she was leaving me all alone. I told myself "Go if you want to go. I won't cry because you're leaving!" I didn't cry either! We drove them to the train in Shellbrook. I said: "Goodbye!" I didn't shed a tear. She must have said to the people in Sedley: "I don't understand it, Irène didn't cry."[95]

When there was no chance of returning to their birthplaces, French-speaking women eventually adapted to the prairie way of life. They really had no choice. Assiniboia resident Madame Babe Lalonde, who came from Quebec, was asked if she had liked it here after all. She answered: "Did you like it here? I had to. I never went back East."[96] Some had sold everything back home; they too had no choice but to stay. Célestine Guillet who arrived in Saint-Brieux from France said: "[I stayed] here. ... I had nothing left in France."[97] It could also mean that Guillet had no one else back home. Financial and familial considerations also dictated the future of Marie Bachelu of Wolseley who came with her father from France in 1910:

> I never thought of going back to France. I came with my father. I didn't have any family. ... There are some who left their families behind, but I came with my father. I didn't have any other choice but to stay here. When you're here without money, you stay.[98]

Asked if she would do the same again, Madame Jean Bonneau, originally from Quebec, and who had eighteen children, was hesitant: "Ah ... I don't know. I dreamed a lot before but once things started to go better, well, it was ok. It took a long time because we came through the drought. The drought was very *hard*."[99] Annette Poissant came with the whole family from Quebec in 1924. She followed her mother. Although she spent most of her life in Saskatchewan, she too was hesitant when asked if she would do things differently: "It's hard to say. I had nothing to say about coming out. Mother came out, so I had to come. ... I had no idea what I would do."[100] Madame Rose Labrecque, on the other hand, did not have to think twice. She had been born in Quebec but lived in the United States before her arrival in Saskatchewan in 1916. If she had had a choice, would she have remained in Saskatchewan? She laughed: "No not me! Him maybe, but not me. I would have stayed where I was: in the [United] States!"[101] Gravelbourg resident Sarah Piché answered indirectly. She arrived from the United States in 1910: "When you're in a certain area you should do your best to

---

95   SAB, R-5209, Interview with Irène Coupal-Trudeau, 1980.

96   SAB, R-162, Interview with Mr. and Mrs. Babe Lalonde, 1973.

97   SAB, R-105(a), Interview with Célestine Guillet, 1973.

98   SAB, R-116(b), Interview with Marie Bachelu-Ferraton, 1973.

99   SAB, R-55(a), Interview with Mrs. Jean Bonneau, 1973.

100 SAB, R-88(b), Interview with Annette Poissant, 1973.

101 SAB, R-118(b), Interview with Mrs. Rose Brulotte-Labrecque, 1973.

adapt to it."[102] Ponteix resident Madame Langlois who arrived from Quebec in 1911, echoed Piché's words: "When one moves to the West, one usually stays."[103]

Prairie life was difficult. In the desire to celebrate the fortitude and contributions made by the French-speaking women who settled in Saskatchewan at the turn of the century, it is easy to forget that these women were homesick for the life that they had known. Despair and loneliness were frequent visitors. As many of their daughters recalled: "but for my mother, it must have been extremely hard." For those who grew up on the Prairies, the pain of homesickness disappeared, but their mothers never forgot what they had left behind. Madame Marie-Jeanne Morin Couture came to understand that when she returned to Quebec:

> *Je suis retournée au Québec et j'ai vu où on avait vécu: une grande maison, un beau terrain. ... J'ai compris maman de vouloir repartir.*[104]

> I returned to Quebec and I saw where our family had lived: a big house, a beautiful piece of land. [Now] I understood why Mama wanted to return [to Quebec].

102   SAB, R-65(a), Interview with Sarah Piché, 1973.

103   SAB, R-88(a), Interview with Mr. and Mrs. Raoul Langlois, 1973.

104   SAB, R-5168, Interview with Marie-Jeanne Morin Couture, 1980.

"A WOMAN OF VALOUR WHO CAN FIND?":
JEWISH-SASKATCHEWAN WOMEN IN TWO RURAL SETTINGS,
1882-1939

Anna Feldman

> *A woman of valour who can find?*
> *For her price is far above rubies.*
> *The heart of her husband doth safely trust in her,*
> *And he had no lack of gain.*
> *She doeth him good and not evil*
> *All the days of her life.*
> *She seeketh wool and flax,*
> *And worketh willingly with her hands.*
> *She is like the merchant-ships;*
> *She bringeth her food from afar.*
> *Her husband is known in the gates,*
> *When he sitteth among the elders of the land.*
> Proverbs 31: 10-14, 23

The first Jewish-Saskatchewan woman I met was the late Branche (Bertha) Feldman, my future mother-in-law, a "woman of valour."[1] The meeting took place about midnight in the middle of harvest, almost fifty years ago. A young Jewish woman from Ottawa, excited by the adventure of my first long train trip, I arrived in Estevan where Keiva, my fiancé, and his brother met me. We drove fifty miles to the Sonnenfeld Jewish farm colony where Branche greeted me warmly and introduced me to the other family members. She took me to the dining room for a Sabbath meal, a feast she had prepared especially for me. This was my introduction to the Feldman family and to the Jewish women of Saskatchewan.[2]

This essay provides a window into the lives of Jewish-Saskatchewan women from 1882 to 1939 residing in two different rural settings in Saskatchewan: some lived in farm colonies, others in small communities.[3] Like other rural women of the Prairies,

---

1   I thank my husband, Keiva Feldman, for his constant support and Georgina Taylor for all her help and Jo-Anne Lee for her insight into valourization. I thank Rabbi Roger Pavey, Gladys Rose, Sidney Buckwold for their help, and D'Arcy Hande and the members of the Saskatchewan Archives Board, and Bonnie Tregebov and the Jewish Historical Society of Western Canada for their assistance. I wish to acknowledge the financial assistance of Multiculturalism Canada and of the History of the Jews of Saskatchewan project of Congregation Agudas Israel, Saskatoon. Finally, I thank my many informants for allowing me to share their memories.

2   The Jews have always constituted considerably less than one percent of Saskatchewan's total population. Comparatively speaking, there were not many Jewish women in this province. However, like other non-preferred immigrant women, they made a contribution and, even without valourization, have an important history to tell. For a discussion of valourization, see: Ruth Roach Pierson, "Experience, Difference, Dominance and Voice in the Writing of Canadian Women's History," in Karen Offen, Ruth Roach Pierson and Jane Rendall, eds., *Writing Women's History — International Perspectives* (Bloomington: Indiana Press, 1991), 79-106.

3   According to the census, only incorporated centres with 500 or more were classified as urban for the years 1901, 1906 and 1911; see John H. Archer, *Saskatchewan: A History* (Saskatoon: Western Producer Prairie Books, 1980), 361. For the years 1916-71 only incorporated centres with 1,000 or more were

these Jewish women, the majority of whom came from urban environments, experienced isolation and loneliness.[4] They also faced additional challenges. Anti-Semitism, cultural tradition and language set them apart from English-speaking, non-Jewish society. Although Jewish women in small rural communities, with neighbours living nearby, were not as isolated as the Jewish farm women, Jewish-Saskatchewan rural women in general used their religion, culture, language and social ties with others of a similar background to help cope with their isolation and anti-Semitism.[5]

Jewish women, for the most part, arrived in Saskatchewan as family members. A higher percentage of women and children among Jews than among other groups of immigrants maintained the family character of Jewish immigration to Canada throughout this period.[6] A letter written by Mrs. Sternberg, a Russian Jew, communicating with her brother in late nineteenth-century Canada, suggests that the process of emigration from Europe and eventually to Saskatchewan was a topic that this family discussed in detail:

> My dear brother — you wrote me that it would cost ninety rubles to bring Gitel to you. Don't forget that is a lot of money. If Gitel became engaged and you put in another ten rubles to make one hundred she would have money for [her] dowry or for a trousseau. You still owe money and Passover is coming soon and you need everything for that so don't forget your circumstances.[7]

---

classified as urban. For historical background to the province of Saskatchewan, see: Archer, *Saskatchewan*; R. Douglas Francis and Howard Palmer, eds., *The Prairie West: Historical Readings*, 2nd ed. (Edmonton: Pica Pica Press, 1992); and Gerald Friesen, *The Canadian Prairies: A History* (Toronto: University of Toronto Press, 1984).

4   The historical literature makes frequent reference to the isolation and loneliness of the new settlers and of the women in particular. See, for example: Georgina Taylor, "'Should I Drown Myself Now or Later?': The Isolation of Rural Women in Saskatchewan and their Participation in the Homemakers' Clubs, the Farm Movement and the Co-operative Commonwealth Federation 1910-1967," in Kathleen Storrie, ed., *Women: Isolation and Bonding — The Ecology of Gender* (Toronto: Methuen, 1987), 79-100; and Eliane Leslau Silverman, *The Last Best West: Women on the Alberta Frontier* (Montreal: Eden Press, 1984).

5   Over the years, I have listened to the family's "olden days" anecdotes, worked in archives, interviewed and taped "oldtimers" and collected reminiscences from letter-writing informants. Few Jewish women have left written records about their experiences; see Gerald Tulchinsky, *Taking Root: The Origins of the Canadian Jewish Community* (Toronto: Lester Publishing Ltd., 1992), 171. I have been unable to find any diaries or journals and have uncovered only a handful of letters. Published works by Jewish-Saskatchewan women include: Molly Lyons Bar-David, *My Promised Land* (New York: G.P. Putnam's Sons, 1953); Ruth Bellan, "Growing Up in a Small Saskatchewan Town," in Jewish Historical Society of Canada, ed., *Jewish Life and Times: A Collection of Essays* (Winnipeg: Jewish Historical Society of Western Canada, 1983); Clara Hoffer, *Township Twenty-Five* (Regina: Saskatchewan Department of Culture and Youth, 1974); Clara Hoffer and Fannie Kahan, *Land of Hope* (Saskatoon: Prairie Books, 1960); Clara Lander, "Saskatchewan Memories or How to Start a Jewish Cemetery," *American Jewish Archives* 26, no. 1 (April 1975): 5-7; Fredelle Bruser Maynard, *Raisins and Almonds* (Toronto: Doubleday, 1972); Sheila Watson, ed., *The Collected Poems of Miriam Mandel* (Edmonton: Longspoon Press, 1984); and Tillie Taylor, "When Anything was Possible," *NeWest Review* (February/March 1991): 15. Also see: C.E. Leonoff, "Wapella Farm Settlement," *Transactions, Manitoba Historical and Scientific Society*, Series 3 (1970-71), 27; and Norman Rosenberg, comp., *Edenbridge, the Memory Lives On. ... A History* (Melfort: Phillips Publishers, 1980).

6   Joseph Kage, *With Faith and Thanksgiving: The Story of Two Hundred Years of Jewish Immigration and Immigrant Aid Effort in Canada, 1769-1960* (Montreal: The Eagle Publishing Co., Limited, 1962), 89; and Louis Rosenberg, *Canada's Jews: A Social and Economic Study of the Jews in Canada* (Montreal: Canadian Jewish Congress, 1939), 138.

7   Jewish Historical Society of Western Canada (JHSWC), P4429, Files 37, 38, Letter from Mrs. Sternberg to her brother, 16 February 1883.

Jewish settlement in Saskatchewan began after Canada's first High Commissioner to London, Sir Alexander Galt, convinced Prime Minister Sir John A. Macdonald that Canada should admit Jewish survivors of Russian pogroms to the "Canadian North-West." Canada needed farmers; the Jews needed a refuge. Many wanted to farm, a way of life denied them because they were barred from owning land in Russia and many other eastern-European countries. With few exceptions, Jews had little farming experience and, unlike most immigrant groups, Jews did not have a peasant background.[8] The initial influx of Jews in 1882 predated Doukhobor, Russian, German, Hungarian and Ukrainian settlements in Saskatchewan.[9] After the Russian Jews' arrival, other Jews came from South Africa, England, Roumania, Poland, the Austro-Hungarian Empire and the Ukraine. This was a heterogeneous group.

Despite their diversity, Jews shared many traditions: their religion; a reading knowledge of Hebrew; Yiddish as a spoken language; a storehouse of religious and secular writings; a thirst for knowledge imbued with a love of learning; a folk heritage of customs, stories, sayings, beliefs and songs;[10] and family values. The latter included a perception of the ideal women as set forth in Proverbs 31 of the Old Testament: "A woman of valour who can find? For her price is far above rubies." Wise, kind and charitable, this ideal woman is also competent in business and a devoted wife, mother and, as my future mother-in-law reminded me, a "help meet."[11] These are some of the cultural characteristics that Jewish women adapted to Saskatchewan's conditions.

Once in Saskatchewan, Jewish women were concerned about the safety of not only their extended families in Europe[12] but also for their own family in their new homeland. In Saskatchewan anti-Semitic meetings objecting to Jewish immigration were sometimes held even before any Jewish immigrants arrived in a district.[13] Anti-Semitic articles appeared in Saskatchewan newspapers.[14] One informant recounted her experience with anti-Semitism:

---

8   Roberto Perin stresses "the overwhelming peasant background of most immigrant groups" in "Writing About Ethnicity," in John Schultz, ed., *Writing about Canada: A Handbook for Modern Canadian History* (Scarborough, ON: Prentice Hall, 1990), 203.

9   Only the Mennonites and the immigrants from Britain and Iceland came to farm in Saskatchewan before the Jews did.

10   Ruth R. Wisse, "Jewish Participation in Canadian Culture," *Royal Commission on Bilingualism and Biculturalism. Research Studies*, 20 September 1965, 40.

11   Genesis 2: 18-24 makes reference to a help meet: "And the Lord God said: 'It is not good that a man should be alone; I will make him a help meet for him'." For the reminiscences of a Jewish woman who adapted to conditions in Germany during the second half of the seventeenth and first quarter of the eighteenth centuries, see: *The Memoirs of Glückel of Hameln*, translated by Marvin Lowenthal, with a new Introduction by Robert Rosen (New York: Schocken Books, 1977). For more information on the role and status of the ideal Jewish woman as viewed in traditional Judaism, see: Shoshana Pantel Zolty, *"And All Your Children Shall Be Learned": Women and the Study of the Torah in Jewish Law and History* (Northvale, NJ/London: Jason Aronson Inc., 1993), 19-39.

12   Simon Belkin, *Through Narrow Gates: A Review of Jewish Immigration, Colonization and Immigrant Aid in Canada (1840-1940)* (Montreal: The Eagle Publishing Co., Limited, 1966), 95.

13   *Regina Leader*, 22 March 1892.

14   In July 1928 Louis Vicker responded to charges from Bishop Lloyd of Saskatchewan that Jews constituted a threat to Canada: "Mr. Editor allow me to say to the Bishop of Saskatchewan that if there is a danger that the Jews and everything also that is Jewish, will prostitute the Canadian nation then I am afraid he will have to abandon Christianity, because I am proud to say that Jesus of Nazareth and all the apostles were Jews and surely the Bishop will admit that the Holy Bible is Jewish and by discarding the Jewish influence, I would like to see what is left for the Bishop and Canadian nation"

> My earliest recollection [is] pre-school. ... It was Easter Sunday and I happened to go for a walk with my brother. ... [People] were coming from church and this young boy, he was five, six years old ... and he started chasing us and yelling "You killed Jesus Christ and I'm going to kill you," and I remember grabbing my brother — he couldn't have been two years old — and dragging him and running and [being] so afraid. I was crying. I was, four and half. I didn't know Jesus Christ. I'd never heard of Him before.[15]

Such incidents did not discourage Jews from immigrating to Saskatchewan. They settled in rural hamlets or villages, or on individual farms within a non-Jewish farming area or in Jewish farm colonies. The individual Jewish farms were spread throughout the province. A relatively large proportion of the Jewish population was classified as rural during the period from 1882 to 1939.[16] In Saskatchewan's five successful Jewish farm colonies (Edenbridge established in 1906; Hirsch, 1892; Lipton, 1901; Sonnenfeld, 1905; and Wapella, 1887), Jewish colonists were interspersed with non-Jewish farmers and each Jewish farm was operated as an independent unit.[17] These colonies were not like those of the Hutterites, for example, who live in exclusive colonies. Jewish rural women in Saskatchewan, unlike Hutterite colony women, have always been in contact with the non-Jewish community. This interaction was easier and more frequent as roads and the means of transportation improved.

Like other early women settlers in Saskatchewan, Jewish women suffered enormously. They faced the shock of adjustment, isolation, loneliness, arduous work, primitive living and working conditions, summers of blistering heat and hordes of mosquitoes, and winters of extreme cold and blizzards. As newcomers to a new land all family members had to contribute to the family survival and farm work.

(L. Vicker, "A Jew Replies," *Western Producer*, 5 July 1928). During the 1920s the Klu Klux Klan (KKK) reached the height of its influence in Saskatchewan. For a discussion of the KKK's activities see: Julian Sher, *White Hoods: Canada's Klu Klux Klan* (Vancouver: New Star Books, 1983).

15   Canadian Centre for Folk Culture Collection, Canadian Museum of Civilization (CCFCS), Feldman Collection, Interview by Anna Feldman with R.G., 14 August 1984.

16   In 1901, 99 percent of Saskatchewan's Jews were rural; by 1931 this had dropped to 21 percent (Rosenberg, *Canada's Jews*, 226).

17   Each Jewish farm colony has its own history. The Young Men's Hebrew Benevolent Society (YMHBS), a Montreal organization founded in 1863 for the purpose of assisting needy Jews, planned and sponsored the colony of Hirsch. Later the Jewish Colonization Association (JCA) took over the management of Hirsch colony. Funded by European Jewish philanthropist Baron Maurice de Hirsch, the JCA was organized in 1891 for the purpose of resettling Jews who suffered from political and other forms of discrimination. Part of the JCA's mandate was to establish farm colonies (Belkin, *Through Narrow Gates*, 64). With the agreement of the Canadian government, the JCA also formed the Lipton colony, whose first settlers were Roumanian Jews (Belkin, *Through Narrow Gates*, 76). Herman Landau, a prominent Anglo-Jewish financier, helped to organize the colony of Wapella. He and a London representative of the Canadian Pacific Railway (CPR) arranged to settle Jewish immigrants in Canada's "Northwest"; see Arthur A. Chiel, *The Jews of Manitoba* (Toronto: University of Toronto Press, 1961), 47. Three graduates of a Slobodka Lesna agricultural college in Galicia established the Sonnenfeld colony; see Anna Feldman, "Sonnenfeld — Elements of Survival and Success of a Jewish Farming Community on the Prairies, 1905-1939," *Jewish Historical Society of Canada Journal*, 6, no. 1 (Spring 1982): 33-52. Two separate groups, one from South Africa and the other from London (England), founded Edenbridge. However, the members of both groups had originally come from the Russian Pale; see Maureen Fox, "Jewish Agricultural Colonies in Saskatchewan with Special Reference to the Colonies of Sonnenfeld and Edenbridge" (MA thesis, University of Saskatchewan, 1979), 26. Jewish farm families, not associated with colonies, were also scattered throughout Saskatchewan.

The position of Ukrainian immigrant women, for example, worsened under pioneering conditions. They had to perform heavier work and spend more time in the fields than they did in the old country.[18] The Roumanian woman who built the family home on her own is an example of what the other eastern Europeans had to do.[19] Although Jewish women in the old country had hard lives, most were not used to heavy physical labour. Nevertheless, in 1902 a deputy minister reported: "eighteen sod houses were built [in the Lipton colony] under the direction of half-breed Indians and plastered by the settlers' wives."[20]

As new settlers, Jewish women also helped with work in the field. The daughter of one Jewish pioneering family recalled:

> my mother told me that my father always worked for other people. He had to. The law said that he had to break, I think it was, forty acres of land within a certain time. When he had a day off he would [work on our own land]. My mother would hang my baby brother from a tree. She would tie him in a sheet. My father would chop [another] tree and she would chop it underneath, to get the stump out, and chop the branches off. They had to milk a cow; they had chickens. They had no pigs. That wasn't kosher. They had all that work to do alongside of raising their family, the housework and everything else.[21]

Farm life was a constant struggle. During the period from 1911 to 1931, approximately six out of every ten homesteaders in Saskatchewan abandoned their claim before securing title.[22] Newspaper columnists acknowledged this rural exodus and blamed it on the harshness of farm life for young people, especially for young women.[23] Although the Jewish colonies appear to have been more stable than most other settlements,[24] there were Jewish women and their families who left their farms. Some moved to rural villages and others to larger centres. One Lipton colony woman committed suicide. On the other hand, there were those who seemed to enjoy the challenge. In 1925, during an on-going discussion in the *Nor'-West Farmer* on what a woman was worth, Mrs. Zelickson, a Hirsch colonist wrote:

> Being a pioneer of Southern Saskatchewan, it is quite interesting to note the value of work which I have performed. Although not having the money in cash, I figure the experience is worth it. I am one of the oldest pioneers in Southern Saskatchewan, coming to this country in 1891 and settling with my husband in our present location in 1892. Having worked here for 33 years you will see in the latter part of this letter what I have done. On remarking the value of my work I do not reckon it as the wage of a maid but I figure it as taking the produce to market. ... I estimate the value of my work for these 35 years as $141,578. I have cooked 361,351 meals, baked

18   Frances Swyripa, *Wedded to the Cause: Ukrainian-Canadian Women and Ethnic Identity 1891-1991* (Toronto: University of Toronto Press, 1993), 30.

19   Anne Woywitka, "A Roumanian Pioneer," *Alberta History* 21 (Autumn 1973): 21.

20   National Archives of Canada (NA), MG30, C119, Vol. 22, p. 8, Report by Deputy Minister M. Thos. Smart to the JCA in Paris, 29 November 1902.

21   CCFCS, Feldman Collection, Interview by Anna Feldman with F.B., 14 August 1984.

22   Vernon G. Fowke, *National Policy and the Wheat Economy* (Toronto: University of Toronto Press, 1957), 78.

23   Alison Prentice, Paula Bourne, Gail Cuthbert Brandt, Beth Light, Wendy Mitchinson and Naomi Black, *Canadian Women: A History* (Toronto: Harcourt, Brace Yanovich, 1988), 115.

24   Maureen Fox, "Jewish Agricultural Colonies," 120; and *Montreal Standard*, 3 December 1938.

> 78,800 loaves of bread, 12,045 cakes, 5,158 pies, preserved 3,300 quarts of
> fruit, churned 13,728 pounds of butter and raised 4,950 poultry. I have put
> in 48,180 hours scrubbing, cleaning and washing. I think this is quite a
> record and will be pleased to hear from any woman who can beat it.[25]

There were those who, by developing other skills, made additional contributions
to the family's income and well-being. A Wapella Jewish farm wife became adept at
printing and developing pictures in her family's special photography tent,
"Idylwylde,"[26] and there were at least two Jewish farm women who traded in furs. One
of the fur traders had formerly been a sweatshop worker from Chicago and a trained
singer. A son described his remarkable mother:

> My mother was a protegée of old Ziegfeld. She played the balalaika,
> mandolin, guitar and piano. She was a soloist, not only in Jewish, but also
> in non-Jewish communities. She would partake in all social events and
> bring the children with her. She was pretty tough. She was a sharpshooter.
> A bear came to the cabin ... and she was afraid it would hurt the children.
> She took the rifle and went out and with one shot she felled it. She was also
> a trapper.[27]

In addition to contributing to the survival of their families, Jewish women were
concerned with becoming "Canadian." As newcomers, they spoke many languages,
but with few exceptions, Yiddish was the one common to all. However, they made a
tremendous effort to learn English as quickly as possible. Branche Feldman of the
Sonnenfeld colony, after her arrival, went to school for a short time because, as she
used to say: "You can't learn pronunciation by reading the *Family Herald and Weekly
Star*." At the Estevan school she attended, the teachers did not know what to do with
her. Without English she could not explain that she was literate: "I brought my
education with me, only it was in a different language." A German boy who acted as
her interpreter was puzzled by her frequent promotions. He made some inquiries
and learned that the teachers judged Branche by her arithmetic.[28]

Love of learning is part of a Jew's heritage.[29] Gabrielle Roy, after visiting
Edenbridge colony, wrote: "To tell the truth, I saw books in all the houses at
Edenbridge; I think the people there buy them in preference to food."[30] The
percentage of literate Jews in Saskatchewan during this period was high in
comparison with the provincial average.[31] Harry Allam noted this emphasis on
learning in his *General Report of the Soldier Settlement Board on the Jewish Colonies*:

> one of the most outstanding things to notice was the desire [of Jewish
> parents] ... to give their children the best education possible. To get money
> for this, most everything else was to go.[32]

---

25   Extract of letter written by Mrs. C. Zelickson published in the *Nor'-West Farmer*, 5 March 1925.

26   "Pioneer Photographs the West," *Vancouver Jewish Bulletin*, 28 November 1991, 27.

27   CCFCS, Feldman Collection, Interview by Anna Feldman with P.G., 24 June 1985.

28   CCFCS, Feldman Collection, Personal Communications, Reminiscences of the late Branche Feldman,
     August 1978.

29   *Pirkei Avot*, 2:6, Hillel (in Hebrew).

30   Gabrielle Roy, "Palestine Avenue," in *The Fragile Lights of Earth: Articles and Memories 1942-1970*, trans.
     Alan Brown (Toronto: McClelland and Stewart, 1982), 55.

31   *Report of Saskatchewan Royal Commission on Immigration and Settlement 1930*, Regina, Table XI-A "Literacy
     of the Population of Saskatchewan, 10 Years of Age and Over, Classified According to Racial Origin," 195.

32   *General Report on the Jewish Colonies* made by Harry Allam, Chief Field Supervisor of the Calgary Office

A former Hirsch Jewish farm colonist said that her mother sold subscriptions for various papers and magazines in order that her children could have reading material.[33] Desire to provide the children with a Hebrew education was so great that despite their having little money to spare and living in small cramped quarters, women gave bachelor Hebrew teachers room and board in addition to wages.

Other aspects of their religion made Jewish women and men different from their neighbours.[34] Judaism is a way of life. For the orthodox Jew, there are traditional customs and religious rules covering the entire year. The home and family are central to many religious ceremonies such as the Sabbath; the Passover *seder*, a ceremonial supper; or the lighting of the candles at *Chanukah*, the Festival of Lights.[35] The "Jewish home" represents the life-giving sustenance of faith and it is in the home that the influence of women is most strongly exercised.[36] Even for secular Jewish women, the birth of a son meant preparations for two events: his circumcision on his eighth day; and *bar mitzvah*, a small coming-of-age celebration in the synagogue, thirteen years later.

With the exception of Wapella, each colony, sooner or later, had a building which its inhabitants used as a synagogue. Like the other colony buildings, it was a small, simple, wooden structure. A few years after it was built, Sonnenfeld's synagogue was enlarged. It had pictures of clouds painted on the ceiling and the star of David painted on an outside end wall. During services men and women were separated. Facing the eastern wall in Sonnenfeld synagogue, women sat at the back on a stage and the men sat at the front.[37] Renovated in more recent years, the Edenbridge synagogue is a beautiful, small building which originally had an outside stairway leading to the gallery where the women prayed. This provided children with access to their mothers without disturbing the men's prayers on the main floor. The men found the arrangement particularly convenient on the Day of Atonement, a fast day for adults, when mothers came prepared with food for their children.[38]

The many rules dealing with what food a Jew is allowed to eat and how food should be handled before it is eaten, compounded the difficulties the Jewish women pioneers had in meal preparations. For example, only certain animals are acceptable as food. The usual practice is that a specially trained ritual slaughterer, a *shokhet*, kills

of the Soldier Settlement Board, Ottawa, March 1937, in Fox, "Jewish Agricultural Colonies," Appendix.

33   Telephone conversation by Anna Feldman with S.S., 23 December 1993.

34   According to Jewish custom, it is necessary to set up a school, build a ritual bath (*mikveh*), consecrate a cemetery and organize a synagogue as soon as possible after a community is formed. However, a synagogue building is not necessary. If there is a *minion*, ten Jewish men, orthodox services for the community may be conducted. In spite of efforts to have *mikvehs* built in other colonies, only Hirsch and Lipton succeeded in doing so. Although the *mikveh* is used by both men and women as an aid to spirituality, it is a necessity for orthodox women. The chief use is to render a menstruant ritually clean. For information on Sonnenfeld's attempt to construct a *mikveh*, see: Feldman, "Sonnenfeld," 43. For an excellent source of information on Jews and Judaism, see: Cecil Roth, editor-in-chief, *Encyclopaedia Judaica* (Jerusalem: Keter Publishing House, 1971). For an analysis of changes in Judaism throughout the millennia, see: Hans Küng, *Judaism: Between Yesterday and Tomorrow* (New York: Crossroad, 1992).

35   Zolty, *And All Your Children Shall Be Learned*, 29.

36   Ibid.

37   Personal communication with K. Feldman, 8 March 1994.

38   CCFCS, Feldman Collection, Interview by Anna Feldman with C.V., 27 September 1983.

the animal. However, when the services of a *shokhet* are not available, Jews may eat the meat if a lay person has the proper knife, is able to recite the necessary prayers, kills the animal according to the rules and handles the meat in a ritually correct manner. In the early years of settlement, the orthodox Jewish family's diet frequently consisted of salted herring and potatoes. There was a welcome relief when a farmer managed to trap prairie chickens alive.[39] This was especially true if the fortunate family could use prairie chickens for the Sabbath.

Sabbath preparations began on Friday with housecleaning, cooking and baking traditional foods including *khallah*, egg bread. Before placing the bread in the oven, my husband's grandmother, the late Sarah Feldman, would throw a piece of the raw dough into the fire. This was to commemorate the tithe originally given to the priests at the time of the temple. To usher in the Sabbath at sundown on Friday night, the woman lit and recited a blessing over the candles. Saturday was a day of rest for the Jewish settlers. They did only the most essential work. Celebrating in the home, colonists enjoyed relaxing, visiting, reading, contemplating and praying for the orthodox. Work for the family began again on Sunday. This did not always meet with the approval of their non-Jewish neighbours. In a letter, Max Heppner noted:

> In the Hirsch Colony this Spring, some of the Ministers of the Church put up a notice in the Post Office warning everybody from working on Sunday with the addition that anybody contravening the law would be prosecuted.[40]

Preparations for such holidays as the New Year and the Day of Atonement were more extensive. The demands on Jewish women's time and energy were even greater. To follow the Passover food rules, for example, it was necessary to change or ritually cleanse everyday dishes. Holiday celebrations also meant visitors. Jewish people from both large and small communities would frequently spend this time with colonists. Should a woman be unable to prepare a necessary food such as *matzoh*, unleavened bread, she ordered it from Winnipeg, or another large Jewish centre. One woman remembered what her parents told her:

> They had [sent their Passover order] to Winnipeg and apparently it didn't arrive. ... My mother and a few of the [colony] ladies [close by] had recipes. One made up a potato kugel, and the other made potato latkes and for breakfast they might have had a baked potato, boiled potato, and someone made potatoes with *smetena* [cream]. For eight days they had potatoes.[41]

Although there was additional work involved in holiday celebrations, this was the time when farm women looked forward to participating in their colony's rich cultural life and having an opportunity to visit. For women, it was one important way of breaking out of the isolation that life on remote farms imposed. Colonists met for dances, box socials, Yiddish plays and a variety of concerts, including those prepared by the Hebrew teacher in which the children celebrated a particular holiday. In Edenbridge, women arranged some of the concerts. One of my most memorable experiences took place in 1980 when I interviewed an elderly, blind, very ill woman and her three daughters. During that extremely long interview they took turns singing Yiddish songs they had performed in Edenbridge. This included a song that the talented pioneer

---

39   Beth Jacob Congregation, *Our Heritage, A History of Regina and Region Jewish Community: A Commemorative Book* (Regina: Beth Jacob Congregation, 1989), 72.

40   Max Heppner, Letter to the Editor, *Jewish Times*, 1 October 1909.

41   CCFCS, Feldman Collection, Interview by Anna Feldman with F.B., 14 August 1984.

had composed. She also recited some of her own poetry. In spite of her infirmities, she glowed with joy as she recalled the years she had spent in the colony.[42]

Colony women had few opportunities to congregate on their own. On occasion, they would have a tea to raise whatever money they could for charity, and various Jewish causes. I heard frequently that such activities not only eased their sense of isolation but also reinforced their sense of identity. They did this even though there were no Jewish organizations in their own community. Their devotion to Jewish life and Jewish causes left a marked impression on Louis Rosenberg. A graduate of the University of Leeds and later a Fellow of both the Royal Economic Society and of the Royal Statistical Society, Rosenberg was one of the most knowledgeable and capable people to have ever worked for the Jewish Colonization Association (JCA). During the years, 1919 to 1934, he worked as the JCA's western agent and travelled extensively throughout his region, which included Saskatchewan. During an interview with David Rome, Rosenberg said:

> The Jew in the small community was much more Jewishly concerned and Jewishly interested than the average Jew who lived in a large Jewish community. Their per capita contribution to Zionist funds was often larger than the per capita contribution of (those from) the large city.[43]

Meeting a guest could be another reason for a gathering of women. On my first trip to Saskatchewan, Branche Feldman held a tea in my honour in the Sonnenfeld synagogue and it was then that she introduced me to the other women of Sonnenfeld. During my research I learned of only one formal group. One informant told me that the members met in the Edenbridge synagogue for a time:

> A group of women had regular meetings. They would raise a little money. [The women] would help if someone needed a little financial help. The money wouldn't be very much. If somebody had to be taken to the hospital, they could see to that sort of thing. They conducted regular business meetings.[44]

The women of Lipton colony, during the pioneering era, sang the music for dances. This was one strategy for getting the young people together.[45] A group of former Edenbridge residents disclosed another way for young people to meet:

> Young people from Kinistino, Naicam, Beatty, Melfort, Star City, Nipawin, Saskatoon [and other places] would visit the colony. Girls would be looking for boys and boys would be looking for girls. It's a funny thing, but the Edenbridge kids, very few married within the colony. They all seem to have wandered. Either they went away for a holiday, went to Winnipeg or Prince Albert and that's where they met.[46]

---

42   CCFCS, Feldman Collection, Interview by Anna Feldman with G.G., L.D., A.G. and M.G., 21 July 1980. For more information on music in the Jewish farm colonies, see: Anna Feldman, "Yiddish Songs of the Jewish Farm Colonists in Saskatchewan, 1917-1939," (MA thesis, Institute of Canadian Studies, Carleton University, 1983).

43   Jewish Public Library (Montreal, Canada), Interview by David Rome with Louis Rosenberg, 11 and 30 January 1972.

44   Congregation Agudus Israel, History of the Jews of Saskatchewan (CAI), Anna Feldman Collection, Interview by Anna Feldman with A.B., 20 August 1987.

45   CCFCS, Feldman Collection, Interview by Anna Feldman with Dr. S.S., 30 July 1980.

46   CCFCS, Feldman Collection, Interview by Anna Feldman with F.B., S.F., S.G., R.G., M.T., A.M., D.P., A.W., I.G. and S.L., 14 August 1984.

The question of finding suitable mates for the young people worried Saskatchewan's Jewish community. A 1925 JCA inspection report on the Hirsch Colony observed:

> There are in the colony [of Hirsch] the following boys of marriageable age: Harry Zelickson, Max Zelickson, Harry Hirt, Richard Frost and the two Schopp boys. There are no girls in the colony. With the arrival of the Barish Hirt family, there will be two girls who may agree to marry [two of the boys].[47]

In January 1939, Jacob Baltzan recalled in *Das Yidishe Vort* the "sad tale" of a Lipton colonist who loved to farm but felt he must leave the land because there were no young men for his daughters who were of marriageable age. Baltzan recounted that the colonist was afraid to allow them to go to the city: "not infrequently he was heard to moan: what does one do for one's children? What should we do with our daughters?"[48]

Statistics on intermarriage are available for few of the years between 1882 and 1939. Of those prepared from census data by Louis Rosenberg for the years between 1926 and 1936, no Jewish women married a gentile in Saskatchewan during the years 1926, 1927, 1929, 1930 and 1936. Although a much higher percentage of men than women usually intermarried, there was a dramatic reversal of that trend in 1933. Only 8 percent of men but 20 percent of women married non-Jewish people.[49] Harry Allam's Soldier Settlement Board Inspector's *General Report on the Jewish Colonies* might supply a clue as to whether the Jewish women who intermarried came from a colony, a rural hamlet or a larger centre:

> I was told there was very little intermarrying between Jews and Gentiles. It is estimated that about one percent of Jewish boys marry Gentile girls, and about two percent of Jewish girls marry Gentile boys ... .[50]

There are many possible theories for the low intermarriage rate. Sociologist G.N. Ramu suggests that residential propinquity acts as an initial filtering device in mate selection.[51] JCA agent Louis Rosenberg reported that there was less intermarriage among members of religious communities which prohibited or limited such intermarriage,[52] while historians Jean Burnet and Howard Palmer state that the Jewish attitude to intermarriage is based on a fear that the Jewish community could disappear.[53] The orthodox Jews, on the other hand, would say that the Jewish-Saskatchewan women were quite successful in their task in educating children to Jewish values.[54]

A wedding was a festive occasion for which the colony gathered and the women

---

47   JCA, Memorandum of Inspection, Hirsch Colony, 22 and 23 October 1925, DB13, Hirsch Colony, Sask., Part 1: First red book 1925-1930.

48   Jacob Baltzan, "My Life as a Farmer," *Das Yidishe Vort*, (In Yiddish) 12 January 1939.

49   Rosenberg, *Canada's Jews*, 107.

50   Allam, *General Report on the Jewish Colonies*, in Fox, "Jewish Agricultural Colonies," Appendix.

51   G.N. Ramu, "Courtship and Marriage," in K. Ishwaran, ed., *The Canadian Family* (Canada: Gage Publishing Limited, 1983), 252.

52   Rosenberg, *Canada's Jews*, 102.

53   Jean R. Burnet with Howard Palmer, *"Coming Canadians": An Introduction to a History of Canada's Peoples* (Canada: McClelland and Stewart Inc. in association with the Multiculturalism Program, Department of the Secretary of State and the Canadian Government Publishing Centre, Supply and Services, 1988), 99.

54   Zolty, *And All Your Children Shall Be Learned*, 29.

looked after much of the preparation. An interviewee described an Edenbridge wedding:

> [It was] one of the fanciest weddings you can imagine. Now how about having it open to the sky? Well, [the building] had a skylight. They opened it up. It was in November, but they opened it up for the time of the ceremony. This was an orthodox, almost Hasidic, wedding in Edenbridge. Everybody took part. The women walked the half-mile with the bride. My mother was so busy, she didn't notice whether I had overshoes or not. And I froze my ankles. The meal was everything you could think of — cakes galore. The cakes had been stored in the little room in the synagogue. They froze! The women didn't know then that you could freeze cakes. … They were horrified. The women used to grow myrtle and they would make bridal wreaths around the veil. My mother used to provide them. They would pinch off branches and make wreaths out of them. The bride would get artificial flowers from a florist in Melfort.[55]

Jewish farm women would meet with their non-Jewish friends in social gatherings in homes, at local dances, chautauquas,[56] fairs, school concerts and sports' days, and public meetings. Reminiscing about political meetings, some former Edenbridge colonists indicated that the women were involved in a lot of the work:

> We used to have money drives … lectures [and] speeches. It was our entertainment, lots of times. And usually the organizers used to come from Melville. … They knew more than us [sic] and they explained … And … read their literature.[57]

A very important connection between the Jewish and non-Jewish women were the midwives of both groups who looked after all the women in their communities. Although some Jewish women also belonged to the Homemakers' Club, it is not easy to determine just how many. This popular rural organization played an important and effective role in helping to overcome the isolation of rural women in Saskatchewan.[58] Membership records of the Homemakers' Club do not usually include information on religious denominations or ethnicity, nor whether members came from a farm or a small community. For example, two such entries are: "Mrs. N.J. Cohen who attended the 1931-32 Kindersley Homemaker's Convention," and "Mrs. I— [who] gave an interesting paper on Dental Care — this is remarkable as Mrs. I— who is Jewish could not read English until the last year or so."[59] Was Mrs. Cohen Jewish and did either Mrs. Cohen or Mrs. I— come from farms? That some

---

55   CAI, Anna Feldman Collection, Interview by Anna Feldman with A.B., 20 August 1987.

56   Chautauqua was a travelling institution with Canadian roots in Methodist temperance rallies. It carried education, inspiration and entertainment across Canada. For more information, see: Sheilagh S. Jameson, in collaboration with Nola B. Erickson, *Chautauqua in Canada* (Calgary: Glenbow-Alberta Institute, 1979).

57   CCFCS, Feldman Collection, Interview by Anna Feldman with F.B., S.B., S.G., R.G., M.T., A.M., D.P., A.W., I.G. and S.L., 14 August 1984.

58   See: Taylor, "Should I Drown Myself?" in *Women: Isolation and Bonding*; Kerrie A. Strathy, "Saskatchewan Women's Institutes, The Rural Women's University, 1911-1986," (MCE thesis, University of Saskatchewan, 1987); and Women's Institutes of Saskatchewan, *Legacy, A History of Saskatchewan Homemakers' Clubs and Women's Institutes, 1911-1988*, (Saskatoon: Saskatchewan Women's Institute, 1988), 149.

59   University of Saskatchewan Archives (AUS), RG11, S.4., Extension Division, Saskatchewan Homemakers' and Women's Institutes, Director's Report, 1939.

Hulda Swedberg in her home in the Marchwell district, 1906. Courtesy Saskatchewan Archives Board R-A 4809.

Swedish-Saskatchewan women celebrating a birthday, c. 1930. Courtesy Broadview Historical and Museum Association Inc.

French-Canadian women near Lebret, Saskatchewan, c. 1920. Left to right: Rose Pilon-Filiatrault, Marie-Anne Pilon-Kilmartin, Eugénie Pilon-Lemire, Marie-Ange Pilon-Henley, Albertine Pilon-Bedel, Mélodie Pilon-Aubin. Courtesy Private Collection, Brian Mlazgar.

Madame Jeanne Boiron (on right) of Val Marie, c. 1900. Courtesy Saskatchewan Archives Board, R-A 20492.

Branche Feldman (far left) just prior to her coming to Saskatchewan with her older sister, Ethel (centre), in 1910. Courtesy Private Collection, Anna Feldman.

Jewish settlers Samuel and Hanna Schwartz with daughter Simma and her husband, Lipton district, c. 1903. Courtesy Saskatchewan Archives Board R-B 1781.

Wives of Jewish refugees working in a garden, Edenbridge colony, 1939. Courtesy Saskatchewan Archives Board, R-B 9851-2.

Originally from Roumania, a Jewish bride (family name of Argenter) and groom (Chaim Mayerowitz) prepare to jump over the *khallah*, Lipton colony, 1916. Courtesy Jewish Historical Society of Western Canada.

IODE float in parade for peace celebration, Kerrobert, 19 July 1919. Courtesy Saskatchewan Archives Board R-A 15549-3.

Appealing for help for women on relief, Saskatoon, 1930s. Courtesy Saskatoon Public Library Local History Room.

Kay Papove cutting grain with a binder, c. 1939. Courtesy Saskatchewan Archives Board
S-B 6578.

Elsie Geppert, daughter of Edward and Bertha Geppert, operating the family tractor on farm near Dafoe in the early 1940s. Courtesy Western Development Museum Collection.

Marie Leclerc washing clothes outside her house, with a washing machine operated by a small motor, Cantal district, 1921. Courtesy Saskatchewan Archives Board R-A 20058.

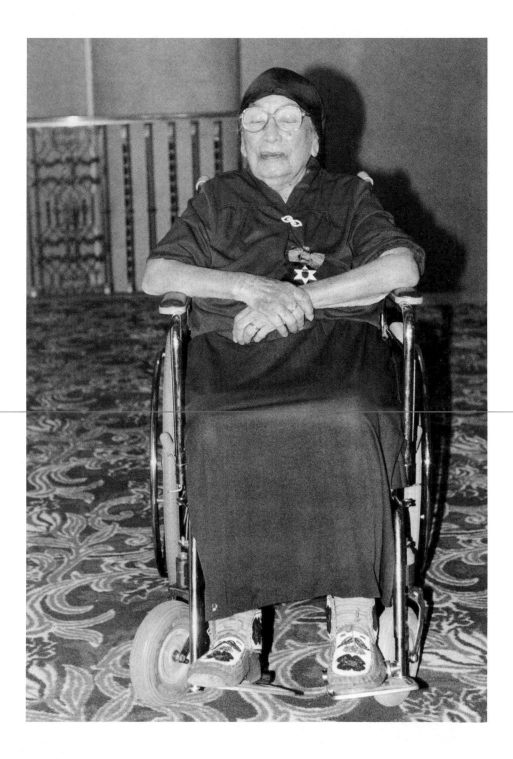

In 1992, Annie Johnstone, an Aboriginal woman from Pinehouse Lake, received the Saskatchewan Order of Merit for her achievements, which included delivering 502 babies. Courtesy Private Collection, Miriam McNab.

Aboriginal woman tanning a hide. Courtesy Saskatchewan Archives Board R-A 4463-2.

Aboriginal women from Pinehouse Lake in Saskatoon, June 1995, because forest fires had forced them to evacuate their homes. Courtesy Private Collection, Miriam McNab.

The drama group of the Regina Chapter, Immigrant Women of Saskatchewan creates, writes and performs plays which create awareness of the difficulties immigrants face when they come to Canada. Courtesy Regina Chapter, Immigrant Women of Saskatchewan.

This group of Saskatoon women graduated from the Immigrant Women of Saskatchewan's Job Reentry Project in 1995. Courtesy Saskatoon Chapter, Immigrant Women of Saskatchewan.

Jewish women living in small rural communities, most of whom were wives of storekeepers, attended the Homemaker's Club was confirmed by the late Harry Buckwold, a former Jewish resident of Admiral, who said that his wife "was the president of the Homemaker's [in Admiral, Saskatchewan], also a member of the Ladies Aid. She wrote plays during Christmas season, also took part in many things."[60]

Socializing was more convenient for Jewish women in small communities than for those who resided in the farm colonies because their neighbours lived close by. These women, most of whom were wives of storekeepers, curled, played bridge, golfed, and participated in the hospital auxiliary, the Red Cross, the Eastern Star and various other community organizations whose membership was predominantly non-Jewish.

In keeping with the role of "help meet," Jewish-Saskatchewan rural women supported their husband's contributions to both the Jewish and larger communities. The men, including Branche's husband Majer, were members of local telephone and school boards, and other organizations. A few became justices of the peace.[61] Some were elected as reeves and councillors in their municipalities.[62] They participated in all phases of the cooperative movement, including the Wheat Pool[63] and they played an active role in politics.[64] When lobbying was required, a community would frequently select a Jew who was skilled in debating and untangling bureaucratic red tape as spokesperson for the entire community. In 1919, for example, a member of Sonnenfeld colony was chosen to lobby Ottawa for a railway line. He succeeded and subsequently one of the stations was named Hoffer, after him.[65]

Hoffer and other hamlets mushroomed throughout the province with the construction of branch rail lines. As rail lines appeared so too did general stores. Often before the tracks reached their chosen communities, merchant families freighted supplies by wagon teams.[66] In hamlets such as Maryfield, Fairlight, Spy Hill, Fox Valley, Admiral, Watson and Big River one might find a Jewish storekeeper and his family.[67] Although some met with success, it was not unusual for others to move from place to place in search of a livelihood. One woman remembered:

> [Her husband] was not a businessman. He was a school teacher. We were in Kinistino, Prince Albert, Elgar, Mildred, Kenwood, Saskatoon, North Battleford, Vermillion [Alberta]. ... I was the businesswoman of the family. I could do anything. I did the buying. I was a good saleslady.[68]

60   Saskatoon Archives Board (SAB), Interview by A.M. Nicholson with Harry Buckwold, 12, 14, 17-20 January 1966.

61   NA, MG30, C126, vol. 1, Israel Hoffer, 1926-49.

62   Rosenberg, *Edenbridge*, 114.

63   A.L. Plotkin, *Struggle for Justice* (New York: Exposition Press, 1964), 63-77.

64   Ibid., 89. Also see: AUS, Interview by A.M. Nicholson with Harry Fenster, 18 November 1970. In a telephone conversation with Anna Feldman in November 1982, Tommy Douglas confirmed that his election of 1935 was not going well until the polls which included Hirsch and Sonnenfeld turned the tide. The same situation was repeated in his successful election of 1940.

65   *Western Jewish News*, 27 November 1975.

66   Louis Rosenberg, *A Gazeteer of Jewish Communities in Canada, showing the Jewish population in each of the cities, towns and villages in Canada in the Census Years 1851-1951*, Canadian Jewish Community Series, Number 7 (Montreal: Bureau of Social and Economic Research, Canadian Jewish Congress, 1957), x.

67   For more information on small businesses in Saskatchewan, see: D'Arcy Kevin Hande, "The Small Businessman in Saskatchewan, 1919-1939," (MA thesis, University of Saskatchewan, 1988).

68   CCFCS, Feldman Collection, Interview by Anna Feldman with M.K., 25 May 1988.

Retailers, non-Jewish and Jewish alike, made important contributions to the villages and hamlets in which they lived. Coming from countries such as Russia, Poland, Austria or Roumania, Jewish storekeepers knew the needs, languages and customs of most of the settlers, who, like themselves, had come to make their new home in Canada. English was soon added to the merchant families' multilingual vocabulary and if there were Natives in the area, merchants also acquired a smattering of one or two Aboriginal languages. The storekeeping couple became friends of their customers and provided them with such services as writing letters or acting as translators and advisors.[69] By giving credit, these business people derived satisfaction in knowing that their customers would have food and clothing and their businesses played a significant role in the province's economy. However, they took the financial risk and many paid the price by going bankrupt during the "Dirty Thirties." Distressed by her memories, one informant lamented:

> *Only* credit. And that brings up a very painful memory for me, because my father extended credit to his customers who were mostly farmers, and when they had any money, they didn't come to pay their bill at the store who had helped them out. Oh no, they went in to Swift Current and bought there. During the Depression we weren't any better off than the other people, but we had a great deal of pride. ... We wouldn't let anybody know that we too were starving, because you can only eat so much from your store. ... If you can't pay your bills, you're not going to get the merchandise.[70]

It was not an easy life. One individual states that her father was in business, but it was her mother who had many careers. She was the secretary, the bookkeeper, saleslady and did the pricing. She also ran the family home and raised the children. Jewish-Saskatchewan rural women were an integral part of the family economy. When talking about her mother, one storekeeper's daughter says she could "remember being upset for her. She worked extremely hard."[71] The load was almost too much to bear for some women. The son of another storekeeper maintains that "women had an awful job. I know my mother was mad all the time. She just hated it."[72]

Living a Jewish way of life in a small Saskatchewan community and providing children with a knowledge of their heritage meant extra work and more responsibilities. A common practice was to hire a well-educated young Jewish man from the city who boarded with the family, worked in the store and assisted with the youngsters' Jewish education. He taught the children various subjects, including Hebrew.[73]

Maintaining the Sabbath as a day of rest and meditation was not possible for members of the Jewish family who had a store. Saturday was its busiest day. But they kept many other rituals and traditions including: on the Sabbath, the mother lit candles, recited the blessing and prepared a special Friday night meal; and, for Passover, families and friends assembled for the *seder*. Like the colony women, the rural women obtained the Passover order from a large Jewish centre. The problem of kosher meat was resolved in different ways. A man who had lived in a small community pointed out:

---

69   Rosenberg, *A Gazeteer*, x.

70   CCFCS, Feldman Collection, Interview by Anna Feldman with D.H., 15 August 1984.

71   CCFCS, Feldman Collection, Interview by Anna Feldman with R.G., 14 August 1984.

72   CAI, Anna Feldman Collection, Interview by Anna Feldman with B.L., 25 May 1988.

73   CCFCS, Feldman Collection, Interview by Anna Feldman with H.F., 27 May 1986.

> [His mother] always prepared kosher meat. In the fall of the year a man
> (*shokhet*) used to come in and [the *shokhet*] would kill about 100 fowl, ducks,
> geese and that they [his parents] processed. [The meat] was kept in a little
> shack, like a freezer. In the summer [my parents] would bring in a little
> meat from Kamsack or Canora. But during the summer months, we were
> actually vegetarians.[74]

For his mother and others, meeting Jewish women from the nearby small communities was a high point in their lives. Watrous, a resort town in Saskatchewan, served as a meeting place for those who could afford the expense. Many people, including Jews, went there during the summer. This vacation also provided young people the opportunity to meet and come to know one another. However, the Jewish holidays were a special time. On the most important ones, the store would be closed and the family would celebrate by visiting with friends or relatives and attending synagogue in a colony or in a larger centre such as Canora, Melfort, North Battleford, Estevan and Rosthern. Or, they might gather in a home with other Jewish families to observe special religious occasions. This was an opportunity for women to break out of their isolation and derive comfort and support from one another. One women recollected that "[the Jews from the surrounding hamlets] came to Wadena for Rosh Hashonah and Yom Kippur. The first services were held in my parent's home."[75] Contributing financially to and working for various Jewish causes was also part of their way of life. In a letter, Belle Drutz wrote that her "mother was an ardent Zionist. Without ever going to a single meeting or attending any functions, she paid dues to Hadassah in Saskatoon diligently. My parents never turned anyone away who was appealing for a Jewish cause, be it in Canada or Israel."[76] When a person in a small community heard that there were war orphans in Europe who needed clothing, she invited Jewish people from neighbouring villages to her home and asked them to contribute money. The women in this group then bought fabric and, after sewing the required garments, forwarded them to a charitable organization in the East.[77]

Isolated in small Saskatchewan hamlets, Jewish women felt the need for support from other Jewish women most keenly when preparing for special occasions such as weddings. But, when one woman's sister was married, all residents in her community participated in the celebration:

> [My sister] was married in [her village] in either 1934 or 1935 and the whole
> village came. ... Five hundred people were at the wedding. ... We bought
> the store that was there and we had the wedding in the store. The Rabbi
> came from Moose Jaw to officiate. It was a Jewish wedding. The whole village
> closed up to go to the wedding. In fact, the poor groom was selling shoes
> and gifts and everything before the wedding. He had to go and get dressed
> and he was selling stuff before the wedding. Oh, it was so funny! But they
> sent out the customers. ... We had forty Jewish people from Moose Jaw and
> another Jewish family from Assiniboia. My mother, may she rest in peace,
> ordered about ten great, big beautiful salmon. She sliced them and made
> pickled salmon and she baked cakes. ... A Chinese man made the salads.
> ... And I guess Mother did most of the baking for the reception. She was a

---

74   CAI, Anna Feldman Collection, Interview by Anna Feldman with B.L., 25 May 1988.

75   CAI, Anna Feldman Collection, Interview by Anna Feldman with R.T., 27 May 1988.

76   Letter from Belle Drutz to Anna Feldman, November 1986.

77   CAI, Anna Feldman Collection, Interview by Anna Feldman with D.P., April 1988.

wonderful cook. ... She put down two barrels of vinegar pickles. Nobody could get over those pickles. There was nothing left in the barrel. ... She had the reception afterwards. Usually the thing was to have a free dance. Well, she didn't want any drunken brawls or anything like that. So that's why we had the reception afterwards.[78]

Although they worked hard and were supportive of their families, Jewish women had their own opinions and their independent views did not always coincide with what their husbands believed. One person remembered that she and her husband had a disagreement during a discussion on politics:

This was our first fight. ... He said, "... and how many people there vote Liberal? They're going to pick you out" ... and he said, "I'm not going to take you." And I couldn't drive the car. And I said, "Well, I'll phone somebody from the Liberal membership and they'll come and get me." Well, that would be worse. That would be more humiliating than taking me. And he took me, but we weren't talking. I killed his vote.[79]

While having one's own view was common, a woman going to a political meeting without her husband was quite unusual. Like many rural people in Saskatchewan suffering from dreadful conditions during the 1930s, one idealistic woman became involved with a communist group:[80]

I was the only Jewish person there. [My husband] was against communism. He didn't like me being involved. At one meeting the secretary was called away. [She asked] me to take the minutes. I said I can't spell [in English] ... so I got the minutes — and here's people talking — so I went in a corner — and I wrote in Jewish spelling [Yiddish script]. [Later the secretary] said "I didn't know you know shorthand!" I didn't answer her. ... She thought that I knew everything.[81]

When I questioned Jewish women about what it was like living in a small community, responses varied from one extreme to the other. A former resident of Saskatchewan replied that she and her family were the first Jews to have ever lived in B. "[The residents of B.] had never seen a Jewish person before we came there, and when I tell you they came to look at us, that is no exaggeration."[82]

Another informant told me that being a member of the only Jewish family in a rural village was not really a happy life for a Jewish girl:

I wasn't allowed to go out. ... I cried. ... I felt very different. ... I had two brothers. [My Dad] wouldn't allow us to stay at the school dance. At 12 o'clock there was always a supper waltz. You chose partners and then they served sandwiches. My Dad made us come home at 12 o'clock because they served ham sandwiches.[83]

Each family found its own method for dealing with differences between Jews and the dominant society. One woman recalled:

78   CCFCS, Feldman Collection, Interview by Anna Feldman with B.A., 29 September 1984.

79   CCFCS, Feldman Collection, Interview by Anna Feldman with R.G., 14 August 1984.

80   For more information on the Communist Party in Saskatchewan, see: Ivan Avakumovic, *The Communist Party in Canada: A History* (Toronto: McClelland and Stewart Limited, 1975).

81   CCFCS, Feldman Collection, Interview by Anna Feldman with M.K., 25 May 1988.

82   CCFCS, Feldman Collection, Interview by Anna Feldman with S.T., 17 September 1985.

83   CCFCS, Feldman Collection, Interview by Anna Feldman with R.R., 3 September 1985.

> My parents did not regard Christmas as a problem. I know they used to take
> great joy in the fact that my sister and I were usually the stars of the
> Christmas program … and I remember my father coming home with a
> couple of dolls for us. It must have been Christmas Eve. I think he said,
> "Well, you know, if you like somebody, you want to give them a present.
> And he was very fond of his little girls, so this was as good an occasion as
> any to bring them a present. We never felt deprived.[84]

A very musical woman, who plays the piano, says that she "never felt different from anybody else. I played for the dances. I played for funerals and weddings [in church]. I played for everything."[85] Several Jewish women expressed considerable warmth when recollecting their relationship with their Doukhobor neighbours: "The Doukhobors had a little word that meant 'Little Jewess,' *zhudishke*, or something like that, but it was done in a very loving way."[86] And one enthusiastic response to my question was:

> I loved those years. We were Jewish in the sense that we knew we were. We
> bought kosher meat from Saskatoon. We were part of the community and
> I belonged to the United Church young people's group. And the reason I
> had been asked to join … [was that] my best friend belonged. I was never
> an outsider.[87]

Branche and most other Jewish women pioneers in Saskatchewan came from eastern-European countries as family members. Their religion, cultural traditions, languages and mode of living were very different from the dominant society. These differences added still more stress to the arduous conditions, isolation and loneliness from which most women settlers suffered. Yet the Jewish women, sustained by their rich cultural life and infrequent visits with women of a similar background, adjusted, learned English and overcame the difficulties faced by all survivors of the "Dirty Thirties." On the other hand, Jewish women who lived in rural hamlets or villages lacked the support enjoyed by colony women. They had to make a considerable effort in order to participate in a Jewish community environment. While some Jewish women living in small communities felt marginal, others believed that they had the best of both worlds. However, it was easier for those who lived in rural hamlets and villages to adapt to the dominant society than their "sisters" who lived on farms.[88] Successfully performing their accepted role as set out in Genesis 2 and Proverbs 31, these Jewish-Saskatchewan rural women were truly "women of valour."

---

84   CCFCS, Feldman Collection, Interview by Anna Felman with R.N., 2 August 1984.

85   CCFCS, Feldman Collection, Interview by Anna Feldman with M.S., 10 August 1984.

86   CCFCS, Feldman Collection, Interview by Anna Feldman with S.C., 4 September 1986.

87   CAI, Anna Feldman Collection, Interview by Anna Feldman with R.T., 27 May 1988.

88   For more information on the Jewish family living in an English-speaking rural community, see: Peter
       I. Rose, "Strangers in Their Midst: The Small-Town Jews and Their Neighbours," in Peter I. Rose, ed.,
       The Ghetto and Beyond: Essays on Jewish Life in America (New York: Random House, 1969), 335-56.

THE "LADY IMPERIALISTS" AND THE GREAT WAR: THE IMPERIAL ORDER DAUGHTERS OF THE EMPIRE IN SASKATCHEWAN, 1914-1918

Nadine Small

When the British Empire declared war on Germany and the Austro-Hungarian Empire in August 1914, Mrs. F.J. Sparling and the members of the Military Chapter, IODE in Saskatoon, Saskatchewan, were ready to spring into action. For years, their chapter and sister chapters throughout the Dominion had been priming themselves to serve Canada and the Empire in time of war by cultivating their imperialism in ways that were appropriate to times of peace. For example, a mere few weeks before the Great War began, the Military Chapter reported that the issue of a recent chapter debate had been, "Resolved that the British Overseas Dominions should forthwith co-operate in the construction and maintenance of an Imperial Navy." The chapter had also been raising funds, some of which were used to help defray the costs of building a drill shed for local Boy Scouts.[1] However, with the onset of war in Europe, the Military Chapter in Saskatoon got down to the serious business of providing practical assistance to the Canadian and imperial war effort.

The Imperial Order Daughters of the Empire (IODE) was a Canadian patriotic women's organization born and bred to serve the British Empire during war. The IODE was organized during the Boer War for women of the Empire who wanted to do war work for that imperial struggle. After the conflict in South Africa, the Order poised itself to play a key role in any future war. Drawing its ranks from the upper echelons of Canadian society, the IODE designed a highly organized and efficient society of women imperialists who were anxious to serve their country and King in time of need. Early efforts tapped the patriotic spirit of the women of Saskatchewan and the other western provinces, and turned the IODE into an elite, coast-to-coast organization that was eager and able to make significant contributions when Britain and Canada became embroiled in the Great War in 1914.

War broke out between Great Britain and the Boers of South Africa in October of 1899. This struggle renewed the interest of many English Canadians in imperialism. When the war began, Mrs. Clark Murray — a Scotswoman, and the wife of a professor at McGill University — was in England where "she met many women who were anxious to help on the home front but were handicapped by lack of channels through which to work."[2] Upon her return to Canada, Mrs. Murray surmised that, while men seemed to be organized and ready to respond to any emergency the Empire might face, women "as a body, had no bond of fellowship, nor opportunity for service, to render effective assistance in time of need."[3] While men could go to war to do their patriotic duty, women had no means by which to express their imperialism. Mrs.

---

1   National Archives of Canada Library (NACL), P 198, *Echoes* (June 1914): 91.

2   Saskatchewan Archives Board (SAB), IODE Records, R 598, file II.6, *The Imperial Order Daughters of the Empire: Golden Jubilee 1900-1950*, 1.

3   National Archives of Canada (NA), Manuscript Division, IODE Records, MG 28, I 17, volume 19, file 9, *Imperial Order Daughters of the Empire: 1900-1925*, 4.

Murray took it upon herself to organize an Empire-wide federation of patriotic women, whose purpose would be to foster a bond of union among the women and children of the Empire and to promote patriotism, service and loyalty to the King.[4] The organization established its headquarters in Toronto in October 1901, and incorporated under the title "The Imperial Order Daughters of the Empire and The Children of the Empire (Junior Branch)."[5] The IODE constitution made provision for primary, municipal, provincial, national and imperial chapters, which allowed for a highly structured, hierarchical organization.[6]

Interest in the IODE developed gradually across the nation. In the first ten years of the twentieth century, imperialists around the world struggled to bolster a waning imperialist spirit in the Empire's subjects. Similarly, the IODE struggled to attract women to its organization in the early years. IODE leaders in Ontario, British Columbia, English-speaking Quebec, and the Maritimes gradually organized more and more IODE chapters in those provinces. However, significant interest in the Order did not begin in the Prairie West until 1909.

In 1909, seven members of the National Executive set out on a western organizational tour. Their goal was to promote the organization of Daughters of the Empire chapters among the women of the West, in an effort to make the IODE a truly national, coast-to-coast women's organization.[7] Financed by contributions from "public-spirited" people and travelling in a private train car placed at their disposal through the influence of Lady Mackenzie, the wife of railway and business magnate, Sir William Mackenzie, the executive members visited Saskatchewan towns and cities during their journey to the Pacific coast. They met with the women who were community leaders in each centre, described the objectives and work of the Order, and organized chapters if interest was shown. The organizers inspired prairie women to form Saskatchewan's first seven IODE chapters — in Battleford, North Battleford, Moose Jaw, Prince Albert, Saskatoon, Regina and Grenfell.[8] Members of these new prairie chapters eagerly encouraged the continued expansion of the Order in the province and across the West. By the end of July 1914, sixty-five chapters organized in the prairie provinces; twenty of these were in Saskatchewan.[9]

The Daughters of the Empire were Canadian imperialists. Like other Canadian imperialists at the turn of the century, their reverence of the history and the institutions of the British Empire was not incompatible with their loyalty to Canada.[10]

---

4   For the most part, the IODE did not reach wide acceptance outside of Canada. SAB, IODE Records, R 598, file II.6, *The IODE Golden Jubilee*, 2; NA, IODE Records, vol. 19, file 10, "Imperial Order Daughters of the Empire: Brief Outline of History: 1900-1949," 1.

5   For information about the original organization of the IODE, and about the Children of the Empire, see: Nadine Small, "'Stand By the Union Jack': The Imperial Order Daughters of the Empire in the Prairie Provinces During the Great War, 1914-1918" (MA thesis, University of Saskatchewan, 1988), chapter 1.

6   Since an Imperial Chapter was never formed, the National Chapter of Canada was vested with its powers.

7   NACL, *Echoes Special Number* (1913): 20.

8   National Chapter IODE Records, "Records of Organizations of Chapters of the Imperial Order Daughters of the Empire According to Charter Number."

9   Ibid.

10   Carl Berger, *The Sense of Power: Studies in the Ideas of Canadian Imperialism 1867-1914* (Toronto: University of Toronto Press, 1970), 9.

They saw Canada as an integral part of the Empire and hoped that the Dominion would come to play a larger role in imperial affairs. The women of the IODE would have agreed with a statement made years earlier by Principal G.M. Grant of Queen's University: "[We] are Canadian, and in order to be Canadian we must be British."[11] The membership articles of the original IODE constitution stated that "all women and children in the British Empire or foreign lands, who are British subjects and hold true allegiance to the British Crown, are eligible for membership."[12] Most of the women who joined the IODE were of British descent, and therefore had a natural interest in an organization devoted to patriotic work for the British Empire.

Until at least the end of the Great War, the membership lists of the IODE in Saskatchewan did not contain names of women of Asian, south European or east-central European descent. This reality was a direct result of the nativist views that the prairie Daughters of the Empire held about "foreign" immigrants. Like most other English Canadians in the West, IODE women believed that non-Anglo-Saxon foreign-born immigrants were not loyal British subjects until they were totally assimilated to the language, customs and beliefs of English Canada.[13] IODE members called all non-British immigrants "foreigners" whether or not they were naturalized citizens. Foreign-born female immigrants who were not completely Canadianized did not qualify to become members of the Order because the Order did not consider them to be loyal British subjects.[14] Furthermore, at the IODE annual meeting in Victoria in 1917, the question was brought forth as to "whether a woman of British birth who was married to a foreigner could be a member of the IODE, and the decision arrived at was that they must be debarred."[15] IODE members even questioned the loyalty of British women who married foreigners.

Although the IODE considered the assimilation of foreign immigrants a top priority before and during the First World War, it was only willing to contribute to the anglo-conformity process from a distance.[16] In the many speeches and reports given by Daughters of the Empire (and repeated in the Order's publication, *Echoes*) about how to solve the immigrant problem, the IODE never considered inviting "foreign" women into its organization as a means to assimilate them into western Canadian society. The group's nativism was stronger than its interest in playing a hands-on role in the assimilation of immigrants into English-Canadian society.[17]

Although most IODE chapters were organized in Saskatchewan's cities and larger

---

11 "G," "Current Events," *Queen's Quarterly* 5 (summer 1898): 328.

12 NA, IODE Records, vol. 18, file 5, "Constitution and Statutes of the Imperial Order Daughters of the Empire," Article IV, Section 1, 6.

13 Howard Palmer, "Strangers and Stereotypes: The Rise of Nativism — 1880-1920," in R. Douglas Francis and Howard Palmer, eds., *The Prairie West: Historical Readings* (Edmonton: Pica Pica Press, 1985), 322.

14 See Small, "Stand By The Union Jack," 14ff for an example of foreign women in Manitoba who the Order accepted into its ranks because they were deemed to be suitably Canadianized.

15 *Saskatoon Phoenix*, 16 June 1917, p. 4.

16 Anglo-conformists believed foreign immigrants were obliged to become Canadians by absorbing the language, culture and institutions of English Canada. Immigrants were expected to renounce their ancestral culture and traditions in favour of the behaviour and values of Anglo-Canadians (Palmer, "Strangers and Stereotypes," 322).

17 See Small, "Stand By the Union Jack," chapter 4, for a discussion of the IODE's efforts to assimilate "foreign" children in Saskatchewan's schools.

towns, rural women were enthusiastic, contributing members of the IODE in the province. The determination of women in small towns and rural areas to organize chapters, to meet regularly, and to participate actively in IODE undertakings despite having to face difficulties such as travelling long distances in harsh conditions to get to meetings, attests to their value as members. Even in cases where they were unable to meet regularly or report substantial amounts of work done, "it meant much to the members [of rural chapters] to be linked with other women of the Empire."[18]

The majority of the IODE's members were urban, married women who had enough leisure time during the day and in the evening to attend meetings and socials, and who had enough money to participate in IODE functions. The IODE was an elite organization as a consequence of the social positions of its members. The position that a woman held in western Canadian society in the first decades of the twentieth century was usually determined by the position that her husband or father occupied in that society. An examination of the occupation of the husbands and fathers of prairie IODE members who belonged to the organization in the first twenty years of its existence indicates that a significant number of these husbands and fathers were professionals, politicians, civil servants and business owners, and that the balance were employed in service industry jobs such as bank managers, office managers, financial agents, newspaper editors and police officers.[19] These groups made up the upper and upper-middle ranks of prairie society, and the respect given to these men was usually extended to their wives and daughters. Because it drew its ranks from the upper echelons of society, the Order represented a relatively small segment of the population; nonetheless, the members did have influence in their communities.[20]

The IODE membership selection process affected the nature of the Order's membership. The process allowed the women of the Order to choose whom they wanted as members in their organization. Women who were interested in becoming members of the IODE had to apply for admission into the chapter that they wished to join. Applicants were nominated and seconded at a chapter meeting, and successful nominees were elected by ballot at the following meeting.[21] If a convincing argument was made against an applicant she would not be nominated or elected a member. This system of membership selection was undoubtedly used — whether or not it was openly acknowledged — to establish the almost exclusively British, middle- and upper-class makeup of the Order.

The method of chapter organization in Saskatchewan also determined the makeup of membership. When the IODE established itself in the West, the people who were asked to organize new chapters were well-known, well-respected women who were active in the community and whose husbands were the civic and business leaders in their respective towns and cities. Once the chapter was organized, these women must have encouraged the women who were in their social circles to apply

---

18   NACL, *Echoes* (June 1917): 82; also see ibid. (October 1916): 48.

19   For a detailed examination of the membership of prairie IODE chapters, see: Small, "Stand By the Union Jack," chapter 1 and Appendix A. Few wives of common labourers or employees belonged to the Order.

20   The IODE's method of chapter organization and its membership selection process had an effect in determining the "elite" nature of the Order's membership. See: Small, "Stand By the Union Jack," chapter 1.

21   NA, IODE Records, vol. 18, file 5, "Constitution and Statutes of the Imperial Order Daughters of the Empire," Article IV, Section 7, 7.

for membership in the chapter. Consequently, women who had friends in the middle to upper ranks of society were more likely to have contact with IODE organizers. Women from the middle ranks of society would have recognized the original members of the IODE as the respected and prominent people in their community, and may have aspired to be part of the organization because of what it could do for them socially. At the same time, it is feasible that women from the lower ranks of society would simply not have been interested in the Order because they belonged to different social circles and because they had different concerns and interests.

Many IODE chapters appear to have had internal oligarchies. IODE members who belonged to the upper echelons of society were expected to become the leaders of chapters. In most cases, this elite group of women held on to the top executive positions in their chapters, and arbitrarily made decisions for their chapters which were almost always adopted by their IODE sisters.

Money was another factor that excluded certain women from belonging to the Order. Women from low-income families frequently had to work and take care of a household, which left no time to attend IODE meetings or functions. It could also be expensive to keep up with the charity and social expectations of the Order. Many women could not afford to spend money on monthly dues and charitable donations. Not everyone could buy a gown for each formal ball, elaborate dinner, or night at the theatre — events that were popular means of fundraising and socializing among the elite members of the organization in most of the urban centres. There were definite financial demands that came with being a Daughter of the Empire; many women would have been unable to fulfill such obligations.

Consistent with their middle- to upper-class composition, prairie chapters of the Order had a paternalistic, condescending attitude toward immigrants and the lower ranks of society. This attitude was illustrated in the 1914 President's address delivered at the IODE annual meeting by Mrs. A.E. Gooderham:

> But Daughters of the Empire have other responsibilities to face. ... [With] little except our own enthusiasm to inspire us, we must look after the lonely, provide means of education for the ignorant, open the doors of culture and opportunity for those in less fortunate circumstances than our own, tend the sick, and do all that lies within our power to make the life of the city or town in which we live healthier, sweeter, noble and better worth living for even the most humble citizen. ... Because we are Daughters of the Empire, we recognize the place that courtesy and consideration must have in the lives of good citizens. We realize perhaps more fully our relative worth as compared to other human beings.[22]

Elitism and nativism were distinct elements of the IODE's makeup.

The Daughters of the Empire were imperialists, and the first years of their existence were spent refining and propounding their ideology. Like other imperialists at the turn of the twentieth century, IODE members feared for the future of the Empire. Because they recognized the potential threat from imperial rivals that Britain was facing on the seas and in conquered lands around the globe, they put their energies into promoting the defence of the physical territories and the cultural and political institutions that made up that Empire.[23] One major characteristic of

---

22   NACL, *Echoes* (June 1914): 8-9, 12.

23   NACL, *Echoes Special Number* (1913): 10.

Canadian imperialism was militarism, and the prewar IODE joined other imperialist groups in rousing public opinion to the necessity and obligation on the part of the Dominion to contribute to the protection of the Empire through augmented naval defence and through increased physical and military training of the nation's boys and young men through the Boy Scout movement and cadet drill corps.[24]

In the early years of its existence, the IODE also strived "[to] promote in the Motherland and in the Colonies the study of the History of the Empire and of current Imperial questions," and to "stimulate and give expression to the sentiment of patriotism which binds the women and children of the Empire around the Throne and the person of their Gracious and Beloved Sovereign."[25] The Daughters believed that it was important for the people of the Dominion to understand why it was essential to defend the culture and institutions of the British Empire and why their patriotic love and loyalty should be expressed loudly and frequently. The women of the IODE searched for ways that women and children could help to unify, improve, protect and strengthen the Empire that already existed — even if their gestures were as small as deciding to bank at the "Imperial Bank" because it suggested the name of the Order, or selling "Be British" pins at local fairs.[26] As stated in the special issue of the Order's magazine, *Echoes*, in 1913:

> Imperialism is the keynote, the driving force of the Organization — as its
> name and the spirit of its Constitution implies. To implant in every
> Canadian man, woman and child the grandeur of our heritage as a British
> people; to make real and practical to every individual the unity of our far-
> flung dominion to the ends of the earth, self-governing within themselves,
> yet bound by tradition, loyalty and gratitude to the Motherland, together
> upholding the ideals of liberty, justice and honour of which the Union Jack
> is the emblem wherever it flies — these are the aspirations which move the
> members to real acts of devotion and enthusiastic work, and make the
> Order an established institution and a power to be courted or feared in all
> matters connected with National or Imperial issues.[27]

The IODE spent its early years, then, propagating imperialist ideals and preparing itself to rally behind the Empire in time of need.

After years of organizational activity and imperialist campaigning, the IODE's stage was set. When the war broke out in Europe in August 1914,[28] the Daughters of the Empire were ready to respond. An IODE history of the Great War claimed:

> The IODE possessed machinery that was probably not equalled and certainly
> not surpassed by any other women's organization in the Empire. In this

---

24 Berger, *The Sense of Power*, 254-55; NA, IODE Records, vol. 3, file 1, Minutes National Executive IODE, 7 June 1918, 37; NACL, *Echoes* (June 1917): 85, 101; SAB, R 766, II.5.b, Minutes of the Golden West Chapter 1917-1920, 9 July 1917, 59; Ibid., II.11.b, Minutes of Saskatoon Municipal Chapter 1918-1921, 29 April 1918, 8.

25 NA, IODE Records, vol. 18, file 5, "IODE Constitution," Article II, Object 1, 4.

26 Private Papers of Mrs. Mary Lynch-Staunton, Minutes of Alexander Galt Chapter, Lethbridge, Alberta, Minutes 1914-1917, 6 February 1914, organizational meeting; SAB R 598, file VI.5.h.i, Book 1, Minutes Victoria and Albert Chapter, Prince Albert, 2 August 1915.

27 NACL, *Echoes Special Number* (1913): 10 — Constance Rudyerd Boulton, former Honourary Secretary.

28 For general background information on Canada's role in the Great War, see: John Herd Thompson, *Harvests of War: The Prairie West, 1914-1918* (Toronto: McClelland and Stewart 1978); and Desmond Morton and J.L. Granatstein, *Marching to Armageddon: Canadians and the Great War 1914-1919* (Toronto: Lester and Orpen Dennys Limited, 1989).

regard they [*sic*] occupied a unique position in Canada. They provided
channels through which patriotic enterprises could reach every part of the
Dominion, and they were able to accomplish many things because they were
prepared and ready when the call came.[29]

The Daughters of the Empire saw the Great War as their opportunity to do the work
for which they had organized. As another IODE history later observed:

> With the advent of the war, the chapters were ready to carry out that clause
> in the Aims and Objects, namely: "to provide an efficient organization by
> which prompt and united action may be taken by the women and children
> of the Empire when such action may be desired."[30]

IODE members boasted that their Boer War experience and over a decade of
preparation for the next imperial war had made the Order the only patriotic women's
group in the Dominion that was organized to respond immediately to the state of
national emergency.[31]

During the fourteen long years before the war, members of the Order had tried
to stimulate patriotism in fellow Canadians through education and symbolic
expression. This kind of effort yielded long-term results that were not always tangible.
Outsiders had suggested that the IODE was serving no useful purpose. In a wartime
article in *Maclean's*, journalist W.A. Craick reported:

> [Some] would have it that [the IODE] was largely a jingoistic, flag-waving
> organization without any real value to the community. Others were inclined
> to regard it as a society affair of an exclusive, high-&-mighty character.[32]

The Daughters were prepared to use the opportunity of war to answer such criticisms.

Canada's involvement in the Great War generated an immediate and enthusiastic
patriotic response among the women of the Dominion, which translated into a new
interest in the work of the IODE, and saw IODE membership and chapter organization
in Saskatchewan and throughout Canada increase dramatically. According to the
Canadian Annual Review, the Canadian IODE had 10,000 members in 1912, and
membership was increasing at the rate of 2,000 members per year. By the end of 1914,
IODE membership was up to 25,000, and by 1918 it was estimated that there were
over 40,000 Daughters of the Empire in the Dominion. The number of Canadian
IODE chapters increased from 300 to 700 during the war years. In the prairie
provinces, the number of chapters increased from 49 at the end of 1913 to 220 at the
end of 1918 — an increase of 171 chapters. In Saskatchewan, 33 new chapters
organized from the time war was declared until the armistice.[33] The IODE argued that
its growing membership — augmented by its ability to reach every part of the country
in any campaign, thanks to its hierarchical, centralized organizational structure —
contributed significantly to its effectiveness during the Great War.[34]

---

29   NA, IODE Records, vol. 33, file 26, "The IODE in Wartime," 4.

30   SAB, R 598, II.6, *The Imperial Order Daughters of the Empire: Golden Jubilee, 1900-1950*, 25.

31   Ibid., 25; NACL, *Echoes* (October 1915): 7 — Mrs. A.W. McDougald, "Annual Meeting Report."

32   W.A. Craick, "A Noble Order — and the War," *Maclean's*, June 1915, 79.

33   J. Castell Hopkins, *The Canadian Annual Review of Public Affairs* (Toronto: The Annual Review
     Publishing Co. Ltd., for 1912 [145], 1914 [233], and 1918 [589]); National Chapter IODE Records,
     "Records of Organization of Chapters of the IODE According to Charter Number."

34   NACL, *Echoes* (October 1918): 13 — Mrs. A.E. Gooderham, "President's Address"; ibid. (October
     1915): 7 — Mrs. A.W. McDougald, "Annual Meeting Report."

One of the IODE's first reactions to the war was to recognize that Canadian men were sacrificing their lives on European battlefields to protect British ideals and British citizens, while civilians in war-torn Europe were hard-pressed to meet the barest of needs. IODE leaders concluded that Canadian women should share in the trials of the Empire and its allies by exercising self-sacrifice and self-discipline on the home front:

> Let us all, each and every one — resolve to deny ourselves something — to practice economy and thrift — for we are indeed fortunate that we have luxuries and comforts, and our pleasures continue undisturbed — we are out of hearing of the din and roar of the Cannon — no Aeroplanes hover overhead to cause us sleepless nights, while those in the war-stricken zones have not even the bare necessities of life — could not every woman and child deny themselves for those weakened infants, the rickety child and tubercular youth of Belgium who simply need food to restore health.[35]

IODE leaders encouraged their members to give up unnecessary extravagance by wearing out their old clothes, trimming their own hats, and dressing their young daughters in simple attire.[36] Women were fined for wearing finery at IODE-sponsored Calico Balls.[37] Food conservation measures were practiced and encouraged.[38]

The most significant sacrifice that IODE members saw themselves making was giving up husbands, sons and brothers to active service. The National Chapter encouraged Daughters of the Empire — as part of their patriotic duty — to give up close relatives to fight for the nation and the Empire. In an annual report for 1916, an IODE sister in Okotoks, Alberta, stated, "We are proud to announce that 4 of our members have given their sons to fight for our liberty."[39] Female relatives of Canadian servicemen were compared to "the Spartan mothers of old," who sent forth their loved ones to battle.[40]

The Daughters of the Empire firmly believed that it was the patriotic duty of every Anglo-Canadian man to fight for his country and the Empire, unless his services were absolutely necessary to the home-front war effort. As a consequence, Daughters of the Empire took an active part in inducing unwilling eligible men to "volunteer." The IODE wanted to make a clear distinction between those men who could not enlist and those who would not enlist, so that slackers could be subjected to public contempt that might coax them to volunteer. Although the IODE did not officially sanction the popularized giving of white feathers to idlers, the records of certain prairie chapters give the impression that some zealous members of the Order took it upon themselves to accost eligible-looking young men in the streets and to demand to know why they were not serving.[41]

---

35   Public Archives of Manitoba (PAM), IODE Records, MG 10, C 70, box 13, file: IODE Municipal Chapter — Annual Reports 1913-1943, "Fifth Annual Report, Winnipeg Municipal Chapter IODE, 1916," 4.

36   Ibid., P 2498, file 1, Fort Garry Chapter Minutes 1913-1914, 10 September 1914, 114; "Military Chapter Would Have Girls Simply Clothed," *Calgary Daily Herald*, 21 March 1918, 10.

37   NACL, *Echoes* (June 1918): 41.

38   For a detailed description of the IODE's involvement in food conservation efforts, see: Small, "Stand By the Union Jack," chapter 5.

39   NACL, *Echoes* (June 1916): 89.

40   "Great Progress Made By IODE," *Manitoba Free Press*, 28 April 1916, 7.

41   PAM, P 2500, file 3, Royal Navy Volunteer Reserve Recruiting Secretary to Mrs. Colin Campbell, 2 April 1917; Private Papers of Mrs. Mary Lynch-Staunton, Alexander Galt Chapter Minutes 1914-1917, 26 October 1915, 95.

The Daughters of the Empire were eager to help the government's military manpower campaigns; they wanted Canada to contribute enough men to ensure a full and victorious war effort, and believed that if more men were sent overseas all Canadian soldiers would be able to return home more quickly. In Saskatchewan towns and cities, recruiting meetings were occasionally held under the auspices of local IODE chapters, often at the request of recruiting officers. When it became known that Wadena, Saskatchewan, was to be the headquarters for the organization of the 204th Battalion, the Michael O'Leary V.C. Chapter "at once directed its energies towards recruiting."[42] The Victoria Chapter in Swift Current had a clever recruitment gimmick. The IODE set up a mysterious "for men only" tent at a local fair. Their interest piqued, men entered the tent only to find that it was a recruiting office. The chapter's records assure that it "secured quite a few recruits" in this way.[43] As the casualty lists grew and recruitment efforts proved less effective, the IODE became a keen supporter of both manpower registration and eventually, conscription.[44]

The Daughters' belief in the rightness of the war and their conviction that it was their duty to make a contribution to the war effort resulted in major IODE fundraising efforts on behalf of the Allied war cause. Although their primary concern was the well-being of Canadian soldiers, the Daughters of the Empire tried to keep in tune with what the general needs of the Empire were during the Great War. The Order was quick to mobilize its forces when appeals were made for assistance — whether the call came from the military or from civilian organizations in war-torn Allied countries.

On 3 August 1914 — the day before war was declared on Germany by Britain — a movement was initiated by members of the IODE to raise money to purchase a hospital ship to be offered to the British Admiralty. The purpose of this undertaking was to give all the women of Canada an opportunity to participate in a project to assist the Empire's war effort. Women across the country rallied around the hospital ship project, and thanks to the outstanding organizational abilities of the IODE, raised over $280,000 in just over two weeks time. Although the money raised was eventually put toward naval hospitals in Britain, the hospital ship idea served as a convenient concept around which the IODE was able to rally women of the Dominion.[45] This early fundraising effort magnified the exceptional organizational system that the prewar IODE had established.

Saskatchewan IODE chapters contributed towards a number of large-scale health-care fundraising projects. The Order provided care for the physical and mental health of the Empire's military forces through the financing of new medical institutions such as the Daughters of the Empire Red Cross Hospital in London, and through donations of money and goods to supply existing hospitals.[46] The Forget Chapter in Regina gave money to a Regina physician — Dr. Morrel, at Valcartier

---

42   NACL, *Echoes* (June 1917): 35.

43   Private Papers of Mrs. Joan Church, Swift Current Victoria Chapter History.

44   See J.L Granatstein and J.M. Hitsman, *Broken Promises: A History of Conscription in Canada* (Toronto: Oxford University Press, 1977), for a history of conscription during the Great War.

45   NA, IODE Records, vol. 33, file 19, "The History of the Hospital Ship Fund."

46   NA, IODE Records, vol. 33, file 26, "The IODE in Wartime," 11.

Camp — to purchase a field bacteriological set and a field water analysis set for use in the Army Medical Corps.[47] During a short-term campaign in 1915, the *Saskatoon Phoenix* assisted the efforts of the local IODE to raise $2,255 for an ambulance to be sent to the Queen's Canadian Military Hospital at Shorncliffe by running articles about the progress of the ambulance fund in its paper everyday for the duration of the campaign. Sympathetic stories were told about the people — many of whom were mysteriously "anonymous" or "contributing their last dollar" — who added to the ambulance fund.[48] The most significant and well-known medical supply effort undertaken by individual IODE members and chapters during the war, however, was their work for the Canadian Red Cross Society. Besides helping to organize Red Cross branches in Saskatchewan cities and donating money to support the war work of the Canadian and British Red Cross societies, Saskatchewan Daughters of the Empire hand-made thousands of pieces of hospital supplies and clothing to aid sick and wounded soldiers.[49]

Early in the war, outside organizations began to recognize the tremendous contributions that the IODE was making to many different wartime causes. Relief funds inundated the Order with appeals for financial and material assistance for the victims and refugees of the European war in Belgium, Serbia and France.[50] In Saskatchewan, the Order answered appeals with the proceeds of fundraising efforts and with actual goods; in Saltcoats and Regina, the IODE arranged for carloads of flour to be sent "to afford some relief to the afflicted Belgian people."[51] The flood of requests from a wide variety of appeals and organizations continued for the duration of the war, and the IODE kept up its remarkable fundraising efforts over this extended period.[52]

The support of Canadian soldiers and the financing of relief efforts required a great deal of money. Even though IODE chapters had raised money before the war, it did not take long for chapter treasuries to be depleted by wartime appeals. During the Great War IODE members became expert fundraisers capable of employing a wide variety of fundraising methods. While they often relied on tried and tested manners of raising money, the women of the Order also displayed ingenuity in their ability to find new gimmicks that encouraged IODE members and the public to continue contributing until the end of 1918.

The women of the IODE contributed substantial sums of their own money to the Order's fundraising appeals. Entertainments and socials held for Daughters of the Empire and the general public were as popular a means of raising money during the war as they had been before. Saskatchewan Daughters of the Empire always paid their share to attend such fundraising social events as swimming galas, ice carnivals, patriotic carnivals, skating parties, picnic fundraisers, box and pie socials, military tournaments, formal balls, informal dances, military socials, vaudeville or burlesque

---

47   SAB, R 598, IV.5.k.i, Forget Chapter Minutes 1914-1916, 30 September 1914, 43.

48   *Saskatoon Phoenix*, "Women's Realm" section, 8 May 1915 to 20 May 1915.

49   *Saskatoon Phoenix*, 28 October 1914, p. 6; SAB, R 598, VI.5.k.iii, Forget Chapter Minutes 1918, 11 June 1918, 63.

50   Shortt Collection, University Library, University of Saskatchewan, *IODE Souvenir 1916*, 36-37.

51   *Manitoba Free Press*, 26 November 1914, p. 2.

52   See Small, "Stand By the Union Jack," chapter 2, for further discussion of the different causes that the IODE contributed to during the Great War.

shows, musical concerts and theatrical presentations. But the most common fundraiser with IODE members was the afternoon tea. To keep teatime contributions interesting, the IODE held theme teas. For example, members who received an apron-shaped invitation to an Apron Tea had to contribute a cent for every inch of their waist measure.[53]

The use of certain entertainments for fundraising was a controversial question for the IODE. At the beginning of the war, the National Chapter indicated that it expected that dances, gala garden tea parties, and bridge parties would be rare in upcoming months because many loyal Canadians would put aside frivolities in the hour of the Empire's great trial.[54] If any attention was paid to these recommendations at first, they were not heeded for long. Indeed, given the fundraising demands made of the Order, the ban on certain social functions was an unrealistic stricture; the Daughters needed to utilize every fundraising avenue available to them.

The Daughters of the Empire would not have accomplished as much as they did during the Great War if they had relied on fundraising within their own ranks; the Order had to look for donations from the general public. Chapters held house-to-house canvasses, and appealed for contributions through the media. Mite or self-denial boxes were placed in public places and schoolrooms so children and adults could drop in what small amount they could spare.[55] Prairie Daughters of the Empire became expert tag day organizers and accumulated thousands of dollars during the war by selling small tags, flags or flowers on street corners — often in the face of harsh winter winds.

Every IODE chapter in Saskatchewan found its own way to raise money during the Great War, and the size and location of chapters had little bearing on their ability to raise money. It is impossible to determine exactly how much money the IODE raised during the five years of the war, although an approximate national estimate was over $5 million.[56] The IODE's significant financial contribution to the war effort illustrated its genuine conviction that the war was fought for the good of the Empire and western civilization, and gave tangible expression to its sense of duty to King and country.

The most important branch of the IODE's program during the Great War was its work for the soldiers of the Canadian contingents. In 1914, the Order readily took up the kind of field comfort work that had been done for Canadian soldiers during the Boer War, but the scope of the organization's Great War soldier support efforts went beyond the commonly perceived images of knitting and sewing that have persisted in the minds of later generations. The Daughters of the Empire put all the time, money and effort that they could muster into caring for the Dominion's fighting men and their dependents before the men left, after they left, and after they returned from active service. Acting under the conviction that soldiers who were of sound mind and body would fight a better battle against the enemy, the IODE hoped to contribute to imperial victory by serving the troops of the British Empire.

The Saskatchewan IODE's work for soldiers began before the men left the

---

53   *Saskatoon Phoenix*, 21 April, p. 6 and 25 August 1917, p. 5; NACL, *Echoes* (December 1918): 25.

54   NACL, *Echoes* (December 1914): 7 — "Entertainment in Wartime."

55   NACL, *Echoes* (June 1916): 87; SAB, R 766, II.11.b, Saskatoon Municipal Chapter Minutes 1914-1917, 1 May 1915; ibid. IV.5.k.i, Forget Chapter Minutes, Book One, 1914-1916, 8 June 1915, 131.

56   NA, IODE Records, vol. 33, file 26, "The IODE in Wartime," 13.

province. IODE chapters did their utmost to make the stay of soldiers in recruiting centres and training camps as comfortable as possible. In many cases, the IODE helped when Canadian military authorities could not get training troops housed and supplied quickly enough in the rush to mobilize the First Canadian Contingent. For example, the Governor Laird Chapter in North Battleford worked diligently to comply with an urgent request — made by a local military officer — to make twenty bed ticks for use in the local armoury where forty-one reservists from the North Battleford area were to be housed temporarily.[57] IODE chapters opened and operated recreation rooms or soldiers clubs, where soldiers could relax, read, write, or play billiards, board games, gramophones or pianos.[58] Daughters of the Empire also sponsored special social events to entertain soldiers in training, including card parties, sports days, military tournaments, and dances, such as the Battleford Chapter's Soldiers Welcome Dance, held "primarily to introduce the soldiers to the town people thereby making them feel welcome and at home in the town."[59]Before reservists and volunteers left Saskatchewan towns and cities, the Daughters of the Empire showed their appreciation to those going to war with farewell celebrations. The IODE organized banquets, farewell balls and huge farewell demonstrations at train stations so that departing soldiers would be properly sent off. Upon departure, the Daughters usually presented soldiers with useful gifts such as housewife kits (which were little packages of necessary articles such as needles, thread, buttons, stationery and first aid supplies), fruit, field comforts and books to occupy spare time.[60]

The IODE's care for the soldiers of the Canadian contingents did not end when the young men left Canadian shores. The Daughters of the Empire knew from their experience during the Boer War that soldiers were never supplied with all of the comforts or necessities that were required to make their lives bearable while in training or on the battlefield. Saskatchewan IODE members met in homes and workrooms to make, collect, bale and ship soldiers' comforts. The Order sent woollen goods, clothes, towels, handkerchiefs, soap, tooth brushes, writing paper, envelopes and other helpful items to men in the trenches and camps in France and England. IODE workrooms frequently served as depots where the general public could donate comforts.[61] On occasion, IODE chapters treated Canadian soldiers in Europe and Great Britain to special foods which were absent from their military diet, including apples, oranges, chocolate, loaf sugar and maple sugar.[62] At Christmas the IODE contributed to official funds which were set up to buy Christmas gifts for soldiers, or sent special Christmas foods and gifts directly to the front.[63]

---

57 SAB, R 766, II.6.b, Governor Laird Chapter (North Battleford) Minutes 1909-1915, 8 November 1914.

58 SAB, R 766, II.6.b.218, Governor Laird Chapter (North Battleford) Minutes 1916-1918, December 1916, 18; Mrs. Mary Lynch-Staunton Papers, Alexander Galt Chapter Minutes 1914-1917, 108.

59 Mrs. C.J. Greenwood Papers, Battleford Chapter Minutes 1909-1927, 10 August 1914.

60 "The IODE to Wave Goodbye to Reservists," *Saskatoon Phoenix*, 19 August, p. 4, and 21 August 1914, p. 4; Mrs. C.J. Greenwood Papers, Battleford Chapter Minutes 1909-1927, 18 August 1914; NACL, *Echoes* (June 1918): 31, (June 1916): 88, and (June 1917): 103; SAB, R 598, IV.5.h.i, Victoria and Albert Chapter Minutes, Book 1, 27 October 1914; ibid., Book 2, 24 April 1917.

61 *Saskatoon Phoenix*, 18 October 1917, p. 4.

62 Mrs. C.J. Greenwood Papers, Battleford Chapter Minutes, 27 November 1917; NACL, *Echoes* (June 1916): 85, and (December 1917): 64; "IODE to Send Sugar to Boys in the Trenches," *Saskatoon Phoenix*, 12 May 1917, p. 4.

63 "An Appeal for Xmas Gifts for J. Canuck," *Saskatoon Phoenix*, 30 August 1915, p. 5; SAB, R 598, IV.5.k.ii, Forget Chapter Minutes 1917, 81.

Early in 1915, stories about the treatment of Canadian prisoners of war (POWs) in Germany began to circulate in Canada; it was believed that the Germans were not feeding Allied POWs adequately. In response, Saskatchewan primary chapters adopted POWs and sent them food directly.[64] Later in the war, the Duchess of Connaught, the Governor General's wife, organized a Prisoner of War Fund. The Duchess's hope was that the women of Canada could contribute to a central fund, and thus provide for the welfare of Canadian POWs in a more satisfactory and economical way.[65] When the war was over, the Daughters of the Empire pointed out, with satisfaction,

> that almost all the Canadians who [had] returned from Germany [bore] testimony to the value of the parcels of food. Many of our men would have died of starvation in a foreign land if it had not been for the packages that reached them with such unbroken regularity.[66]

Knitting was the one IODE comfort activity that continued from the beginning to the end of the Great War and perhaps has left the greatest impression on the minds of subsequent generations of Canadians. IODE members knit no matter what other projects their chapters undertook. When it seemed like the hours spent knitting were endless, when they wondered if their time would be better spent elsewhere, or when interest in knitting slackened, IODE leaders encouraged members not to grow weary. The Daughters were regularly reminded, "as long as our brave soldiers are on the march, or in the trench, they will need all the comforts that women can supply."[67] Knitted soldier comforts that Daughters of the Empire made for servicemen included sweaters, mittens, scarves, wristlets, caps and helmets, "kneecaps," cholera belts and, of course, socks.

If there was ever any suggestion that the Order's sock-knitting efforts were a waste of time, the significant number of appeals for and testimonials to the value of a steady supply of clean, hand-knit wool socks — requests and tributes made by both officers and men in the field — shattered such doubts. In 1916, a despatch from England was printed in the *Saskatoon Phoenix* "IODE Notes" column to encourage women to continue knitting socks:

> The statement made by General Sir Edwin Alderson to Canadian journalists who visited the front, to the effect that "trench foot" has practically been eliminated from the Canadian troops, bears out what has been said in letters addressed to the Daughters of the Empire in connection with the sending of socks. ... [They] have contributed not only to the men's happiness but to the maintenance of health under bad climatic conditions. ... [T]he socks sent had proved invaluable in saving the men's feet.[68]

There is no way to determine or even estimate the number of pairs of socks that the Saskatchewan IODE and Daughters across the country knit and sent to Canadian troops during the Great War, although one IODE history remarked, "[T]hat the number of pairs of socks shipped overseas was probably larger than the population

---

64   NA, IODE Records, vol. 26, "The IODE in Wartime," 15; SAB, R 766, II.9.b, Military Chapter (Saskatoon), Chapter Day Book, 1917; ibid., II.5.b.i, Golden West Chapter (Saskatoon) Minutes 1914-1917, 175.

65   "Duchess of Connaught's Prisoners of War Fund," *Saskatoon Phoenix*, 20 September 1916, p. 5.

66   NA, IODE Records, vol. 26, "The IODE in Wartime," 15-16.

67   NA, IODE Records, vol. 31, file 4, "How Can We Help Most, Now!" circular letter, n.d.

68   *Saskatoon Phoenix*, 13 May 1916, p. 6.

of Canada, and the Daughters of the Empire prepared, collected and despatched a large proportion of them."[69]

The IODE also faced several soldier-related concerns on the home front during the Great War. One of the constitutional objectives of the IODE was "to care for the widows, orphans and dependents of British soldiers or sailors during war, sickness, accident or reverses of fortune."[70] The women of the IODE believed that if the men in the trenches knew that their dependents were cared for in Canada, they might be better able to concentrate on the task at hand. The Order was frequently the first organization in prairie towns and cities to take on the responsibility of caring for the wives, children, widows, orphans and mothers of Canadian servicemen.

The Daughters of the Empire provided a variety of services to soldiers' families. Members of the Order tried to brighten the lives of soldiers' dependents whenever possible. Some chapters organized wives' and mothers' social clubs or provided entertainments for such clubs that were already in existence.[71] At Christmas, the IODE held parties, provided dinners, bought gifts for children, and frequently gave Christmas trees to soldiers' families. More importantly, before local committees of the Canadian Patriotic Fund were in working order, members of the Saskatchewan IODE joined their sisters across the country to do relief work to meet the needs of soldiers' dependents who had been left destitute because recruits often did not have time before they left for active service to provide an adequate living for their families.[72] Daughters of the Empire offered friendship and advice to women who were left alone with the full responsibility of caring for their homes and children while their husbands were away. IODE chapters made it their cause to visit these families, to give moral support, companionship and "practical guidance."

The "practical guidance" given by certain IODE chapters and individual members was very paternalistic, and was undoubtedly offensive to the soldiers' wives who were being "guided." Some Daughters of the Empire used their visits to "counsel in matters relating to general questions of child-rearing, household health and hygiene."[73] Other IODE members tried to dictate how Patriotic Fund money should be spent by soldiers' families.[74] In their own misguided opinion, these Daughters of the Empire believed that they should use their visits to teach soldiers' families how to be better "imperial citizens." In reality, these condescending, middle- and upper-class members of the IODE were attempting to impose their views on the working-class soldiers' wives. Other IODE members were angered by this type of unnecessary,

---

69   NA, IODE Records, vol. 26, "The IODE in Wartime," 15.

70   NA, IODE Records, vol. 18, file 5, "Constitution of the Imperial Order Daughters of the Empire," Article II, Object 5, 5.

71   SAB, R 598, VI.5.k.ii, Forget Chapter Minutes 1917, 14 November 1917, 93; Provincial Archives of Alberta (PAA), IODE Records, Acc. 74.1, box 1, item 182, Report of Visiting Committee IODE, 22 March 1915.

72   Philip H. Morris, ed., *The Canadian Patriotic Fund: A Record of its Activities from 1914-1919* (Ottawa: The Canadian Patriotic Fund Executive Committee, n.d.), 7. See this volume for further information about the Canadian Patriotic Fund. Once this fund began to provide allowances, the Daughters helped local Patriotic Fund committees administer the fund ("Soldiers' Families To Be Well Looked After By Citizens," *Saskatoon Phoenix*, 26 August 1914, p. 2).

73   PAA, IODE Records, Acc. 74.1, box 6, item 179, Relief Committee Minutes, 9 September 1914.

74   PAA, IODE Records, Acc. 74.1, box 6, item 179, Relief Committee Minutes, c. September 1915.

overbearing interference in the lives of soldiers' wives, and chastised such women for being overly harsh and judgmental.[75]

IODE volunteers offered comfort and condolences to the families of soldiers who were killed or wounded in action. In Saskatoon, the Military Chapter's Active Service Committee wrote sympathy letters to mothers, wives and sisters of soldiers who were killed or wounded. Committee members also sent letters of congratulation to soldiers and families of soldiers who received promotions or won Military Crosses and other such awards for valuable and patriotic services performed on behalf of the Empire.[76]

The IODE's work for Canadian soldiers did not end when they had completed their active service, whether as a result of injury, death, or when released from duty at the end of the Great War. The Daughters of the Empire wanted to do what they could to make the veteran soldiers' return to Canada a positive experience. Most IODE chapters in the larger western centres organized committees or had representatives on Returned Soldiers Welcome and Aid Leagues that were formed in their city to assist newly returned soldiers.[77] This work began as soon as returned men arrived at their western destinations, where they were met and warmly greeted by Daughters of the Empire. The Saskatoon Active Service Committee met returning soldiers at the train and took them to their homes or to the hospital, and entertained those who were going beyond Saskatoon. In some locales, the IODE organized homecoming celebrations to welcome returned soldiers.[78]

The Daughters of the Empire felt a strong obligation to care for the convalescing maimed and wounded men who returned to Canada before and after the armistice. Saskatchewan IODE chapters frequently assisted the military agencies that ran soldiers' convalescent homes or hospitals in western cities by equipping the facilities with beds, linens, hospital clothes and other hospital supplies.[79] They attempted to satisfy the physical needs of particular patients, and supplied hospitals with special culinary treats or hard-to-get foods. For example, the Golden West Chapter in Saskatoon set aside ten dollars each month for buying fruit or greens for the local Soldiers' Convalescent Homes, and sent cases of oranges, plums, tomatoes, apples, grapefruit, grapes and even chocolate, on a regular basis.[80]

Although its material donations to the hospitals were valuable, the IODE's ability to meet the human needs of the convalescing men was also a significant contribution. Most IODE chapters in the West had a hospital-visiting committee, which sent visitors to the hospitals to pay regular visits to invalid soldiers. As the war progressed and the

75   *Calgary Daily Herald*, June 1918, 57.

76   *Saskatoon Phoenix*, 12 September, p. 6, and 13 October 1916, p. 5.

77   "Practical Work Done by IODE for R.S.W. League," *Saskatoon Phoenix*, 22 March 1917, p. 5; SAB, R 598, VI.5.h.i, Victoria and Albert Chapter (Prince Albert) Minutes, 8 February 1916.

78   *Saskatoon Phoenix*, 15 May 1917, p. 5, and 12 June 1917.

79   SAB, R 598, VI.5.k.ii, Forget Chapter Minutes 1916-1917, 27 January 1916, 15; *Saskatoon Phoenix*, 25 March 1916, p. 6. In Saskatoon, the IODE was given charge of the official opening of the Returned Soldiers' Home on 21st Street ("IODE To Make Arrangements to Open Soldiers' Home," *Saskatoon Phoenix*, 10 June 1916; "IODE to Have Charge of Opening Soldiers' Home," *Saskatoon Phoenix*, 13 June 1916, p. 6; "Large Attendance at the Opening of Soldiers' Home," *Saskatoon Phoenix*, 16 June 1916, p. 6).

80   NACL, *Echoes* (June 1916): 75-84; Mrs. Joan Church Papers, History of Fitzgerald Chapter, Saskatoon; SAB, R 766, II.5.b.ii, Golden West Chapter (Saskatoon) Minutes 1917-1920, 53, 65, 69.

number of wounded men who returned to Canada steadily increased, the work of these committees grew to the point that every member of most chapters was needed to make regular visits to convalescing men.[81]

The IODE in Saskatchewan gave special attention to another group of returned soldiers — those who were mentally affected by their wartime experiences and consequently hospitalized in the Battleford Provincial Asylum. At first, members of the Governor Laird Chapter in North Battleford paid visits to the patients. The Superintendent quickly decided that the visits only disturbed the patients more, and the visiting ceased.[82] The Governor Laird Chapter continued to donate its own money, as well as donations received from throughout Saskatchewan, to provide treats for returned men who were patients of the institution.[83] The IODE's willingness to work for mentally afflicted veterans indicates that it believed that it had a responsibility to provide for all returned soldiers, even if the situation proved awkward or difficult.

The final effort that the IODE made for Canadian soldiers was to honour and commemorate their heroism and sacrifice. When soldiers died while in training in prairie towns and cities or were killed in action in Europe, the women of the IODE attended funerals and organized remembrance services, decorated graves with flowers or potted plants, and created monuments or honour rolls in memory of men who died for the Empire but were buried overseas.[84] For example, the Military Chapter in Saskatoon sponsored a unique memorial after the war. Elm trees were individually selected and paid for by the next-of-kin or friends of fallen soldiers and planted along the three miles of Next-of-Kin Memorial Avenue in Woodlawn Cemetery.[85] After the war, the Daughters of the Empire in Canada collected $200,000 in a fund to promote the educational work of the Order, a lasting and practical memorial to the Canadian men and women who had died in defence of the Empire during the war.[86]

In his *Canadian Annual Review* for 1916, J. Castell Hopkins assessed the Great War activities of Canadian women's groups by stating:

> The greatest of these organizations, as far as war-work was concerned, was the [Imperial Order Daughters of the Empire]. It's [*sic*] 500 branches or chapters were in closer cooperation, its policy more precise and clear, its practical effort better co-ordinated, than in other cases.[87]

Hopkins's tribute helps to explain why the members of the IODE were successful in

---

81   PAM, IODE Records, MG 10, C 70, box 18, Queen Victoria Chapter Minutes 1912-1916, 4 February 1915, 61; ibid., 7 October 1915, 94; ibid., box 11, Winnipeg Municipal Chapter Minutes 1912-1916, 23 February 1916, 193.

82   Mrs. Joan Church Papers, Governor Laird Chapter History, 7; SAB, R 598, IV.8.a, Saskatchewan Provincial Executive Minutes 1914-1921, 18 September 1918, 119.

83   The Governor Laird Chapter hoped to receive $2.50 from each chapter in Saskatchewan, so that there would be $1 per week to spend on each returned soldier in the asylum (SAB, R. 766, II.6.b, Governor Laird Chapter Minutes 1916-1918, 9 July 1918, 140, and 21 October 1918, 161).

84   *Saskatoon Phoenix*, 15 May 1917, p. 5.

85   Shortt Collection, University of Saskatchewan Library, pamphlet entitled "Imperial Order Daughters of the Empire Military Chapter Next-of-Kin Memorial Avenue," c. 1951, 1-3.

86   For further information about the details of this program, see NA, IODE Records, vol. 19, file 9, "IODE 25th Anniversary History," 21-2.

87   J. Castell Hopkins, *The Canadian Annual Review of Public Affairs, 1916* (Toronto: The Annual Review Publishing Company Ltd., 1917), 419.

their wartime endeavours. During the war, the IODE had a large and growing membership of women who were dedicated to making a significant contribution to the imperial war effort. Members learned to recognize the power of small deeds in the aggregate: if they all contributed their little bit to a common cause, great things could be done.[88]

The IODE in Saskatchewan was a smaller part of a greater whole during the Great War. In essence, the province's IODE chapters focussed on the same issues as chapters in other regions of Canada. The singleness of purpose and the centralized organization of this national women's society contributed to the continuity of IODE aims throughout the Dominion.

Because it was waiting and prepared for another imperial war by 1914, and because it was prompt, efficient and focussed, the IODE was able to make a significant contribution to the Canadian Great War effort. By the outset of the war in 1914, the IODE was looking for an opportunity to prove its value as an organization. War allowed the women of the IODE to prove that they could do more than talk about their ideals. The Daughters of the Empire put their highly structured organization into action and gave tangible expression to their beliefs. Furthermore, although other women's groups took up war work in 1914, they were not able to operate in the prepared and efficient manner of the Daughters of the Empire during the First World War.

In 1916, J. Castell Hopkins suggested that one of the IODE's strengths was that its policies were precise and clear. The Daughters of the Empire had a well-defined set of ideologies and objectives which were established before and upheld throughout the Great War. The Order was motivated primarily by its imperialism, which consisted of two major components: patriotism and militarism. The Daughters believed that they had a duty to their country and Empire that they were obligated to fulfill. They answered this call to arms with an unswerving patriotic devotion that was openly displayed in their symbols and their acts. The IODE also sincerely believed that the Empire was fighting a righteous war and that the battle had to be fought to a victorious conclusion in favour of the civilized British world. This deep-rooted militaristic conviction influenced the Order's entire wartime agenda. The Daughters of the Empire realized that the war could not be won without fighting men. Consequently, the objective of most IODE endeavours during the war was to recruit and assist Canadian soldiers so that the Dominion would have a strong contingent of men in peak physical and mental condition who were able to give their best in battle.

When Mrs. Clark Murray organized this federation of imperialist women during the Boer War, her hope was to give women a channel through which they could express their own brand of patriotism. The Daughters of the Empire grasped this opportunity, and expressed their imperialism in ways which were frequently maternal in nature. The Daughters cared for Canadian soldiers and their families like a mother cares for a child: they clothed them, they fed them, they nurtured them when they were ill, and they provided for their special needs and wants. When they interfered in the lives of soldiers' dependents, some Daughters of the Empire acted like the typical, overbearing parent who offers unwanted, even unwarranted, advice to his or

---

88   PAM, IODE Records, MG 10, C 70, file "IODE Municipal Chapter—Annual Reports 1913-1943," "Seventh Annual Report — Secretary's Report for the Year 1918 Municipal Chapter Winnipeg IODE," 1.

her child. The IODE idea of wartime sacrifice was clearly that of the Edwardian middle- and upper-class woman's realm, where concessions included trimming your own hat, cooking without rationed ingredients, and allowing your husband and sons to join up and put their lives on the line for the Empire. IODE fundraising methods made the most of women's skills, and social activities that appealed to women of the time doubled as IODE fundraising events.

The women of the IODE had two distinct class advantages that helped them make a difference in the Canadian war effort: influence and money. For the most part, Daughters of the Empire were from the upper echelons of society, and they had relatives or friends who were in positions of power: newspaper editors who donated space for advertising in the local paper, military officials who welcomed IODE recruitment efforts, and civic politicians who encouraged the social-welfare assistance that the Order volunteered to soldiers and their families. Most IODE women could afford to donate substantial sums to fundraising efforts, and they had friends or associates who could make financial contributions to the war cause. Furthermore, the women of the IODE could afford to stay at home rather than go to work, which allowed them leisure time that could be devoted to the Order's wartime projects. However, although the Daughters' social position did allow them to assist the war effort, it also engendered a patronizing, elitist attitude that permeated much of the Order's war work.

Ironically, the Great War proved to be the zenith of the IODE's existence as an imperialistic, patriotic woman's organization. The IODE was born of an imperial war and flourished in a period of imperial optimism. The Boer War gave the Order life and established its patriotic and militaristic aims and ideologies. In the years after the South African conflict, the IODE gradually expanded and developed at a time when imperialism was on the rise again. By 1914, the Daughters of the Empire were prepared to serve their King and country in the hour of need — and they did. Four years later, however, it was clear that the Great War had brought a close to the imperialist Edwardian era in Canada. By the end of the war, the very values for which the Order stood were thrown into doubt. Disillusionment set in and the organization's imperial zeal was undermined. The IODE did survive to serve in another world war from 1939 to 1945 and to the present day undertakes philanthropic, educational and nationalist endeavours. Nevertheless, the Order never recaptured the patriotic ardour of its first twenty years. The Daughters of the Empire can only look back with longing at the days of the Great War when, in their words, their work had been both "interesting" and "spectacular."[89]

---

89   SAB, R 598, II.6, *The Imperial Order Daughters of the Empire: Golden Jubilee, 1900-1950*, 25.

ENGENDERING RESISTANCE:
WOMEN RESPOND TO RELIEF IN SASKATOON, 1930-1932

Theresa Healy

The Mayor and Aldermen,

Since November 18th 1931 until date My husband has had two turns for work each time was nineteen days not three full weeks. It averages Since November of 1931 6 weeks work for money in six months and winter months. During that time I have received three orders of coal each order was half a ton, That is one and a half tons of coal to heat a four roomed bungalow which has no furnace or heating and [has] plumbing installed which would have frozen solid had I not brought [extra] coal to prevent such. Now I am supposed to pay $30.00 a month rent. Now when we received the little money I had to buy coal pay light and water Bills buy food where do you suppose the rent was going to come from? I couldn't begin to pay rent for six months, out of that I am very wide awake to relief. ... if we don't help those out of this struggle we will have a terrible revolution. I see it coming I have every opportunity to see it coming.[1]

Mrs. William N. Watson wrote this letter in Saskatoon on 2 April 1932, after attending a meeting of the Westmount Ratepayers Association where she "heard that the council was ready to accept any suggestions made to enlighten the burden of relief to the people."[2] Her six-page letter, in addition to the clear-cut descriptions of the inadequacies of relief and her warnings to council of trouble ahead, also included strong moral and political opinions on the nature and place of relief in government.

Her warnings were prophetic. On 15 November 1932, six months after she had written to council, the city police had surrounded Saskatoon's city hall. Inside, forty-eight women and their children, instituting the city's first sit-down strike,[3] were occupying council chambers. They were protesting the introduction of a compulsory relief agreement that had to be signed under the threat of suspension from relief.

---

1   City of Saskatoon Archives (COSA), City Clerk's Records, box 5887b, Relief-S, 1932, file 308, #20. Mrs. Watson's letter is reproduced here exactly as she wrote it. I would like to thank the women who read and edited earlier versions of this essay: Antonia Botting, Anne-Marie Di Lella, Margaret Little, Alex Maas, Shelley McNab, Donna Morgan, Bonnie Murray, Joy Parr, and Veronica Strong-Boag. Their criticisms and insights strengthened this essay; any remaining weaknesses are my own. A special thank you to Saskatoon City Clerk Janice Mann and her staff who make me welcome in their office, share cake and coffee and generally support this work above and beyond the call of duty. And finally to all those wonderful women who share their stories of the 1930s with me and inspire me with their own courage and humour — I could not have done it without you.

2   Ibid.

3   This description was used by Don Kerr and Stan Hanson in *Saskatoon: The First Half Century* (Edmonton: NeWest Press, 1982). Many thanks to Don Kerr, who first introduced me to this incident when I was a fledgling historian. See also: Joan Sangster, *Dreams of Equality: Women on the Canadian Left, 1920-1950* (Toronto: McClelland and Stewart, 1992), 141. Sangster points out that, apart from an emphasis on women's roles, feminine passivity was not a hallmark of local relief protests. The Saskatoon city hall sit-down strike illustrates this thesis.

The women were not alone in their protest. Outside, an angry crowd confronted the police, who refused to allow representatives from various labour organizations to deliver bedding and mattresses, though local restaurants had been allowed to send in meals for the sit-down strikers. An editorial in the Saskatoon *Star Phoenix* denounced the requirement to sign the relief agreement as "blackmail."[4] Nearby, members from the Saskatoon Trades and Labour Council, who were representing the women, met with city council members in an attempt to end the standoff. Yet, nearly forty-eight hours passed before the women and children left city hall, satisfied that their demands had been addressed and that changes would follow.

This episode and Mrs. Watson's letter demonstrate the extent of the involvement of women in the political protests of the 1930s, representing two extremes on a continuum of women's strategies of resistance to the control of the state inherent in its relief policy. The harsh provisions of relief alone might have been a catalyst for political action. But beyond the inadequacies of relief, these women were experiencing the intrusion of the state into their homes and family lives in a direct and unpleasant way. Because of relief policy, the state became an invisible, brooding presence at every inadequate meal served in the home of those on relief. This new context resulted in a shifting of working-class women's boundaries. Especially, notions of respectability/shame and independence/state assistance took on different meanings.

As a result of the state's more tangible presence in the home, women began taking action outside the home. Women began to intrude into the sphere of political activity generally considered the preserve of men: public protest which risked confrontation with the police.[5]

Working-class women responded, then, to a middle-class male policy built on both traditional "feminine" strategies and they adopted more public — and more risky — roles. The failures of relief and the inability of various levels of government to correct those failures ensured a fertile spawning ground for political activities ranging from collective to individual, from violent political protest to individual acts of accommodation or rebellion. Organized women's groups, like the Women's Labor League and the Women's Section of the Saskatoon Unemployed Association argued with city council over the forms and methods of relief.[6] Individual women, like Mrs. Watson, also expressed their dissatisfaction with council's methods. Both individuals and groups also manipulated the system to their own ends. These approaches, sometimes disorganized and poorly planned,[7] and at other times highly developed

---

4   Although the newspaper disapproved of the women's methods, it supported their aims. See: Editorial, *Star Phoenix*, November 1932, p. 5.

5   Engendering, then, is used in this essay in both senses of the word. Resistance was engendered by a provocative and overt intrusion of the state into the home. That resistance also took gendered forms, both traditional and new.

6   Well known and respectable local women's groups, like the Local Council of Women and the Young Women's Christian Association (YWCA), were also involved in provoking changes to the relief system. While some of their arguments derived from, and benefited, working-class women, these groups are beyond the scope of this essay which focusses on the less well known and, perhaps, more suspect and less respectable, women's groups. It may be that these lesser known groups were more suspect because, though gender-based, they were purely political. Groups like the Local Council of Women had a charitable purpose which tended to make them a little more acceptable, though no more powerful, to the power brokers.

7   It was in direct interaction with relief policy that many working-class Saskatchewan women came to

and well thought out, forced changes to the relief system of immediate benefit to those on relief in the first two years of the decade.

Clearly, relief — or, rather, its failure — was the reason the women of Saskatoon complained so vociferously. The occupation of city hall chambers resulted from the culminated frustration of women with city hall's refusal to act on their suggestions and needs. Why was city hall unable to respond to such unanimous and clear calls for change?

City hall was trapped by the assumptions which had framed relief policy in previous years. Originally, relief was a religious and charitable duty: the provision of basic necessities for those unable to provide such things for themselves. In Britain, from whom Canada inherited its relief provisions and mechanisms, relief had devolved to a municipal responsibility provided for through city taxes and, because of associations with the workhouse, had become a hated institution, a place of last resort. In Canada, the relief system was complicated by the belief of most Canadians that there was always work. One could always "go west" and support oneself on the land. Therefore, relief provisions were minimal. Recipients were supposed to prove their fitness and genuine need, and to pay for relief by working for it. Yet, relief was always a part of the Canadian city landscape. Apart from times of economic depression, it remained a small and often invisible landmark.[8]

The city's relief policy was gendered. It was based on an assumption that men worked and women did not and that women and children were provided for through marriage by the labours of employed men committed to their responsibilities as married men. Relief policy was blinkered by firm ideals of proper role behaviour for men and women. This gendered vision of relief was middle class in origin. Middle-class policy makers believed that if the working class used thrift and forethought its need for relief would only be minimal and temporary. Thus, relief was a measure to provide the minimum basic necessities for a minimum period until normal family circumstances — a working male head of household providing for his dependents — were restored.

Within this approach was a covert agenda — to punish deviance and reward conformity. Prior to the widespread unemployment of the Depression, relief applicants were screened. Only the "genuinely" deserving, those unfortunate enough not to be able to provide for themselves because of unavoidable circumstances, were entitled to receive relief. To qualify, applicants had to prove their suitability. Beyond this, relief's greater role in English Canada was to reinforce notions of the independent family with a working male breadwinner and a home-making female as the norm.[9]

---

terms with the inequalities of their society for the first time. Relief activities were, in many respects, a unifying political training ground for many women in the same way suffrage was for women a generation earlier. Veronica Strong-Boag makes a similar argument in *New Day Recalled: Lives of Girls and Women in English Canada, 1919-1939* (Toronto: Copp Clark Pitman, 1988).

8   See Mary Theresa Healy, "Prayers, Pamphlets and Protest: Women and Relief in Saskatoon, 1929-1939" (MA thesis, University of Saskatchewan, 1990), 1-11, for a full discussion of the construction of municipal relief in Saskatoon.

9   The gendered nature of relief policy is further illustrated by the neglect of unemployed women. Unemployed single "girls" were expected to return home and help their mothers, and married women were not supposed to be working anyway. See: Helen Gregory MacGill, "The Jobless Woman," *Chatelaine* (30 September 1930): 5. As MacGill pointed out, little governmental attention was given to the problems facing unemployed women: "an unemployment conference does its whole duty … when it discusses the difficulties and seeks the relief of workless men."

Working-class realities were often far from the ideals framing relief policy. Working-class women and sometimes their children frequently found themselves working for cash or other resources in order to contribute to the financial survival of the family.[10] Men were not always working or independent. Periods of unemployment — particularly the seasonal unemployment of the Canadian labour market — illness, personal problems or economic downturn often meant men were not able to fulfill their role as sole financial supporter. Rural families, recently arrived immigrants or Aboriginal families whose stake in the Canadian economy was often fragile, also found it difficult to conform to idealized models of the family. Further, even those families which did conform to the model or would have liked to found maintaining the ideal family difficult.

Even in the best circumstances, male working-class earnings would not ensure even minimum standards of living.[11] Families could not afford to save in order to provide for periods of increased economic hardship. As a group of "housewives and mothers" wrote to council:

> Our husbands and those of us responsible for the welfare of our children have for many years been able to earn a living in this city. Surely it is not our fault that we are unable to do this now. The statements have been made that the workers are shiftless and we should have saved and prepared for times like this. We wish, however, to point out that wages received even in the best of times do not allow very much saving. Nevertheless many of us did manage to save a little which we invested in homes and furniture and which we are gradually losing.[12]

Making ends meet, providing for basic necessities, was difficult enough "even in the best of times." For the working class, long-term goals were more pragmatic and included educating the children, or paying for health care or insurance. Working-class women needed the skills to make $10 do the work of $20.

In times of unemployment, even the $10 cash income disappeared. These realities of working-class life ensured that relief, no matter how unpalatable and difficult, was a fact of life — even before the Depression. In response to the need for government help, municipal governments established relief departments responsible for the provision of relief. Relief rolls, the lists of those receiving municipal provision, existed year-round. These were the "deserving poor," mostly women with no male support. Reflecting the gendered nature of relief, the statistics define these women by their status in relation to the male household head: "widowed," "deserted," "husband in jail," "husband in bush."[13]

---

10 See Christina Maria Hill, "Women in the Canadian Economy," in Robert Laxer, ed. *The Political Economy of Dependency in Canada* (Toronto: McClelland and Stewart Ltd., 1973), 84-106, for an interesting overview of the various forms women's labour has taken in Canada. Also, see the Canadian National Council of Women's (NCW), "Survey of Three Hundred Married Women Working in Industry." Of these 300 women, 79 percent reported their husbands were still at home. NCW, *Year Book for 1929*, Report of the Trades and Professions Committee, 108-11.

11 In the NCW survey women reported reasons such as paying off doctor's bills or supplementing husband's irregular employment as reasons for their employment. Though 54 percent of the women reported their husbands were steadily employed, when asked how long they intended to work, 45 percent reported they would work always or indefinitely.

12 COSA, City Clerks' Records, box 5887b, Relief-S, 1932, file 308, #19, Mrs. Pasha, Mrs. Allen, Mrs. McKenzie, Mrs. McKague, Mrs. Reeves, Mrs. Squires and Mrs. Hall. Letter to the mayor and aldermen, 2 July 1932.

13 For example, see: COSA, D500.III.895, Relief — Unemployment Relief, (370), 1929-1931, Monthly

However, relief rolls did not only consist of women. In the winter months, even during the "roaring twenties," the numbers of those receiving relief rose, increased by families with unemployed male heads. This unemployment was seasonal and temporary. City finances easily handled this seasonal expansion and the city was secure in the knowledge that with spring the male unemployed heads of families would return to work in construction and agriculture. In spite of the overall small numbers of people on relief, the process of applying for relief was not easy, nor was it intended to be, because the gender and moral strictures of relief were still paramount.

In the years before the 1930s, then, given the understanding of the "natural" cycles in employment, and of gendered and class patterns to relief support, Saskatoon's relief adminstration was generally complacent. In the 1920s, Saskatoon was a booming, industrializing city. New buildings, new industries were opening and the pages of the local paper confidently reported local achievements.[14] With its role as the "Hub City" of the West, an economic base rooted in agriculture and a fledgling industrial base, Saskatoon's coffers could afford the minimal charge of relief costs in the 1920s. Further, the city's leaders believed the city had nothing to fear from the temporary disruptions ensuing after October 1929. For example, in 1929 and 1930, while editorials and stories in the local paper referred to the New York stock market crash and the international problems it was causing, the writers did not seem to believe these events would affect Saskatoon. The Saskatoon *Star Phoenix* generally led a chorus of praise for a self-satisfied "Saskatoon is growing" theme. The paper also tended to castigate those who did not believe in the picture of a prosperous Saskatoon unaffected by the "temporary mild disruption" caused by events in the "East."[15]

This sense of invulnerability meant a slow reaction to the realities of the Depression, especially to the needs of unemployed residents. The Depression did not have an immediate impact on Saskatoon's economy. Because of this, the city council was anxious not to attract the needy from other locations. While expressing his support for any plans the city council might have, the Chief Constable said: "do not publicize any scheme, unless other cities have similar arrangements. The first city that does anything definite towards helping out the unemployed, will be flooded with unemployed from other cities."[16] The Council heeded his appeal and placed advertisements in newspapers in other cities warning the unemployed not to come to Saskatoon looking for work and warning relief would not be given.[17]

Until the summer of 1930, the inactivity of city hall appeared justified for it seemed that nothing had changed. Certainly, relief numbers had been slightly higher over the winter of 1929-30. People had been slower than usual to go off relief in the spring.

Relief Officer Reports, Distribution of Relief and Causes of Appeal for the City of Saskatoon, December 1929-December 1930.

14   For example, the value of building permits, another sign of economic well-being, had nearly reached $6 million in 1929, and was still over $5.5 million in 1930. Among the new buildings were a nurse's home, a new power plant, a new federal building, and a new police department. There was a darker side to urban growth: as population grew, so did crime. For example, see: "Police Have More to do as Population Increases," *Star Phoenix*, 18 October 1929, p. 6.

15   "Saskatoon Keeps Growing," *Star Phoenix*, 6 September 1929, p. 4.

16   COSA, D500.III.893, Relief — Relief to the Unemployed (378), 1929-1930, Letter from the Chief Constable to the City Clerk, 20 December 1929.

17   See, for example, the classified ads in the *Star Phoenix*, 2 November 1929, p. 21. Note that the paper contains a similar ad from the municipality of Trail, British Columbia.

But by November 1930, the problem was evident as over 100 families, three times the figures for November 1929, were on the relief roll. Five months later, over 500 families were on relief, and the figures stayed in the hundreds throughout the summer. By early 1932, city relief was costing $1,000 a day and the monthly cost was almost equal to the yearly total for 1929.[18] The average monthly total of families in 1929 was thirty-six.[19] By January 1932, the average was 1,800 families,[20] and at the end of that month 2,000 families were on relief.[21] At this point the city threatened to cut relief for everyone.[22]

The members of Saskatoon city council, immediately responsible for delivering relief in the city, had not intended to be cruel, oppressive or politically provocative in their response to the demands created by the mass unemployment in the city. They simply had few other choices. The first two years of the Depression saw public work projects as relief work. Funded by money from the federal and provincial governments, these projects included the building of the Broadway Bridge, the completion of the Bessborough Hotel, construction of the Nineteenth Street subway, improvements to the riverbank, and substantial work on the city's infrastructure, such as the sewer system.[23]

These sturdy, functional and aesthetic contributions to the physical face of the city reflected the middle-class ideology of relief. These were the sources of relief work Mrs. Watson mentioned in her letter. Unemployed men like Mr. Watson supported their families by working on these projects. Regardless of their personal work experience or physical suitability, the physical labour of unemployed men "paid" for their relief support. This expectation was clear in the language of the policy. The relief work provided was supposed to provide each male relief applicant with the opportunity of earning sufficient cash to support his family.

For single women or women heading families, there was no similar work test. The gendered vision did not expect women to prove their willingness to work. Instead, the test of women's qualification was moral and behaviourial, not physical: if they were seen as respectable, they had earned their relief. Respectability was domestic: married women with children would be at home looking after and raising children and single women would be at home helping their mothers.

The language of the relief hiring policy reveals the hierarchy of preferable relief recipients for relief work. For example, first priority was given to men who were British-born subjects or in the process of becoming naturalized Canadians, married

---

18   Statistics drawn from the reports of the relief officer to city council, recorded in City Council Minutes, from the week ending 5 October 1928 to week ending 11 January 1932. Saskatoon City Hall Records, Microfilm.

19   "Unemployed in West Will Be Advised to Stay Clear of City," *Star Phoenix*, 15 October 1929, p. 9.

20   "1,800 Families on Relief List," *Star Phoenix*, 7 January 1932, p. 3. This figure comprised 6,791 individuals.

21   "City Relief Bill is $1,000 Daily," *Star Phoenix*, 27 January 1932, p. 3. Of these families, 750 were supported by relief work on the Broadway Bridge.

22   "May Have to Slash Relief for Families," *Star Phoenix*, 29 January 1932, p. 3.

23   Initially, the funding from the upper levels of government reflected the same relief priorities as the municipal government: all relief money was temporary and had to be dispersed through relief work. Public work projects were abandoned as the preferred method of relief delivery when the upper levels of government realized that direct relief is a much cheaper method of supporting vast numbers of people in need.

and with children. Of these, Council would only consider *bona fide* Saskatoon residents, that is, those who had been resident in Saskatoon prior to 31 December 1929. City council applied these criteria, not only to its own relief work projects, but also on any construction work in the city.[24]

Unfortunately, sheer numbers affected the suitability of public works projects as joint work-test and relief-earning outlets. The work made available through public works projects was not enough to go round. Mr. Watson, as Mrs. Watson pointed out, received only nineteen days work in six months. The aldermen attempted to maintain some kind of criteria for determining who would be hired on the public works projects. As a result, men worked far less than promised and what work they were paid for was not sufficient to support their families.

Because of this inability of public works projects to provide work for everyone who needed it, the city manufactured other make-work projects in order to maintain the work test/relief earning principle in its relief program. The Mayor explained why these relief work projects were in place: "only for the purpose of testing their willingness ... as the services being rendered are of no value to the city as the Engineering Department would not employ men to do the work in the absence of the present situation. In other words the work is entirely created for test purposes."[25] For example, men were expected to work at the city's wood yard, each hour of labour worth a certain amount towards the family's light bill. Even these programs were not without problems. The city's fuel merchants argued the city's wood yard was unfair competition.[26] There was a level of humilation to the city's relief program: "Yes, put a man doing all the dirty work they can show him up, like sweeping the streets, digging ditches."[27] The public nature of these make-work projects made receiving relief a public affair.

In the absence of a working economy, the state then betrayed its own principles. In failing to provide meaningful work, the moral lessons of earned relief were lost. In this context, the provisions of relief by the municipality became a focus for a broader discontent. The activities of Saskatchewan women in the 1930s must be seen within the environment of this double failure. The concrete problems which engaged recipients during the first two years of the 1930s were related to the everyday administration and policies of relief, but compounded by the bitterness of unemployment itself. The activities of the state in trying to cope with the problems generated by unemployment, through the control mechanisms of relief and the responses of

24   The city clerk, on the council's instructions, wrote to every contractor in the city who held a city relief project contract with city council. In this letter he asked for the completion of a statistical survey on the nationality, length of residence, marital status and number of dependents of all men employed by the private contractors on the public relief contracts. See: COSA, D500.III.895, Relief — Unemployment Relief, (370), letters and replies re: Status of Men Employed on Relief, Unemployment Projects.

25   COSA, D500.III.875, Letter from Mayor Hair to Mr. Molloy, Deputy Minister of Railways, Labour and Industry, 30 January 1930. The city may have been additionally adamant about the "useless" nature of the work and its function as a work test because of the provincial government's unwillingness to fund any normal city costs, such as sanding streets. These costs the cities would have had to undertake and pay for themselves.

26   Ibid.

27   COSA, City Clerk's Records, box 5887b, Relief-S, 1932, file 308, #20, Mrs. Wm. N. Watson, letter dated 2 April 1932.

those supposedly controlled by relief policies, are an object lesson in power in a contested terrain. Both the governed and the governors engaged in a complex and problematic process of negotiating compromise and influence through the bureaucracy of relief.

However, the first concern for many working-class women was to stay off relief entirely. They developed a variety of responses derived from long-standing experiences of balancing household budgets. While working-class men's notions of masculinity may have been tied up in their ability to provide for their families through arduous and difficult work, working-class women's notions of femininity were engaged in their household management skills and their abilities to make ends meet.[28] Even in "good" times, in order to reconcile competing demands and to contribute to the family's survival, women had developed an underground economy, an exchange of goods and services that often generated cash. Women's labour in this regard has been consistently underrated and underestimated. Considered "domestic" labour, the financial and emotional importance of women's work rarely counts in census or other terms.

What a woman undertook in the informal economy was decided by the resources available to her both inside and outside of her home, as well as an assessment of what she could afford of her time or skills. For example, part-time or full-time work opportunities available locally would be weighed against what resources were available within the home. Additional rooms for lodgers or child minding, or the skills to provide in-home hairdressing or cooking may have been attractive cash-generating sources for women already burdened with the heavy labour of running the home and family.[29] Outside the home, women offered reliable cleaning services, spring cleaning or domestic help. Marcels, a special kind of wave applied to the hair with curling irons, and child-minding services were portable, that is, they could be available in either the home of the woman giving or receiving the service.[30] Small animal husbandry guaranteed a source of food and income for the family, though not always without problems.[31]

Involvement in the informal exchange of goods and services was compelled by need,

---

28   See: Mark Rosenfeld, "'It Was a Hard Life': Class and Gender in the Work and Family Rhythms of a Railway Town, 1920-1950," in Bettina Bradbury, ed., *Canadian Family History* (Toronto: Copp Clark Pitman, 1992), 241-80, for a fascinating discussion of masculinity and work.

29   Part-time work was preferable to full-time, and women looked forward to the time when they could afford not to work, because of the demands made on the full-time wife and mother; see Elizabeth Roberts, *A Woman's Place: An Oral History of Working-Class Women, 1890-1940* (Oxford: Basil Blackwell, 1984), 136-39. Even where paid work opportunities existed locally, women's choices were also informed by other factors, such as number and ages of children at home, and the husband's attitude to "his" wife working. See also: Jane Lewis, *Labour and Love: Women's Experiences of Home and Family* (Oxford: Basil Blackwell, 1986); and Lenore Davidoff, "The Separation of Home and Work? Landladies and Lodgers in Nineteenth and Twentieth Century England," in Sandra Burman, ed., *Fit Work for Women* (London: Croom Helm, 1979).

30   Drawn from the classified advertising columns of the Saskatoon *Star Phoenix*, 1931-39. It is still possible to see similar advertisements in the *Star Phoenix* today, everything from child minding to perogies, a Ukrainian food speciality.

31   One woman had her flock of chickens stolen not once, but twice. After the police found and returned all of them after the first theft, they were stolen a second time. She was not so lucky the second time; when the police returned them after the second theft, half the flock was missing (*Star Phoenix*, 28 April 1930, p. 3).

charitable impulse or sisterly solidarity.[32] But these strategies were strained in the 1930s because the spare income and cash to fuel the underground economy was short.

Women had to use other skills, which they normally used to stretch household income to the absolute limit, in order to keep their families off relief. Women not only prided themselves on their ability to "make something from nothing." In many cases they had no other choice. Under women's hands and creative skills, the ubiquitous flour sack made many reincarnations as pillow cases, tea towels, even articles for trousseaus. Adult clothing was remade into children's wear. Thus, women's traditional handcraft skills became vitally important in clothing their families.[33]

Women had to make other sacrifices in order to stay off relief. There were less respectable ways of generating income.[34] Stories of bawdy houses and bootlegging also found their way into the local paper, though local people were aware that sacrificing respectability in this way was a means of rejecting the dependence of relief. As Mrs. Watson put it: "I know of many cases where there are people bootlegging rather than face the struggle [of living on relief]."[35] Selling household possessions was another sacrifice. As one woman, a mother of six, reported:

> my husband for the past five weeks has been hundreds of miles from home hunting work, and still is, while I, myself, am having to sell various things to keep my young family going, of whom five are under school age, and I guess there are quite a few in the same position.[36]

Women also left home to seek work elsewhere or to "ride the rods," though not in such large numbers as men.[37]

Unpalatable as relief might seem to middle-class policy makers, there came a time when relief became the only source of survival for a family struggling against unemployment. Therefore, when all else failed, those in need applied for relief.

The process of applying for relief was difficult and demeaning. Applicants needed witnesses, *bona fide* city taxpayers, who could verify they had been residents of Saskatoon since before January 1930. The application form itself was intimidating: a gigantic document, 11 by 17 inches, it included enquiries on political affiliation, military service, membership in organizations, alcohol and narcotic use, and a section asking for a list of all household possessions.

In applying for relief, all sections, including a newly introduced section "the

---

32   Roberts, *A Woman's Place*, 141.

33   Women make this point in oral histories repeatedly, and with great pride. For example, see the collection of oral histories "Port and Prairie: Vancouver and Saskatoon, 1929-1939," deposit in archives in British Columbia and Saskatchewan, forthcoming.

34   For example, see a story detailing council's refusal to deal with anonymous complaints about "such scandalous goings-on" (*Star Phoenix*, 5 Februaury 1932).

35   COSA, City Clerk's Records, box 5887b, Relief-S, 1932, file 308, #20, Mrs. Wm. N. Watson, letter dated 2 April 1932.

36   A Mother of Six, "Married Women Workers," *Star Phoenix*, 24 May 1930.

37   Riding the rods or the rails was the practice of hitching rides on the railway by lying on the rods under the railway cars or on the roofs of the box cars. There have been few reports of women doing this, but there is some evidence that women did take to the rods in this way disguised as men. See the Saskatoon YWCA report of young girls greasing their curls flat and hiding them under caps ("Girl Hoboes Problem for Traveller's Aid Officer," *Star Phoenix*, 13 October 1932). Also see: Honor Wells interview by Leslie Wells, Vancouver, May 1986 (copies of interview held by interviewer and author).

agreement," had to be completed. In applying, a family had to declare destitution, meaning they had exhausted all possible sources of funds, including selling anything of value.

The Relief Agreement, the new section of the application form, directly precipitated the city hall sit-down. (For the complete text of the Relief Agreement see Appendix 1, p. 112.) The language and policies of the agreement illustrate the assumptions of middle-class policy makers. The response it engendered — the city hall sit-down strike — exemplifies the frustration of the working class with relief.

In the sit-down strike the women's response was clear. They refused to sign away their rights as part of the process of applying for relief. Women on relief had their own standards of behaviour which conflicted with the assumptions of the relief policy.

The women made clear demands from their sanctuary. They wanted to be reinstated on relief (they had been cut off for refusing to sign), and they articulated their problems with the agreement. They spelled out the changes they wanted made to the agreement section of the relief application.

For example, the notion of working-class independence was based on the sanctity of the home, the privacy of the family. This meant keeping the state out of their homes. Women did not want the state, in the shape of relief investigators or "visitors," prying into their homes and lives. Yet, if they signed the relief agreement, they gave permission, under Clause 2, for "any member of the Civic Relief Board or any of its duly authorized employees" to enter any reliefer's home at any time of the day or night, in order to ascertain the truthfulness of the declarations made on the relief application.[38]

The concept of relief as a loan rather than a right was officially formulated in the agreement. Clause 3 required the repayment of any sums "loaned," whenever the city requested. Further, the city would determine how much was owed. By signing the agreement, reliefers promised to "on demand pay to the City of Saskatoon the value of relief supplied to me or my dependents after the date of this agreement" and agreed that "a certificate by the Civic Relief Board of the City of Saskatoon or by the treasurer of the said City of Saskatoon shall be conclusive evidence as to the making of such advance and the amount thereof." The women in the city chambers made it clear that they considered this clause an insult. The sit-down strikers argued reliefers had every intention of repaying. Reliefers were not "bums." They did need, however, to be able to determine fair repayment schedules.[39]

Though the relief agreement they were protesting did not address the provisions of relief, the women in council chambers did not allow the opportunity their protest generated to go by without expressing their dissatisfaction with other aspects of relief. They used the publicity to air other complaints derived from their experiences with relief.

By 1932, women on relief had two years of intimate experience with the shortcomings and attitudes of relief. They argued that they could barely keep their families warm and fed on what the relief system allowed (see Appendix 2, p. 113).

---

38 "Reliefer" was the common term used to refer to any person receiving relief.

39 These comments were made during the sit-in, and after the sit-in was over. Women did not object, *per se*, to repayment of relief. They wanted some control over repayments, especially how much and when. They also argued that the city had no right to recoup money it had never spent, as two-thirds of relief money came from the provincial and dominion levels of government, which were not demanding repayment. See the *Star Phoenix*, 18 November 1932, for the stories covering the agreement and the reaction to it.

The relief system was hampered. While the city's relief system tried to integrate the provision of necessities with the preservation of the "moral character" of recipients, the major concern of council as the decade progressed was reducing costs. Theoretically, a person on relief received direct assistance to cover the basic necessities of life. In practice, relief came in various forms. Qualifying families received relief for shelter (a term that covered rent, water and light), for clothing, for fuel (wood or coal or coal oil), and for food.[40]

While the relief policy of the city provided for fuel, shelter, clothing and food, when individuals or families applied for relief, they did not necessarily receive relief in all these categories. Applicants were given relief only in the categories the city decided they needed it, that is, bureaucratic decisions restricted access to needed provisions.[41] Furthermore, the city tried to ensure applicants paid for any relief given, wherever possible. For example, while light and water came under rent relief, electricity and water bills were "paid" for by work performed for the city by the household head.[42] Excess consumption required cash.

While promising shelter as part of relief, the city actually shifted the onus of providing these needs onto the landlord. The relief department routinely refused to pay relief for rent costs until a family was faced with eviction.[43] The renter-leaser relationship was strained by the inability of the reliefers to pay their rent, and the refusal of the city to grant relief for rent. Further, the type of quarters designated, and the amounts of rent permissable restricted relief families to inadequate homes.

Clothing was rationed and given according to what the clothing bureau had in stock. The clothing bureau was in the basement of city hall and was supported by both public and private agencies. The city provided an annual grant. The six service clubs involved in founding the bureau canvassed for donations of cash but, more usually, used goods. The bureau was also another site of the work test. For example, unemployed cobblers would repair and renew donated shoes. Women were "employed" in the sewing room, repairing donated clothes or cutting yard goods into garments. Clothing relief was a major source of discontent. Not only were there continual shortages but also the new relief clothing was readily identifiable as "relief" issue, while the donated goods were "shameful." As Mrs. Watson wrote:

> The relief Bureau for clothing is not what the press makes believe it is. I know for a fact some of the clothing given out to be an absolute insult to the receiver, garments filthy and almost impossible to wear. They may give

---

40   Saskatoon Public Library, "Schedule I," *Report of the City Commissioner,* 1934.

41   For example, the needs of school-age children were ignored in the relief calculations and, if the children were not in school, they were expected to be working and contributing to the family's income.

42   Water was supplied by tickets, $1.00 for one month. Tickets were issued in the winter, but this relief service was "almost entirely discontinued" in the summer. Women were expected to use the free water taps in the summer, regardless of the distance involved. Even as late as 1937, many homes in Saskatoon were not connected to the water mains (COSA, City Clerk's Office, file 307, (1937), Water — Relief Recipients — Summer Period, Report of the Relief Officer, Adopted by Council, 10 May 1937).

43   This was the rent relief policy established by the provincial government. Landlords were pressing city council to change this because of the difficulty many of them were facing in living on, and paying taxes from, their rental income. For many, especially widows, this was their only income. See: Alma Lawton, "Urban Relief in Saskatchewan During the Years of the Depression" (MA thesis, University of Saskatchewan, 1969).

out some good articles but what I have seen given to some people rather
than wear such the parties went cold and did without.[44]

The provision of clothing, especially for children, was a constant source of friction
between reliefers and the council.

Food was probably the most crucial category of relief. "Diets" (see Appendix 3, p.
114), or lists of food allowances for families, were carefully calculated according to
strict lists prepared by experts. These lists were introduced as the basis of the relief
voucher in 1932.[45] Every meal became a nightmare of inadequacy. With diet lists
determined by experts, the most fundamental home-making task was limited and
reduced. The women argued the diets provided nutritionally inadequate amounts of
food.[46] Women on relief were faced with the unenviable task of converting
inadequate and unappetizing food supplies into family meals.

Another major source of discontent was the method of providing food relief.
Before the introduction of the relief store, food relief in Saskatoon was in the form
of vouchers.[47] These spelled out on the face of the coupon the value of goods a woman
could "purchase" at her local store. By 1931, this was a closed-face food voucher —
that is, clearly specifying types and quantity of food rather than cash value — issued
to relief recipients.[48]

Women deeply resented the intrusion into the management of their households
represented by the closed-face voucher. Their responses took two forms. On a direct
and individual level, women simply manipulated the system. They came to private
arrangements with the stores authorized to accept the vouchers. Under these private
agreements, the shopkeepers would not fill the quota of specified goods but would
allow housewives to substitute small necessaries not permitted, such as matches,
sewing thread, or candles. This benefited both parties. Stores could make a small
profit on the difference between the value of the foods paid for by the city and the
value of the goods the housewife had actually taken. Housewives had access to
additional nonapproved goods.[49]

---

44   COSA, City Clerk's Records, box 5887b, Relief-S, 1932, file 308, #20, Mrs. Wm. N. Watson, letter dated
      2 April 1932.

45   As one of the changes achieved around the delivery of relief, the Saskatoon Local Council of Women
      was later consulted in the preparation of these lists (COSA, City Clerk's Office, Box 5865, M — Relief,
      1936, file 303, Relief, Increase in Cash Allowance, Report on Diet Basis of Cash Food Relief, 9 April 1936).

46   Studies in other cities showed the women's views were justified. Nutritional requirements provided
      for by relief budgets were below the minimums required for the long-term maintenance of health.
      A study completed by L.C. Marsh, *Health and Unemployment*, published in 1938 as part of the McGill
      Social Research Programme pointed out most relief programs in Canada did not meet basic
      requirements. See: A.E. Grauer, *Public Assistance and Social Insurance: A Study Prepared for the Royal
      Commission on Dominion-Provincial Relations* (Ottawa: King's Printer, 1939). A study of relief services
      in Saskatoon argued "the diet schedules given to relief recipients in Saskatoon could be substantially
      improved" and recommended consultation with the "Inter-Provincial Nutrition Advisory
      Committee," a group comprised of the directors from the household science departments at the
      Universities of Saskatchewan, Manitoba and Alberta. This group had already assisted relief officials
      in other prairie provinces. See: *A Study of Community Welfare Services in Saskatoon: A Report Prepared for
      the Community Council of Saskatoon, 1937* (Ottawa: Council House, 1938), 12.

47   It was presumed working-class people on relief could not be trusted with cash.

48   COSA, City Clerk's Office, Box 5865, M — Relief, 1936, file 303, Relief, Increase in Cash Allowance,
      Data on Relief Diets, 30 March 1936.

49   This activity was reflected in the litany of complaints of "abuses" of the system brought before council.
      For example, see the appeal of the Save-More Grocery and Fruit to be re-instated for relief orders. It

The second form of response was more political. Either as individuals or through organizations of the unemployed, women began to protest directly to council. Protests regarding the inadequacy of the voucher system began to increase. Complaints were so frequent and vociferous that council meetings were increasingly taken up by deputations from various organizations and individuals.[50]

Beyond the food allotment, women began to agitate for items such as household linens or the renewal of household objects such as pots and pans, or lino (oil cloth). As the Depression continued, articles such as furniture and pots and pans reached the point of needing replacement but relief was only designed as an interim measure. Replacing necessary items for the family's daily life was not part of the short-term nature that informed relief policy as survival provisions only.

Without surrendering control or accepting the right of recipients to influence the system, the council tried to revamp the system to address the complaints. The relief officer was one innovation. Always male, and usually with a military background, he was supposed to free council from the time-consuming and unrewarding work of administering the relief system.[51] One of the earliest acts of the relief officer and the Civic Relief Board, established as part of the same innovation, was to abolish the voucher system of relief and establish a relief store.

City council had originally considered the possibility of establishing its own relief food depot as a cost-saving measure. Opposed by unemployed organizations and representatives from the city's merchants, the idea had been rejected in June 1931 but was reintroduced in 1932.

There was still opposition. The Women's Section of the Saskatoon Unemployed Association, for example, had made a presentation to council opposing the establishment of the relief store. It predicted the opening of the store would mean the layoff of clerks and the closure of independent stores. The group also argued that it infringed upon the rights of relief recipients to shop where they chose for the best bargains. Furthermore, they argued that practices the Council described as abuses of the voucher system, such as bargaining and trading arrangements, were an important role of the housewife and should be permitted by the system "in the interests of the health of the family."[52]

In fact, if any change was to be introduced to the system, the women wanted one that would increase, not reduce, their autonomy. They wanted cash relief. In the absence of this, they wanted certain rights under the voucher system. For example, the right to ask for substitutions in the diets in the interests of the health of the family. They also believed that the range of articles the store proposed to carry was not wide enough.[53]

---

based its case on the fact the manager was not aware of the substitutions being made on relief orders (COSA, Minutes of City Council, 23 May 1932). See also: Lawton, *Urban Relief,* 119.

50   Lawton, *Urban Relief,* 119. The groups represented a diverse array of interests, including ex-servicemen's associations, neighbourhood groups, political alliances, as well as women's groups.

51   The Local Council of Women and the YWCA had lobbied the council to hire women relief officers as there were "some things a woman could only tell another woman." It also argued for the inclusion of women on the Civic Relief Board when it was established. Neither of these attempts were successful.

52   COSA, Minutes of City Council, 19 May 1932. Mrs. Carr led the delegation.

53   COSA, City Clerk's Office, file 358, 1932, Relief Store, Delegation of Women's Branch, Saskatoon Association of Unemployed.

In spite of these arguments against the relief store, the promise of central control as a means of increasing efficiency and controlling the "abuses" inherent in the voucher adminstration made the scheme irresistible. (See Appendix 4, p. 115, for a plan of the relief store.) After the hours of council meetings spent dealing with angry reliefers and questions related to vouchers, council believed the answer to its problems lay in a city-owned and operated food relief depot. The city established a depot a year after the original motion had been defeated.[54] In addition to increasing control over suspected abuses, the city expected to be able to save money with the relief store, a belief the city treasurer justified when he reported, on request of council, a "net saving of $5,631.93, in respect to grocery orders, as compared with the month of May when there was no store."[55] In fact, the city accomplished more than a saving. The women who occupied city hall suspected the city had been making a profit out of their misery. They were right; the city turned a profit on the operation of the relief store.[56]

Once in operation the city-owned and operated relief service met universal condemnation. Market Square was packed by hundreds of "jobless men and women" to protest the store the day after it opened.[57] There was an emotional and political component to the rejection of the store. As the letter from the housewives and mothers stated, "Perhaps you cannot visualize the humiliating influence that such an institution has on people who have, up to the past two years regarded themselves as free citizens. We still feel we have a right to ask for and receive decent treatment."[58] Relief recipients also had concrete objections. Travel to one central location — not easy in good weather — was especially difficult during the winter months.[59] The "housewives and mothers" objected to carrying their groceries home, not because the task was beyond their capacity, but because:

> Many of us have no-one to send and it is indeed humiliating to carry away our parcels from the Relief Store in beer cases. We do not wish to advertise the Liquor Traffic and we do not think you should expect us to do so. The Street Cars are running almost empty and if we were allowed to take our parcels home from the Store in the street cars, it would be most highly appreciated.[60]

Streetcar tickets for reliefers to use when going to pick up grocery orders would have

---

54   COSA, City Council Minutes, 8 June 1931.

55   Saskatoon City Council, City Clerk's Office, microfilm, Report of the City Treasurer, 25 July 1932, City Hall Records, Minutes of City Council, 1 August 1932, Item 1307.

56   The city council made a profit from the operation of the relief store: $1,122.54 reported in December of 1932, and $1,038.75 expected in January of 1933 (Civic Relief Board Minutes, 21 December 1933; cited in Lawton, *Urban Relief*, 122). Also see: COSA, City Clerk's Office, file 358, 1933, Relief Store.

57   *Star Phoenix*, 1 June 1932. The newspaper report legitimized the protest by stressing "No Hint of Communism Tinges Gathering" in the headline.

58   COSA, City Clerks' Records, Box 5887b, Relief-S, 1932, file 308, #19, Mrs. Pasha, Mrs. Allen, Mrs. McKenzie, Mrs. McKague, Mrs. Reeves, Mrs. Squires and Mrs. Hall, letter to the mayor and aldermen, 2 July 1932.

59   Saskatchewan winters are notoriously cold and difficult. Without sufficient food and clothing to survive they become more so.

60   COSA, City Clerks' Records, box 5887b, Relief-S, 1932, file 308, #19, Mrs. Pasha, Mrs. Allen, Mrs. McKenzie, Mrs. McKague, Mrs. Reeves, Mrs. Squires and Mrs. Hall, letter to the mayor and aldermen, 2 July 1932.

had other benefits. There were reports of butter melting into rice in the summer, or eggs freezing in the winter, because of the time involved in picking up and transporting groceries.[61] Additionally, the city's desire to cut costs meant, in the opinion of reliefers, that food of questionable quality and limited selection was sold.[62] Women complained that they were not allowed certain items such as eggs, jam and fruit which "would seem to be a necessity, at least for the children."[63] Adding such essentials to the relief store supplies, women argued, would not add greatly to the cost but would aid them immensely in maintaining the health of families and "carrying on our homes under great difficulties."[64]

The reliefers were not alone in protesting the city store. The city's storekeepers had organized a petition in April to oppose the opening of the relief store.[65] City merchants objected to the loss of business and unfair competition represented by a city monopoly of relief business. Many shopkeepers relied on the reliefers' patronage to stay in business. Without it, they feared they would join the ranks of the reliefers. Many shopkeepers were already carrying customers who could not afford to pay their grocery bills. The city, at least, paid the reliefers' grocery bills. It was a general opinion that the city should share the little money to be made from relief among the tax-payers, such as those paying business licenses.[66]

For women, the operation of the relief store provided an immediate focal point of concern. Ironically, in its attempts to control "abuse" of the system, the city had ensured a greater commonality of experience and a sense of even greater sharing of the relief experience. With less power over what they were purchasing, and with everyone receiving exactly the same goods, there was an escalation of complaints.

The women in the sit-down strike expressed much of the contempt felt for the relief store. Again, the notion of corruption or dishonesty, of the city profiting from reliefers, was clear. Women stated they were receiving second-class goods, including butter smelling strongly of fish.[67] Shared hardship fuelled a groundswell of protest.

The city hall sit-down was the beginning of change in the relief system. The negotiations with the Trades and Labour Council resulted in city council resolving that no reliefer would be "asked to repay any relief given or relief for which that person is liable until a period of four months has elapsed since he or she went off relief, and further that the maximum amount of repayment required will not exceed

---

61 Many of these complaints were reiterated by the women involved in the sit-down strike (*Star Phoenix*, 18 November 1932).

62 "City Hall Vigil," *Star Phoenix*, 9 November 1932, p. 3.

63 COSA, City Clerks' Records, Box 5887b, Relief-S, 1932, file 308, #19, Mrs. Pasha, Mrs. Allen, Mrs. McKenzie, Mrs. McKague, Mrs. Reeves, Mrs. Squires and Mrs. Hall, letter to the mayor and aldermen, 2 July 1932.

64 Ibid.

65 The business owners were no more successful in preventing the opening of the relief store. For the collection of petitions, dated April, 1932, see: COSA, City Clerks' Records, Box 5887b, Relief-S, 1932, file 308, #13. The signatures represent the owners of businesses such as the Save-More Store, Broadway Meats, Safeway and Bert's Grocery. One of the petitions provides a breakdown of the annual taxes and license fees paid by the business owners.

66 Lawton, *Urban Relief*, 122. Also see: COSA, City Clerk's Office, file 302, Joint Conference of City Council and Civic Relief Board at Canadian Legion.

67 *Star Phoenix*, 20 November 1932.

ten percent of the salary or wages earned in any one month."[68] This resolution was to be conveyed to the unemployed women in council chamber and, if they found it satisfactory, they would be issued relief that night. The council also wanted the Relief Board to publish a statement saying that "they [the relief board] had not intended to be too harsh in the enforcement of the provisions of the agreement."[69] A further resolution was passed rescinding all signed relief agreements.[70]

The women left city hall victorious. Though they were accused of political behaviour — there were suspicions that the women were communists and had carried out the sit-in to disrupt upcoming civic elections — they did achieve their stated goals of changes to the relief agreement.

While the women did not achieve great success in overturning the relief system in 1932, they did achieve incremental changes to the system over the next two years. By 1934, the composition of the Civic Relief Board changed; the control of relief adminstration returned to the hands of council where reliefers had a greater chance of influencing policy.[71] The relief store, in spite of its profits, was discontinued and a cash system for food relief was instituted after a plebiscite among the unemployed voted in a cash-for-relief system.[72]

Through the relief policy, women experienced state control in a new way. Families sat down to eat with the state as an invisible guest at the dinner table because of the very direct control the city exercised through food relief. The inadequacies and control of the system were felt in a very real way.

The relief agreement the women were expected to sign was the straw that broke the camel's back. The agreement spelled out the state's expectations of behaviour for the working class — both female and male. The reaction of the women to the relief agreement in particular, and relief policy in general, speaks to the willingness of working-class women to act in defence of their own standards and expectations. Women brought their notions of respectability and of what was expected and acceptable, which differed sharply from local government policies. The mass unemployment, the inability of all levels of government in Canada to correct the economy or even mitigate the effects of the Depression, revealed inadequacies in relief programs that recipients had long known. Soul destroying, physically and mentally debilitating, morally corrupt, the realities of relief became a political catalyst for the increasing numbers who were subjected to its administration.

It was the clash of the realities of the Depression with comforting gendered and class notions which instituted the first serious challenge to the construction and place of relief in society and the assumptions which informed relief policy. While the

---

68   COSA, City Clerks' Records, box 5887b, Relief-S, 1932, file 308, Minutes of a meeting held Saturday, 19 November 1932 at the Saskatoon Public Library Auditorium.

69   COSA, City Clerks' Records, box 5887b, Relief-S, 1932, file 308, Letter to the chairman and members of the Civic Relief Board, 22 November 1932.

70   COSA, Minutes of City Council, 16 November 1932, Clause 2790.

71   Appointed in October 1932, the Civic Relief Board was originally composed of seven prominent citizens and the mayor (COSA, Minutes of City Council, 3 October 1932). The new Civic Relief Board, consisting of council members, was established May 1934 (COSA, Minutes of City Council, 7 May 1934).

72   COSA, Minutes of City Council, 10-24 September 1934, cover the debates on the cash system and the plebiscite and the results. See also: COSA, City Clerk's Records, Uncatalogued, box 5864, file 308, Plebiscite Among the Unemployed, September 1934.

council tried to balance financial and moral claims to its efforts, it often worsened the situation, unintentionally solidifying resistance.

As with many other state policies, the articulation of objectives did not necessarily mean wholesale achievement of those objectives. Much of Canadian social policy still needs to be examined for the extent to which it was able to impose on the lives and beliefs of those it sought to control.[73] The activities of the women and others in Saskatoon suggest that the state policies designed to control became a source of increasing resentment and a focal point for resistance. Rather than control, such policies were manipulated, ignored or contested.

Regarding relief policy, women worked at several levels. First, women tried to manage the household so as to keep the family off relief. Second, women worked against the policy in order to improve the conditions and quantity of relief and to instill more dignity into relief services. This, in turn, directly challenged the class and gender assumptions of the policy. Third, women worked towards changing the political and economic system which they believed was responsible for the entire debacle of the 1930s.

The action of the women occupying city hall and other activities and protests during the decade were a declaration of relief as a right and a rejection of the moralistic class and gender assumptions of the policy.[74] The groundswell of change was at the grass-roots level. Through shared experiences, a notion of rights, of what individuals could expect from the state, developed and emerged.

The mass unemployment of the 1930s was a new face to the poor who had always been a part of the urban landscape. They would prove a critical mass that would change the shape and nature of relief. The women of Saskatoon who protested relief policies were an integral part of that change. These women, both as individuals and as groups, rejected relief. Their intimate relationship with the everyday shortcomings of relief gave them vital ammunition to critique and challenge the system on a pragmatic basis that instituted important and meaningful changes to its delivery. Their intimate relationship with the economic reality of employment and unemployment also ensured they attacked the very existence of relief. Women brought forward and supported ideas which were political re-conceptions of the role and nature of relief in Canadian society. In doing so, they challenged other boundaries, writing their ideas into a new and emerging national script on the place of the state and relief in Canadian society. While many of the actions and individuals involved in this change have been written out of the records — and we know little of women like Mrs. Watson, Mrs. Pasha and Mrs. Carr — fragments do survive. In reading these, we can understand the basics of changing unemployment relief from a necessary but unpleasant charity to an inherent component of a society unable to provide full employment:

> But to be so unfortunate as to have a wife and children to provide for and a home to pay for and be on relief is not at all pleasant. And furthermore

---

73 James Struthers makes a similar argument for the examination of Canadian policy at the level at which it happened, that is, the local level. See: James Struthers, "The Provincial Welfare State: Social Policy in Ontario," *Journal of Canadian Studies* 27, no. 1 (Spring 1992): 136-56.

74 The Saskatoon city hall sit-down strike was only one of many public protests and demonstrations during the decade. The *Star Phoenix* records many demonstrations across the province; many turned violent.

it's terribly hard at times just to exist. Life is too short to live it this way. And I think insurance whereby everyone working be made to pay so much into it according to salaries the larger the salary the more they will pay and not only the tax payer would pay but all receiving money. And should anyone be let out of a job he would know he would not be in need or go deeply into debt to live. And be threatened with actions, seizures, collectors, sheriffs and tortured with threats of all kinds because you were so unfortunate to lose your job, not because you were disqualified, but because times were abnormal.[75]

75   COSA, City Clerk's Records, box 5887b, Relief-S, 1932, file 308, #20, Mrs. Wm. N. Watson, letter dated 2 April 1932.

Appendix 1
Relief Agreement for the City of Saskatoon

I/we, _____ of Saskatoon hereby covenant, promise and agree to and with the City of Saskatoon that should the said City of Saskatoon by itself or by its Civic Relief Board give to myself or my dependents relief either in kind or in money;

(1) That I will diligently seek and will take any position that presents itself or is offered to me either in the City of Saskatoon, in the bush or on a farm outside of Saskatoon.

(2) That any member of the Civic Relief Board or any of its duly authorized employees may at any time enter and inspect any and all premises occupied by me or my dependents.

(3) That I will on demand pay to the City of Saskatoon the value of relief supplied to me or my dependents after the date of this agreement, and I agree that a certificate by the Civic Relief Board of the City of Saskatoon or by the treasurer of the said City of Saskatoon shall be conclusive evidence as to the making of such advance and the amount thereof.

(4) That should the said City of Saskatoon or its Civic Relief Board either now or at some future date require a mortgage or deposit of title or a bill of sale of any of my assets as security for relief advanced after the date of this agreement I will on demand give such bill of sale.

(5) I further agree that all monies advanced to me or which come into my possession, except for statutory exemptions, shall be the property of the City of Saskatoon and I hereby transfer, assign and set over unto the City of Saskatoon all such monies to the value of relief advanced after the date of this agreement by the said City of Saskatoon or its Civic Relief Board to me or to my dependents.

(6) And I further agree that I will from time to time, or as required by the Civic Relief Board report all monies earned by me or my dependents.

(7) It is also agreed that wherever the singular pronoun is used throughout this agreement the same shall be construed as meaning the plural where the context so requires.

Source: Editorial, "The Agreement," *Star Phoenix,* 19 November 1932, p. 4.

Appendix 2
Saskatoon Relief Provisions, 1937

VOUCHERS:

Fuel:	On inspection, requirements estimated.
	Summer: 1/2 cord wood or kindling every 3 mths
	Winter: 1 cord wood every 3 mths for cooking
Light:	$1.50/mth where there are school age children
	$1.00/mth where children are not of school age
Water:	$1.00/mth
Oil:	1 gal. Coal oil (increased in times of sickness or for very large families).
Clothing:	Investigated by Family Welfare Association.
Milk:	4 pints per week per adult or person over 12

CASH PAYMENTS:

Food:	1 adult $6.93/mth; 1 adult & 1 dependent $10.72/mth; 1 adult & 2 dependents from $10.94-$11.70; 1 adult & 3 dependents $13.22-$15.70. Scale for dependents determined by age.

Taken from: *A Study of Community Welfare Services in Saskatoon*, 9-10.

Appendix 3
Diet List

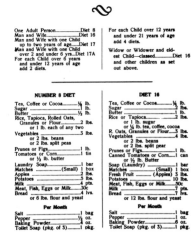

DIET 30

Tea, Coffee or Cocoa	¼ lb.
Sugar	5 lbs.
Butter	3 lbs.
Rice or Tapioca	2 lbs.
or 1 lb. sugar	
or ¼ lb. tea, coffee, cocoa	
R. Oats, Granules or Flour	6 lbs.
Beans or Split Peas	3 lbs.
Canned Tomatoes or Corn	2 cans
or 1 lb. Butter	
Syrup	2 lbs.
or 1 can peanut butter	
Flour	4 lbs.
Soap (Laundry)	6 bars
Jam (4 lbs.)	1 tin
Matches (Small)	1 box.
Vegetables	5 lbs.
Fresh Fruit (Apples)	8 lbs.
Potatoes	24 lbs.
Bread	20 lvs.
or 30 lbs. flour and yeast	
Meat, Fish, Eggs or Milk	$1.00
Milk	14 qts.

Per Month

Salt	1 bag
Pepper	1 oz.
Baking Powder	6 oz.
Toilet Soap (pkg. of 3)	1 pkg.

DIET 31

Tea, Coffee or Cocoa	¼ lb.
Sugar	6 lbs.
Butter	3 lbs.
Rice or Tapioca	2 lbs.
or 1 lb. sugar	
or ¼ lb. tea, coffee, cocoa	
R. Oats, Granules or Flour	6 lbs.
Beans or Split Peas	3 lbs.
Canned Tomatoes or Corn	2 cans
or 1 lb. Butter	
Syrup	2 lbs.
or 1 can peanut butter	
Flour	4 lbs.
Soap (Laundry)	6 bars

Jam (4 lbs.)	1 tin
Matches (Small)	1 box
Fresh Fruit (Apples)	10 lbs.
Vegetables	6 lbs.
Potatoes	26 lbs.
Bread	20 lvs.
or 30 lbs. flour and yeast	
Meat, Fish, Eggs or Milk	$1.00
Milk	14 qts.

Per Month

Salt	1 bag
Pepper	1 oz.
Baking Powder	6 oz.
Toilet Soap (pkg. of 3)	1 pkg.

DIET 32

Tea, Coffee or Cocoa	¼ lb.
Sugar	6 lbs.
Butter	4 lrs.
Rice or Tapioca	2 lbs.
or 1 lb. sugar	
or ¼ lb. tea, coffee, cocoa	
R. Oats, Granules or Flour	6 lbs.
Beans or Split Peas	3 lbs.
Canned Tomatoes or Corn	2 cans
or 1 lb. Butter	
Syrup	2 lbs.
or 1 can peanut butter	
Flour	4 lbs.
Soap (Laundry)	6 bars
Jam (tin)	4 lbs.
Matches (Small)	1 box
Fresh Fruit (Apples)	10 lbs.
Vegetables	8 lbs.
Potatoes	30 lbs.
Bread	24 lvs.
or 36 lbs. flour and yeast	
Meat, Fish, Eggs or Milk	$1.20
Milk	14 qts.

Per Month

Salt	1 bag
Pepper	1 oz.
Baking Powder	6 oz.
Toilet Soap (pkg. of 3)	1 pkg.

Diets for Unemployment Relief
As Approved by Saskatoon Civic Relief Board
August 31, 1933

One Adult Person	Diet 8
Man and Wife	Diet 16
Man and Wife with one Child up to two years of age	Diet 17
Man and Wife with one Child over 2 and under 6 yrs.	Diet 17A
For each Child over 6 years and under 12 years of age add 2 diets.	

For each Child over 12 years and under 21 years of age add 4 diets.	
Widow or Widower and eldest Child—classed	Diet 16
and other children as set out above.	

NUMBER 8 DIET

Tea, Coffee or Cocoa	¼ lb.
Sugar	1 lb.
Butter	½ lb.
Rice, Tapioca, Rolled Oats, Granules or Flour	2 lbs.
or 1 lb. each of any two	
Vegetables	3 lbs.
or 2 lbs. beans	
or 2 lbs. split peas	
Prunes or Figs	1 lb.
Tomatoes or Corn	1 tin
or ½ lb. butter	
Laundry Soap	1 bar
Matches (Small)	1 box
Apples	2 lbs.
Potatoes	5 lbs.
Milk	4 pts.
Meat, Fish, Eggs or Milk	50c
Bread	4 lvs.
or 6 lbs. flour and yeast	

Per Month

Salt	1 bag
Pepper	½ oz.
Baking Powder	4 oz.
Toilet Soap (pkg. of 3)	1 pkg.

DIET 16

Tea, Coffee or Cocoa	¼ lb.
Sugar	2 lbs.
Butter	1 lb.
Rice or Tapioca	2 lbs.
or 1 lb. sugar	
or ¼ lb. tea, coffee, cocoa	
R. Oats, Granules or Flour	3 lbs.
Vegetables	4 lbs.
or 2 lbs. beans	
or 2 lbs. split pear	
Prunes or Figs	1 lb.
Canned Tomatoes or Corn	1 can
or ½ lb. Butter	
Soap (Laundry)	1 bar
Matches (Small)	1 box
Fresh Fruit (Apples)	3 lbs.
Potatoes	10 lbs.
Meat, Fish, Eggs or Milk	50c
Milk	7 pts.
Bread	7 lvs.
or 12 lbs. flour and yeast	

Per Month

Salt	1 bag
Pepper	1 oz.
Baking Powder	6 oz.
Toilet Soap (pkg. of 3)	1 pkg.

Source: City of Saskatoon Archives, City Clerk's Correspondence Series, 1069-1565 (2), Relief Store, 1934.

Appendix 4
Draft of Plan for City Relief Food Store

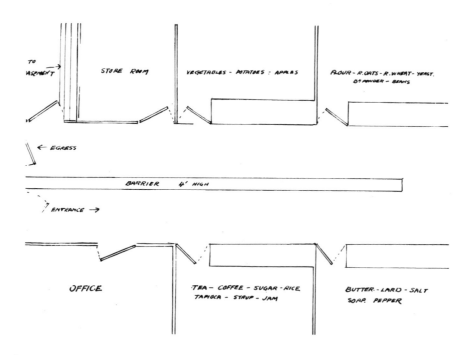

Source: City of Saskatoon Archives, City Clerk's Correspondence Series, 1069-1602 (27), Reports of the Standing Committee on Relief, 1932.

"YOU JUST DID WHAT HAD TO BE DONE": LIFE HISTORIES OF FOUR SASKATCHEWAN "FARMERS' WIVES"

Julie Dorsch

> I can remember when Sue was small, I would put her in the car, so I knew nothing would happen to her, and then I would go down to the pasture to get the cows and bring them up. Then I'd drive the car out by the barn, where I'd check on her and I'd milk the cows. There was no baby-sitter. You had to work around these things. You had to figure everything out. … The car always seemed like the safest place. Because you know, there's very little that she could get into and hurt herself. And I think all farm wives did that if they worked outside.

Valerie, a Saskatchewan farm woman, now in her late sixties, describes how as a "farmer's wife" in the 1940s, she balanced the frequently conflicting demands of farm work and child rearing.[1] A fascinating tidbit of information revealing an individual's ingenuity and ability to "make do," this story has wider significance. While her child-care method may surprise non-farm women, perhaps Valerie is correct and this story will strike a chord of recognition in other farm women, particularly those who worked outside and had no easy access to child care or helpful neighbours. Other women, while developing their own solutions, will find a universal motif: the need to juggle work and child care. Valerie speaks with both uniqueness and commonality. Her experiences convey patterns and themes that have relevance for Saskatchewan farm women, rural women and women as a whole.

The personal histories that this essay discusses demonstrate the dual character of oral history interviews and what makes them so compelling: while they can stand on their own as rich individual testimony, oral histories also provide an avenue to explore and interpret the lives of a larger group. Surprisingly, very little is known about Saskatchewan's farm women. Even the most basic information is lacking. In what kinds of work were farm women involved? How did they do that work? How did changes in technology alter their work? Without this sort of knowledge, the contributions of rural women to the development of Saskatchewan have gone either unnoted, or have been celebrated in vague, mythical terms.

Academic studies about farm women focus almost exclusively on the political and social reform activities of an early and elite group of women. While their activities were important, because of their effect not only on women of their own time and also on those of later generations, these women were exceptional. History must go further; it must also consider the daily lives, activities and beliefs of "ordinary" women. Who were these "ordinary" women, these women who were not public figures? What

---

1   I would like to thank the four women who shared their stories with me. I have altered their names to respect their privacy.

were their daily routines? What did they think of the world around them? Did these women wish to break through the social, political or economic boundaries enclosing them? How did they expand, evade and cope with those boundaries? How did their different viewpoints influence their behaviour and beliefs?

To answer these kinds of questions about "farmers' wives" an obvious starting point is talking directly to these women.[2] Locating them in conventional historical materials is simply not an option as these are not the type of women found in newspapers and similar public records. However, the challenge of discovering historical sources about this group of women is not the only stimulus in conducting this study. Interviewing women has another significance. In the words of Susan Armitage, an American oral historian, "[t]he very act of focusing on women and asking them to 'speak for themselves' is a challenge to traditional male-centered history. We, the interviewers, make that challenge explicit by articulating the values we find in our interviews, and by locating them in an historical context."[3] In other words, "women are asked to speak for and about themselves — about their own work and their own lives, rather than about 'history' or the activities of their fathers, husbands, sons."[4]

While acknowledging the diversity of experiences of Saskatchewan farm women, this essay focusses on one particular group — the often historically invisible group of contemporary, non-elite, Saskatchewan "farmers' wives," now in their sixties and seventies. Analysis of the women interviewed for this study suggests that farm women were not a homogenous group: there was great variety and scope in the work that they performed. What emerged, too, from these interviews, was the discrepancy between the invisibility of their work and the reality of their importance on the farm. This evidence contradicts the traditional view of agriculture as a male domain, wherein a women's contribution outside the home, as well as inside, is assumed to be of little importance.

In a series of interviews, I spoke with four women: Valerie, Cynthia, Judy and Margaret. All were in their sixties and seventies. All were born in Canada. Three of

---

2   By making women the subject of inquiry, contemporary feminism has contributed postively to the postmodernist undermining of Enlightenment "certainties." By invoking women's different experience to challenge the grand narratives of Western history, feminism has valorized women's own narratives — women's stories of their own experience. This valorization, Canadian historian Ruth Roach Pierson explains, has pushed women's historians in the direction of oral history. Along with autobiography, oral history promises to bring the researcher closest to the "reality" of women's lives. See Ruth Roach Pierson, "Experience, Difference, Dominance and Voice in the Writing of Canadian Women's History," in Ruth Roach Pierson, Karen Offen, and Jane Rendall, eds., *Writing Women's History: International Perspectives* (Bloomington, IN: Indiana University Press, 1991), 90-91. Indeed, the greater the past subjugation of women, the greater the need to collect oral histories. Such a record vouchsafes to women that idea of history critical to their own sense of identity. And, because it allows women to construct their own representations of their past lives, oral history has the benefit of offering at least a partial solution to the postmodernist/feminist controversy surrounding representation and "voice." The debate revolves around the question of who is entitled to speak on behalf of women of different racial origins, see Gail Cuthbert Brandt, "Postmodern Patchwork: Some Recent Trends in the Writing of Women's History in Canada," *Canadian Historical Review* 72, no. 4 (December 1991): 468.

3   Susan H. Armitage, "The Next Step," *Frontiers: A Journal of Women Studies* 7, no. 1 (1983): 4.

4   Ibid., 3. Armitage differentiates between women's history and oral history: "Woman's history is not necessarily the same thing as an oral history interview with a woman, as local history projects with old settlers sadly illustrate. ... The women talk about the activities of their fathers, brothers, husbands, and sons. ... They believe history was made by men. ... The result is that most old settler local history projects tell us very little about women."

the women grew up on farms, one in town. The four became "farm wives" at roughly the same time, in the period 1936-45. With their husbands, the four farmed in the same community in southern Saskatchewan, their lives tightly wound together with the ties of friendship, kinship and community. The interviews themselves were shaped by a number of questions: How did rural women perform their work? Of what did their tasks consist? What help did they have? How did work change over time as families acquired "labour-saving" devices? How did the work of farm women change with the mechanization of the farm itself? In what ways did women contribute to the financial support of their households? What rewards did they receive? What sort of relationship did they have with their husbands, with other women? Did the latter relationships help women cope with the limitations of their lives? While the sample size is too small to generate definitive conclusions, the interviewees' answers do expand our knowledge as well as raise more questions for future research.

One area in which the respondents increase our knowledge is the issue of "women and work," a popular focus in Canadian women's history for nearly two decades. Astonishingly, little is known about the occupation which absorbed the energies of a vast number of Canadian women: farm work. Most studies of rural women concentrate on an earlier generation of farm women and consider their political and reform activities. But the vast majority of women had little or no time for these sorts of occupations; they were simply too busy doing all that farm life required of them. For every Agnes McPhail or Violet McNaughton, there were thousands of Valeries juggling the responsibilities of work and motherhood. For them, the accomplishments of middle-class women with supportive husbands, leisure time or the inclination to participate in reform were a remote experience.

While it was not the only issue to surface in the interviews, work recurred as a theme. Three of the women had worked for wages before marriage: one as a teacher, another as a hairdresser, and the last as a domestic. The fourth worked for board as a domestic so that she could finish her grade twelve:

> I went to the local school and then I did grades nine, ten and eleven by correspondence — they weren't taught there. I didn't get three of my grade eleven courses and my Dad felt really bad I think because one of them was French. He was French and never taught this at home. So I think that was why they sent me to Notre Dame in Wilcox, where I did French, Algebra and I think, Social Studies. … The next year, Mom and Dad didn't have enough money to send me to school so I worked for my board as a maid. I tell you I learned a lot of things. What a terrible job. She [the woman I worked for] never did a lick of work during the day — [she never] picked up or washed a dish. I'd get home and I'd have to work like crazy to get the work done. I had spares during the day so I could get most of my homework done then.

Despite getting her grade twelve, this woman and the other three interviewees followed social conventions of their day and gave up their jobs when they married, exchanging financial independence (of a sort) for the expectation and need for economic support. This meant becoming a financial dependent. Judy commented on the change: "It was really hard when you got married. [Before] you had your own life. I had money. I felt awful having to ask for money." Two of the women considered joining the armed forces in the 1940s because of the pay. One of them said: "It was better than anything you could get anywhere else. At that time I was doing hair for fifteen dollars a week and by the time they got done taking everything they wanted — taxes — you maybe had five or eight dollars." Why did they not join up? One replied: "I had a birthday and Dad came to town that day and he said there's no way you're joining the forces. You do, and that's the end. You can't come home again. He didn't want any of his daughters to be in the forces. He thought they were really wild."

The two women did not join the military ranks; instead, as was the case for the other two women, their work life after marriage revolved around the farm. This subject was a much discussed issue in the interviews, not surprisingly, given the centrality of farm work in these women's lives. Consider one woman's description of a typical summer day:

> The men had to be on the road on their way to the fields by 6:00-6:30 [a.m.].
> So you got up around 5:30 because you had lunches to make. You made
> breakfast — porridge and eggs and bacon or sausage or whatever — it was
> a real meal. My husband got up and usually he'd build the fire in the
> cookstove, get it going, go do his chores and then come in and have
> breakfast. While they were eating I would pack their lunches and then
> they'd be on their way. And noon was always a big meal cuz they'd already
> been up and done their work and they'd expect a big meal — it was meat
> and potatoes. Then my day would start with getting the kids up, fed and
> dressed and doing ironing or laundry or baking or canning or gardening
> or whatever the season required. In the summer the days were very long.
> We rented some land that was quite a ways away and if the men had to get
> to that you'd get up at 5:00. It was daylight so you got up; the day had started.
> There were lots of days you could've stayed in bed but that was life, you
> accepted it. Everybody else did it so you didn't feel different. Evenings
> always had mending or sewing; I hated darning and patching but there was
> always a basket with mending in it — lots of socks to darn and overalls to
> sew patches on. Always. That, I think, was one of the unpleasant things in
> life. But I used to do it at night. I used to do mine in the summertime when
> I was waiting for the men to come home because they wouldn't get back till
> late. They would have had their dinner — lunch — and they'd take
> something for the afternoon or if I wasn't going to town I'd take coffee and
> sandwiches out to them in the afternoon about 4:00 so they could continue
> to work while it was light. By the time the men got home for supper, around
> 9:00, I'd have the cows milked, the cream separated and the calves and other
> animals fed.

As with most women of the interviewees' generation, farm women were responsible, first and foremost, for the family home and those who occupied it. The work of these four farm women clearly divided into two categories — household maintenance and sustenance.[5] The first, household maintenance, involved the routine activities of cleaning, washing and cooking — tasks which are familiar to most women today.[6] But

---

5   These categories correspond to the ones delineated by historians Susan Armitage and Sara Brooks
     Sundberg. See Armitage, "Household Work and Childrearing on the the the Frontier: The Oral History
     Record," *Sociology and Social Research* 63, no. 3 (April 1979): 469; and Sundberg, "Farm Women on
     the Canadian Prairie Frontier: The Helpmate Image," in Veronica Strong-Boag and Anita Clair
     Fellman, eds., *Rethinking Canada: The Promise of Women's History* (Toronto: Copp Clark Pitman, 1986),
     95-106.

6   Several historians have noted that oral history methodology is particularly suited to research on
     domestic work. For example, "The general usefulness of oral evidence for women's history increases
     sharply when research focuses on domestic work. Here, in the daily routines, the automatic
     movements and gestures, and the unconscious thought processes, historical experience is most
     universal yet least consciously acknowledged, hence rarely recorded by any means. Again, oral history
     can help to reveal the acts and the interrelationships which make up this experience. ... Women have
     left few written or published accounts of their daily round; they seldom recorded what they thought
     about the domestic role, nor did they note and explain the reasons for changes in domestic routine
     and responsibilities"; see Barbara Reilly, "Domestic Work: Oral History and Material Culture," *Journal
     of the Canadian Oral History Association* 8 (1985): 9, 10.

without the labour-saving devices we now take for granted, these activities were far more physically demanding and time-consuming. This remained the case not only for frontier women, but for the vast majority of those who toiled on the farm in the 1930s, 1940s and 1950s. The key to the new domestic technologies was electricity, and while it became available in a majority of built-up areas in Canada by the end of the 1920s, its arrival on farms came much later. According to the 1941 census, nearly all urban homes had electricity, some 60 percent of rural non-farm homes used electricity, but only 20 percent of farm households had it.[7] The respondents in the study attested to the slowness of electrification — it was 1953 before their four farms were "hooked up" by the "highlines." Nevertheless, by 1951-52 all four farms were using wind- or motor-powered generators to provide some electricity. As one of the women noted, however, this technology was inferior to the "highlines" hook up:

> In 1953 we all got power and of course then most farms got an electric fridge. I was fortunate because I had a coal oil fridge before. It was run from kerosene. … And I had a propane stove. But my husband and a neighbour went down to the [United] States and they bought these wind chargers and then on our farms we had electricity (32-volt). They got them cheap, secondhand, from some American farmers who'd been hooked up. We had an iron and vacuum cleaner and even a waffle iron. The neighbours didn't generally have these things. [My husband] and that particular neighbour were that way. In the basement you had twenty-four of these great big glass batteries. These batteries stood about two feet tall and they were probably about eighteen inches square. They had to be serviced and tested and the water kept up. They were a lot of work to maintain.

> And then sometimes you'd get a period of time when there wasn't any wind. So then you bought auxillery motors and then they hooked these motors up and they could charge the batteries and that way we always had power. We didn't have to wait for the wind to blow. Some people used the motors all the time, not wind. Then we had, from that, running water. They put in pressure tanks because we could have electric motors run through the batteries. But not everyone had this sort of thing. There's lots of people [who] didn't have running water [un]til way into the [19]60s. There were people who just did not have anything. We didn't have indoor toilets until we built the new house in 1964. We had running water and everything but not an indoor bathroom.[8]

Even without electricity, domestic technology was starting to become available, though the rate of its acquisition varied. For example, two of the four women

---

7   Alison Prentice, Paula Bourne et al., *Canadian Women: A History* (Toronto: Harcourt Brace Jovanovich, 1988), 246.

8   Oral history is not necessarily the best method for determining the rate of electrification and buying appliances. The interviewee may be right about the dates and when other people obtained electricity and appliances; on the other hand, she may not. The feelings of good fortune could be due to the importance she places on the arrival of these technologies. Oral historians have noted that there may be inconsistencies in a respondent's report, particularly with regard to temporal sequence of events. Does such inconsistency reduce the validity of oral history? In reference to the work of oral historian Alessandro Portelli, Paul Thompson explains: "[A]s Portelli argues… '[t]he facts that people remember (and forget) are themselves the stuff of which history is made.' The very subjectivity which some see as a weakness of oral history can make them uniquely valuable. … [A]s Portelli puts it … '[t]he importance of oral testimony may often lie not in its adherence to facts but rather in its divergence from them, where imagination, symbolism, desire break in.' … Their imagination of an alternative past and so an alternative present … may be as crucial as what did happen"; see Thompson, *The Voice of the Past: Oral History*, 2nd ed. (Oxford: Oxford University Press, 1980), 102.

interviewed had grown up in households with a motor-driven washing machine. Three of the women had one of their own after marriage. The fourth continued to do laundry by hand until the early 1950s. But even with this machine, laundry remained a heavy task:

> I was lucky I had a washer with a motor on it. Definitely it made washing easier than scrubbing by hand on the board. I never had to do it by hand and I never grew up in a home where you did because my mother had one [with a motor]. She got hers way back in 1931 or '32 before the Depression came. Still the water had to be hauled. You had to put it on the stove. You heated it up in big boilers. Then you carried it over and put it in the machine and you did all your laundry in the same water. You started with the white clothes and washed them. Then you got down to the work clothes. You maybe did five or six batches of clothes in that water. There was no dryer. You hung it on the line. Then you brought it in, sprinkled it and ironed it.

> Then you carried it [the water] out and if you had flowers you put it on that or you scrubbed out the toilet or you did a lot of things with that water — it was very valuable. Maybe you even took some of it and scrubbed your kitchen floor. You just never wasted water. When I was married we each had a cistern with a pump on and the pump was in the house. This was drinking water and water for cooking. But laundry water came from the dugout. My husband hauled it. And in the winter it was snow. We had these big barrels and the snow was put in that.

Although laundry was clearly still hard work with this early appliance, its value was not doubted, as another woman recounts, "I remember when the machine broke down and we couldn't get parts — they had to come from out east — and I had to do the laundry by hand. Well, that opened my eyes to what my Mom used to do."

While acknowledging that some of the early appliances were labour-intensive to look after, and not as good as later models, the women valued the new machines. As Margaret explained: "I loved them all." However imperfect or expensive the equipment, the women I interviewed awaited its purchase eagerly. They believed these appliances lightened some of the heavier and most time-consuming labour:

> We didn't have fridges or anything till later so everything had to be figured out in proportion so things didn't spoil. We had basements and my husband would put up ice. We had an ice house. In the winter we'd put up ice and then we would use that. We had a hole dug in the basement and then a barrel set in. And then we'd put the ice in that barrel and you'd set the milk and cream and things in that. But then you see I had this kerosene fridge. It was a real job to take care of it — you had to fill it with fuel and keep the wick trimmed — but it was worth it to have it. You didn't mind. Then you could go to town and buy meat. Before that what we all had was a freezer box in town. You rented these. They were in a big room — a refrigerated room. You put your meat in that and it was frozen. It was all wrapped in packages then when we went to town that was the last thing we did before we left to come home. We'd go to this freezer and you had a key for your particular box and you would take out whatever you wanted to last for two or three days. That's all you could bring because you had no place to put it at home and then you had your meat.

None of the women noted reservations about the appliance's efficiency when they were considering its purchase.[9] Rather, affordability was the determining factor.

---

9   These women showed none of the reluctance to embrace household technology suggested by Angela

Margaret explained: "We bought the new appliances that came out as we could afford them. We weren't ones to use credit — we paid cash." Cynthia echoed this sentiment: "We waited [un]til we had the money."

Who made the decision regarding the purchase of a household technology? The evidence is not conclusive. One woman said several times that she was fortunate that she had the appliances: her husband was "just that way." Another said the decision was "up to her." In all cases the women mentioned the involvement of their husband in the decision-making process. In most instances it appeared this involvement was not reciprocated when the time came to buy farm equipment. It seemed farm women still had to convince their husbands of the need for these household helpers. Cynthia explained: "It was my decision what I wanted, needed, in the house but we talked it over." But as for the purchase of the farm equipment, she replied: "Mostly I just saw it as it came in the yard for the first time. Well I was more or less told 'What do you know what goes on outside'." Margaret concurred with Cynthia: "My husband made all the decisions about outdoor equipment — I didn't know anything about that."

The second category of work is sustenance, which Susan Armitage defines as "work which contributed directly to the family economy by making cash expenditure unnecessary."[10] Cost-cutting activities the interviewed women engaged in included sewing, mending and darning, harvesting the garden, picking wild berries for jam, preserving and canning a wide range of foods. Valerie described her household production activities:

> I'd can as much as 400 quarts before we had a freezer. There'd be vegetables — peas, beans, tomatoes — [and] fruit — peaches, apricots, pears and plums. As far as fruits and vegetables those would be the main ones; and I made all kinds of pickles and relish and jams. I'd use anything I could find to make jams — even wild chokecherries. My husband's mom gave me her jars. I even canned chicken and beef because we had no freezer. We canned everything. Everybody did. Otherwise you wouldn't have it. You couldn't buy stuff like you can now. And what they [the stores] had was expensive. Of course after we got the freezer we froze things — vegetables, meats.

> I sewed everything as far as children's clothes until the boys were old enough to wear jeans. And the girls I always sewed for. All the baby clothes. Then I did a lot of my own; none of my husband's though. We all had a machine for sewing, mending and patching.

The lasting utility of the categories Armitage developed to describe the activities of frontier women suggests much continuity between their work and that of the women interviewed. These women remained responsible for the care of their families and they still carried on sustenance activities. Like many earlier farm women, the four interviewees had large families — made larger by the presence of hired men and, in one case, two boarders — to cook, clean and wash for. The women who grew up on farms saw that continuity, while noting the significant difference technology made: "Really it was the same stuff. Though the 1950s — power — changed our lives. Once you had power then it was not long before you had running water. You can't imagine the difference." Though as another woman noted, some of the work may

---

Davis in "'Valiant Servants': Women and Technology on the Canadian Prairies 1910-1940," *Manitoba History* 25 (Spring 1993): 33-42.

10   Armitage, "Household Work," 469-70.

have become less physically demanding but it still seemed endless: "Ironing was the worst. When the boys were in school and they wore those white shirts, it was twenty-one shirts a week." Child care remained a twenty-four hour a day responsibility for the women: "There were no babysitters, not like today. You took your kids everywhere, even to dances. We'd lay our coats in the corner and they'd sleep on them. They slept and we danced."

The women suggested, then, that circumstances had changed for the farm women who came after them. For one, there was a suggestion that the younger generations of farm women did not seem to be continuing many of the activities associated with being a farm wife: "Now what you see is that women don't can or freeze like what we did. And they don't sew as much." Valerie suggested that this may have implications for the role of women on the farm: "So many of the women work off the farm, they have jobs off the farm. In my day that was unheard of. You were a partner in farming. Now women aren't to the same extent. Though I suppose their paycheques go into the farm."

To an already heavy household workload these farm wives added field work, barn chores, fixing machinery and buildings (usually as helper and parts "go-fer") and they were constantly on call to chase cattle or fill in when needed. Taken together, this group of farm women did all the tasks that farm men did. These women were clearly involved in activities usually defined as "farming." The oral evidence contradicts the usual division of labour that describes the farm wife as responsible solely for the nurture, maintenance and reproduction of farm labour. Their responses suggested another pattern: while women's labour might be flexible, — women doing "women's work" and "men's work" — men's labour was not flexible. Except perhaps in the rarest cases, men did not do "women's work." Women might willingly or through the force of circumstances take on "men's work" but the responsibility for such "female" tasks as housecleaning, the processing and preservation of food and child care belonged solely to women. "They [men] were the rigid ones," commented one of the respondents. However, all the women noted, quite incredulously, that the division of labour between men and women appeared to be changing. As Cynthia described it: "Men do a lot more in the house. It still floors me when my son calls and invites us for dinner at their [his and his wife's] house and he's made the dinner." Valerie commented that her one son does laundry, cooks and looks after the kids. Her other son does not perhaps do as much this way but, "he helps out much more than men used to."

A seasonal variation is also apparent in farm women's work. The women tended to do the outside work primarily in the May-November period, when their own work was at its busiest. The extent to which the women worked outside varied considerably, ranging from very little on an *ad hoc* basis, to a substantial amount on a regular basis.[11] Cynthia explained her participation:

> Valerie was out hauling grain and stuff like that more than I was. Oh once

---

11   A national study of farm women by the Council on Rural Development Canada found the average work per week for those who do only housework is fifty-three hours. For rural women who also work on the family enterprise, the average is eighty-one hours; see Council on Rural Development Canada (CRDC), *Rural Women, Their Work, Their Needs and Their Role in Rural Development* (Ottawa: CRDC, 1979), cited in "Keeping Women Down on the Farm," *Resources for Feminist Research/Documentation sur la recherche féministe* [*RFR/DRF*] 11, no. 1 (March 1982): 13.

in a while I'd do that [haul grain] — not too often. Doing outside work wasn't a regular part of my schedule — I had too many kids to look after and a hired man. Once we got a hired man, I didn't get asked to do too much outside. It was not specifically my job to look after the gardens, chickens, turkeys, pigs, but then again if they were out in the field or something you were just told that they wouldn't be home and it was your job. You did whatever came along — you just did what had to be done. Some [women] did [a lot].

She noted, too, that women felt differently about this kind of work:

I think some liked being outside. I was raised in the city and when I moved to the farm it was a whole new world. It took me quite a while to get used to all that, and of course I'd never been around machinery. So I think they were afraid I'd run into the barn or something. I drove the truck and drove the tractor around once in a while. My husband and a brother farmed together and one fall, when we first moved out here, he [the brother-in-law] was in the army and he didn't get home for harvest for a couple weeks. I was joed into going out on the tractor for two weeks and I thought I'd never think the farmer had an easy job after that. They were the two most boring weeks in my life — such long days. I don't think I would ever have made a work-outside farmer. I was quite happy in the house with my job. I think if you could just work outside and not have to worry about the inside it might be alright but to try and do both jobs. ... Sometimes you used to wonder how some women did it. Like Valerie, she kept everything up as well as doing that.

Given the varying predilections for farm work as well as the variance in farm work done by the women, the interviews raised the issue of how much agency women had when it came to determining what work, outside their "female tasks," they would take on as their responsibility. Judy suggested that one reason behind her never learning to drive was her desire to limit her work so that she did not have to drive machinery or be a "go-fer." Another of the women, however, felt that women did not have much choice and that when it came to driving, if the husband wanted a woman to drive so she could help out, she would learn how to drive. As she explained: "If he didn't think it'd be useful, however, it'd be darn tough to convince him to take the time to teach you. I'm very thankful I know how to drive otherwise I'd have been so isolated and dependent." Another respondent commented:

It would drive me nuts if I had to sit in the house and wait for my husband to have time to take me in [to town]. You would never get out. I just wasn't made that way, well I was raised in town and my mom lived in there and I had friends I wanted to see. I just decided if I wanted to go to town I was going to town. I hadn't driven that much before I moved down here but I soon learned. We had an old Model T truck that you couldn't drive very fast in. It went twenty-five miles per hour.

For another woman learning to drive a car became a basis for a belief in equality. "When I was twelve my father announced he was going to teach me to drive. I said, 'But neither mother or my two older sisters know how.' He said, 'Yes, but your brothers can and so can you'."

Oral history, as well as providing information on what tasks women did, provides unique information concerning how women carried out those tasks. For example, how did farm women, with no access to child care or easily accessible neighbours, combine outdoor work with child rearing? As the story at the beginning of this essay illustrates, those two tasks were blended in some surprising ways. Valerie's situation suggests that farm women who worked outside faced special challenges when combining child care and farm work:

> All the kids spent some time in the grain truck with me, particularly the two oldest. I made one bed on the floor of the truck and another on the seat — because we'd combine till nine or ten at night. I'd pack a lunch and take things to do. They all learned "Twinkle Twinkle Little Star" and we'd read. When they were really small you watched them so they didn't get backed over by the equipment but they all learned early the danger of the machinery.

> It wasn't a pleasant thing — all the chaff from the grain and dirt. We'd get in at nine or ten and we'd all have to have a bath. Then there was no bathtub or running water. I'd make supper and get the kids bathed. My husband and the hired man would do the chores. That was if I hauled grain. If I didn't, I'd do the chores.

Farm work complicated the carrying out of other "female tasks," too. Valerie recounted:

> I had my housework to do, too, and while I was out in the fields it wasn't getting done. I'd have to get up early and do laundry. If we were going to have potatoes I'd peel them and put them in cold water. While the grain was unloading I'd start something. Later when we had an electric stove I could start something, a roast say, but not before, you couldn't leave the fire. You had to plan everything. You just made do.

While planning was essential for Valerie when she was hauling grain in the fall, Cynthia found that the sudden demands of farm work made her planning impossible:

> Sometimes you'd end up baking bread, doing laundry and ironing on the same day. You had a schedule of sorts but it was flexible because if the men wanted you to go to town for something you had to go. Sometimes you had to sit and wait for the bus to come down with a part and bring it home and you had to have dinner on the table at twelve. You did your work around what they wanted you to do. I can remember for my mother it was one day for each chore and you didn't change it. But if something else came along that I had to do I'd rearrange my chores and go. Your work was scheduled around their meals, too. 12:00, 6:00 they wanted their meals. They walked in the door and it was supposed to be on the table ready to sit down and eat. Because they didn't have the time to wait, did they? That was the hardest thing for me to learn because I grew up in town without a father around the house and mom sorta catered to us kids when we were in school. When you get out on the farm it's different.

Cynthia's response suggests a difference between the work of farm women and that of non-farm women.[12] While some women, like Cynthia's mom, may have organized their work into regular schedules, this appears to have not been an option for farm women. The degree of planning may have depended on the degree of women's integration into the farm's outside work, but even the woman who was most involved in the outside work could not plan her schedule with the same certainty as her urban counterparts.

Did the women feel that their husbands recognized their contribution to the

---

12   For more on schedule and planning of housework by urban working-class women, see Meg Luxton, *More Than a Labour of Love* (Toronto: The Women's Press, 1980), 118-21.

family enterprise? Two of them strongly asserted that they and their husbands were partners. This was balanced by the acknowledgement that this was not always the case in other families: "I felt that we were partners. I don't think that was typical — though farm men were pretty good at treating and thinking their women were partners — I know that some women didn't feel that way. It'd come up, if there was a bunch of women sitting around. They'd bring it up." The other two women hesitated to describe their situation as an equal partnership and one voiced resentment because she did not feel that she had received recognition for her work, that she had not been treated as a partner.[13]

Two of the interviewed women — those who felt their marriages were partnerships — earned their own incomes. One, after twenty-two years of marriage, took a job off the farm as a reporter for the local newspaper (she had also worked briefly as a waitress in the 1940s and for expenses for the Farmers Union in the early 1950s). The other, as early as 1950, had her own considerable income from a cattle herd. Her husband felt that it was important that she be financially independent so he co-signed a loan for her that she then used to start her business. The importance of this financial independence was something she emphasized:

> I felt like a person once I had my own money, my own income, my own income tax to pay. I felt sorry for women who didn't have that security and there were lots of them around; most women didn't have it. There was a woman I curled with. [She] and her husband were farmers. He drove her to the rink when she curled. She couldn't drive. When it was her turn to buy the team coffee, he'd buy it. When they bought groceries, he was always there to pay for them. He paid all the bills. When he passed away she suddenly had to deal with the money. She'd never even written a cheque, never managed a bank account. How could she manage her finances? There were a lot of women like that. Even my mom had to ask for money when she had to buy groceries or gifts or anything. This was in the late 1970s! I can remember asking dad to give her some money for gifts. Money was always an issue for women. When the family allowance came into being it was the first time many women had a bit of money of their own; it was paid to mothers and it gave them a little bit of freedom to go to town and shop without having to ask their husbands for money. I think it was $5 a child when it first started but it increased slowly and I think if you had a little older child in their teens you got a little more, but you only got this till they were eighteen or finished school. You didn't necessarily spend it on the kids. But in those days $5 went a long way and it probably went towards [getting] everybody a little something. At Christmas time they always sent it early and people had it to buy little gifts or whatever. That was a big step for a lot of women. I once asked my husband why it was so important to him that I have my own money. He said it was because I worked on the farm, too. I think it had a lot to do with his mother. As long as his parents had been on the farm she'd managed to hold onto a little money from the chickens she raised. That was gone when they moved into the city. She had worked so hard and I think it hurt him that she had no money. I remember one time she asked him for some to buy a belt because her husband wouldn't give her any. He was so sad about that.

---

13   For a discussion of economic contribution and partnership, see: Linda Graff, "Industrialization of Agriculture: Implications for the Position of Farm Women," *RFR/DRF* 11, no. 1 (March 1982): 10-11; and Gail Grant, "That Was a Woman's Satisfaction: The Significance of Life History for Woman-Centred Research," *Journal of the Canadian Oral History Association* 2 (1991): 29-38.

Margaret also described her situation as unusual. She could not think of any of her contemporaries who worked off the farm (nor could the other women interviewed): "No, I can't really think of anyone else that did. A lot of women made crafts and sold them. Some women were clever that way. Most women didn't have time to work off the farm. There was so much work to do. But I was lucky because mother lived with us and she was there to help out."

While financial independence allowed Valerie some "sway and say," it did not make her completely "liberated":

> I may have had financial independence, but my husband was still the boss. I spent one year as an instructor for 4-H and I really enjoyed it. But when I went to do it the next year he said no. He could do all the things he wanted to do — curl and belong to his clubs — but not me. If supper was late or if he had to wait to pick me up because the weather was bad or the gravel roads a mess that was it. Our daughter didn't take 4-H and I didn't teach, because he didn't want to be bothered. He didn't really have a good reason. (I think, too, he might have been embarrassed if I worked — people might have talked and thought he wasn't a good provider.)

How Valerie chose to manage this financial independence was not always acceptable to her husband, as this story illustrates:

> Our oldest daughter wanted to go to university to study to become a biochemist. She loved the sciences and she really wanted to do that. Well, her father told her she could go to work at the hospital and become a nurse's aide. He didn't want her to leave home and he didn't see any point in girls going to university — girls got married — that was his way of thinking. In my mind if she didn't want to be a psych nurse why should she? Why should she be something she didn't want to be?
>
> The result was a family feud. My husband's sister-in-law had a friend in Saskatoon where she could board while going to school. I had enough money to buy her suitcases and pay for her tuition, though not enough for university, only the technical school. That same sister-in-law and I were going to drive her up to Saskatoon. When it got to be that morning and my husband saw that we weren't going to back down, he finally gave in. He drove us and he went in with her to register and to pay for her tuition. But you know when she graduated it wasn't even important to him. We didn't even go. He was happy she passed but it just wasn't important to him. Two years later our son wanted to go to university and there was no question of him going. We went to his convocation, too.

She did add, however, that her husband's opinion later changed: "Years later, when our youngest daughter wanted to go to university, there was no question in his mind that she should go. He was very supportive."

None of the money these women earned went to support the farm unit. The women used this money for themselves. This is a different pattern than that which some other scholars have described which sees women donating "pin money" to help keep the family unit going. The difference here is that the two women described above had steady incomes — one woman worked as a reporter for nine years and the other woman had a cattle herd. Their money was by no means "pin money."

Whatever their contribution to the family farm, however, most farm women were in an ultimately precarious position. Cynthia noted one difficulty: "When I wanted something I had to ask. If he wouldn't give it to me I pouted. You'd hope it drove him crazy and he'd give in." Declarations of partnership aside, there was a tenuousness in their family partnerships that all these women acknowledged. Yet, by and large these women seem to have accepted without much anger or resentment the legal and other disadvantages that they experienced. This is not to say they did so with complete passivity or without knowledge of the constraints put upon them. For example, in 1944 one of the woman participated in a raid on a local bar to protest its exclusion of women:

> It was after the provincial election, [in] 1944, I believe. There was a group of us women who had worked for the CCF [Co-operative Commonwealth Federation] and some women who were in the armed forces and stationed nearby. It all tied in with the election — we had worked hard for the CCF and their message was about equality and all that stuff and those service women, well, they could serve their country but they couldn't go to the bar. We were good enough to do a lot of hard work for the party but not to go to the bar. The men could go but our option was to go home and drink coffee — well we drank coffee all day and we were damn well put out. We wanted comradeship. We wanted to go to the bar and have a drink to celebrate. It was so ridiculous: all through the war if you were eighteen and had a coupon you were allowed to buy so much beer — it was rationed like everything was then — but you couldn't go into the beer parlours and have a drink. We felt we should have the same privileges as the men, so we made a raid on this beer parlour. We were really feeling like big wheels … we walked in — a pack of young women, some in uniform — and sat down like we did this everyday. Some men came over and told us it was the law that we couldn't be there. They rounded us up like cattle and showed us out the door. We had no choice. They would have called the cops. We were just like minors today, and worse. It's easier to hide the fact you're underage; we wore skirts and couldn't hide the fact that we were women. I can always remember that — now it seems so stupid — but I suppose it was things like that which changed the world.

In the course of the interviews, the women indicated repeatedly that they felt that they had no choice: "What could you do? … It was different then." This story, told by Cynthia, illustrates these sentiments:

> Women used to sit in the car for hours on end waiting for their husband who was in the beer parlour. The wife, even the kids, would sit out in the car and wait and if he was having a good time he'd just forget them after two, three beers. … A lot of these women couldn't even drive. It's just different now and it's hard for you to visualize. Women wouldn't even go to town for that simple reason: they knew they'd have to sit in the car and wait for their husbands. So they didn't even go to town. They didn't go nowhere.

"Going nowhere" is part of Cynthia's oral history, her personal document — indeed, her personal statement. Many oral historians note that almost all the women that they interviewed have felt positive about their lives and activities, even in the face of poverty and sexism. Certainly this was true of the subjects of this study. As oral historian Armitage states, "the question then arises: what is the relationship between the reality of sexism and a women's personal reality?"[14] The answer, some historians of women suggest, lies in the notion of the female subculture. For example, Canadian historian Eliane Leslau Silverman declares in her historiographical essay published

---

14   Armitage, "The Next Step," 6.

in 1982, that "[f]ar from being peripheral, the issue of a women's culture is central to the writing of women's history."[15]

Certainly in these interviews female friendships figured prominently. The women discussed in great detail their card games, visits for coffee, telephone chats and daily summer excursions. One woman declared that their coffee visits were "essential for survival"; another said that the telephone was her "lifeline." In emergencies the women turned to each other for support, for someone to look after their children. These women also seemed to derive a great deal of sustenance from the community-building and community-sustaining activities in which they participated, activities considered particularly female.

As well as possessing a variety of skills that are essential to the survival of the family unit, rural women have always been, and continue to be, responsible for the vitality and stability of rural communities. Without a doubt this kind of activity is work. It may even be called politics at its most basic level because it keeps communities going. This work could be quite formally organized and happen within clubs or churches or some other structure, or, it could be quite informal, women phoning friends and plotting a wedding shower, a work bee, card games to raise money for a local project or the food and entertainment for a community dance. It might even involve getting the local school ready for the new school year. Together three of the women described this activity:

> When school would start in the fall we would all have to go one day with mop, pail and scrub brush and clean up the school. And the women did that. In our school it was hardwood floors and so you scrubbed and scrubbed and scrubbed and then you waxed and waxed and then you polished and polished. You'd be scrubbing your head off and the one next to you wouldn't be doing such a good job and you'd look at it and then think, "My God, somebody's gonna have to do that over." So you'd probably come back the next day when she wasn't around to do hers over again. And you'd always have somebody who'd come late and have to leave early. Then they'd complain that they didn't see why they had to come at all. There was one in particular, she didn't know why she had to come; she was baking bread, doing this, doing that. I said, "Well, what else is new, the rest of us have to do that, too." But there was always one of those.

As close as some of the friendships were, and as critical to these women's well-being this socializing was, these women did not bare their souls to one another. One of the interviewees put it this way: "There were some things you never talked about. It just wouldn't have been right." Sexual relations or problems in the marriage were not discussed, nor did women make negative comments about their husband.[16] Whether talking with friends or with an oral historian, the "good wife" is the uncomplaining wife.

---

15   Eliane Leslau Silverman, "Writing Canadian Women's History, 1970-1982: An Historiographic Analysis," *Canadian Historical Review* 63, no. 4 (December 1982): 521. In her synthesis of the interwar period, Canadian historian Veronica Strong-Boag argues that women developed and relied on female networks of friends and organizations as a source of empowerment in a society in which they were denied equality: "A predisposition to intimacy, rooted in patterns of socialization, helped sustain a female culture without which lives would've been poorer and harder"; see Veronica Strong-Boag, *The New Day Recalled: Lives of Girls and Women in English Canada, 1919-1939* (Markham: Penguin Books, 1988), 218.

16   Gail Grant describes the same selectiveness among her informants in "That was a Woman's Satisfaction," 31.

While much more evidence is needed concerning women's culture, by their own admission, these women's relationships were critical to their lives. This is a serious claim. Oral history is the primary tool for the reconstruction of women's subculture and the discovery of how women shape their lives.

This is not to say that written material — diaries, letters, reminiscences, fictional accounts, club and organizational records — is useless for uncovering information about women's lives. Historians of women have used these with great success. Ultimately, the best chance of seeing women's lives as they truly were and are lies in using written and oral sources together.

For Saskatchewan rural women, the results of such comprehensive research will be knowledge and acknowledgement of the variety and importance of their lives and work on the farm and in the community and province. For long enough historians have ignored rural women's contribution outside as well as inside the home and have left the impression that men alone built Saskatchewan's agricultural society. In this sense, oral history will benefit Saskatchewan history in general. The outcome will be a more complete history, a history that begins to reveal more accurately how a modern agricultural society developed.

FROM THE BUSH TO THE VILLAGE TO THE CITY: PINEHOUSE LAKE ABORIGINAL WOMEN ADAPT TO CHANGE

Miriam McNab

> They have dreams but they're just stuck there. They're just trapped. They
> don't know how to get out. I didn't know how. I consider myself so lucky
> to be out of there![1]

The words of this Aboriginal woman from Pinehouse Lake, Saskatchewan, reflect her relief at escaping from the depressed conditions of the northern village where she grew up. Typically, northern Saskatchewan communities suffer high rates of unemployment and welfare dependency which the traditional bush-harvesting activities can no longer alleviate. Women and men in these communities, driven first from the bush to the village by the conditions of the larger economy, are now forced to seek work and education opportunities in the larger urban centres in the south.[2]

Urbanized and substantially acculturated Aboriginal people in southern Canada often view with sadness the cultural changes their people have undergone in the past. As a result, they call upon northern Aboriginal people to resist the intrusion of southern cultural influences. In the south, First Nations have seen many of the same cultural changes and impacts on their societies that northern Aboriginal people presently experience, but these changes generally took place a generation or two earlier and over a longer period of time. Today many southern First Nations people grieve over their two greatest losses: their former close link with the land and their indigenous languages. It is, therefore, surprising that many northern Aboriginal people actively and eagerly anticipate the future and the changes it has in store for them and their children. In some ways, women are at the forefront of these changes. For the northern Saskatchewan Aboriginal women considered in this study, this may represent a continuity of successful adaptive strategies and flexibility which characterized the northern Metis in the last century and may continue to do so today.[3]

---

1   Verbal testimony in this paper was obtained from interviews with six women held in Pinehouse and in Saskatoon. Their names are withheld to protect their anonymity. The older women were interviewed in Cree with the assistance of female interpreters known to the informants. The author acknowledges the invaluable assistance of the women and men of Pinehouse Lake, Saskatchewan, and Winona Stevenson, Department of Native Studies, University of Saskatchewan.

2   Northern Saskatchewan refers to the Subarctic boreal forest north of the city of Prince Albert. South of that city, the parkland belt and the northern plains are the more densely populated regions of the province.

3   Aboriginal, an inclusive term used interchangeably with Native, refers to Inuit, Metis, and registered/ status Indians in Canada (Inuit are not discussed in this essay). First Nations are bands of registered Indians. Metis are not as easily defined. Originally they were offspring of mixed Euro-Canadian and Indian marriages and were excluded from Indian status. Today, they are mixed bloods, descendants of mixed bloods, and may or may not be registered Indians as well. Northern Saskatchewan Metis communities are very similar to the cultural-linguistic groups (Cree and Dene, for example) of which they are a part.

For a student of Aboriginal cultures and history, the relatively recent and rapid changes of the north offer a fascinating, telescoped view of how life changed for the ancestors of southern Aboriginal people. Learning the history of Aboriginal peoples is vital for Aboriginal people to understand current situations. However, learning the history of Aboriginal women has not been easy. Most literature on Aboriginal peoples neglects, either by accident or by design, the contributions of Aboriginal women and, in doing so, silences them. It is only recently that scholars such as Eleanor Leacock, Jennifer S.H. Brown, Sylvia Van Kirk, Karen Anderson, Ron Bourgeault and Carol Devens, have begun to give an historical voice to Aboriginal women, and it is clear that the contributions of these women are considerable.[4] While more literature exists on eastern Indian women, Patricia Albers and Beatrice Medicine's book *The Hidden Half*, is a useful collection of historical and ethnohistorical works on Plains Indian women.[5] But little has been published regarding northern Aboriginal women's history. Mary Crnkovich's *"Gossip": A Spoken History of Women in the North*, Julie Cruikshank's *Life Lived Like a Story*, Freda Ahenakew and H.C. Wolfart's *Our Grand-mothers' Lives As Told in Their Own Words*, and Dolores and Irene Poelzer's *In Our Own Words*, are a few.[6] The journal, *Canadian Woman Studies*, which in 1989 published a special issue on Aboriginal women, is currently compiling a special issue on the North. The number of works is growing and perhaps most important are those of Aboriginal women scholars, such as Freda Ahenakew, Priscilla Buffalohead, Patricia Monture-Okanee, Winona Stevenson and M. Annette Jaimes, who offer woman-centred perspectives on the past and on many matters concerning Aboriginal people today.[7] It is hoped that this work adds to this women-centred perspective on the subject of cultural change and northern Native women.

Based on field research conducted in a Cree-Metis village in northern Saskatchewan

---

4   Eleanor B. Leacock, "Montagnais Women and the Jesuit Program for Colonization," in Eleanor B. Leacock, ed., *Myths of Male Dominance: Collected Articles on Women Cross-Culturally* (New York: Monthly Review Press, 1981), 43-62; Jennifer S. H. Brown, *Strangers in Blood: Fur Trade Company Families in Indian Country* (Vancouver: University of British Columbia Press, 1980); Sylvia Van Kirk, *"Many Tender Ties": Women in Fur Trade Society in Western Canada, 1670-1870* (Winnipeg: Watson and Dwyer, 1980); Karen Anderson, *Chain Her by One Foot: The Subjugation of Women in Seventeenth-Century New France* (London: Routledge, 1991); Ron Bourgeault, "Race, Class and Gender: Colonial Domination of Indian Women," in J. Vorst et al., eds., *Race, Class, Gender: Bonds and Barriers* (Toronto: Published by Between Lines in Co-operation with the Society for Socialist Studies/Société d'études socialistes, 1989), 87-115; Carol Devens, *Countering Colonization: Native American Women and the Great Lakes Missions, 1630-1900* (Berkeley: University of California Press, 1992).

5   Patricia Albers and Beatrice Medicine, *The Hidden Half: Studies of Plains Indian Women* (Lanham, MD: University Press of America, 1983).

6   Mary Crnkovich, ed., *"Gossip": A Spoken History of Women in the North* (Ottawa: Canadian Arctic Resources Committee, 1990); Julie Cruikshank, *Life Lived Like a Story: Life Stories of Three Yukon Native Elders* (Lincoln: University of Nebraska Press, 1990); Freda Ahenakew and H.C. Wolfart, *Kôhkominawak Otâcimowiniwâwa/Our Grandmothers' Lives: As Told in Their Own Words* (Saskatoon: Fifth House Publishers, 1992); Dolores T. Poelzer and Irene A. Poelzer, *In Our Own Words: Northern Saskatchewan Metis Women Speak Out* (Saskatoon: Lindenblatt and Hamonic, 1986).

7   Ahenakew and Wolfart, *Kôhkominawak*; Priscilla Buffalohead, "Farmers, Warriors, Traders: A Fresh Look at Ojibway Women," *Minnesota History* (Summer 1983): 236-44; Patricia Monture-Okanee, "The Roles and Responsibilities of Aboriginal Women: Reclaiming Justice," *Saskatchewan Law Review* 56 (1992): 237-66; Rhonda Johnson, Winona Stevenson, and Donna Greschner, "Peekiskwetan," *Canadian Journal of Women and the Law* 6 (1993): 153-73; M. Annette Jaimes with Theresa Halsey, "American Indian Women At the Center of Indigenous Resistance in Contemporary North America," in M. Annette Jaimes, ed., *The State of Native America: Genocide, Colonization, and Resistance* (Boston: South End Press, 1992).

and in the southern city of Saskatoon, this essay examines some of the relatively recent socioeconomic changes experienced by northern Aboriginal women. It encompasses the shifts from the bush to the village and from the village to the city, and examines the major causes of these shifts. This essay contends that the major external influences encouraging village settlement are found in the larger market economy, especially external markets for bush commodities, and the intrusion of the state, in the form of its programs, services and regulations. These combined forces — elements of the capitalist mode of production — intrude into the lives of the northern peoples, producing change in the "traditional" or "bush" mode of production and its social relations.

The major shifts experienced by women are increased sedentization in villages, less dependence on, and less involvement in, family-oriented production of bush economic commodities, and greater dependence on social welfare programs and wage labour. Combined, these changes do not successfully reproduce the same social relations characteristic of the traditional bush activities.[8] Taken to its culmination, capitalist intrusion results in urbanization in the south and adaptation to a waged labour or welfare-dependent lifestyle in the city. This essay also examines some of the push-pull factors involved in the move from village to city.

The women featured in this discussion are all Cree-speaking, ranging in age from twenty-three to ninety-two (at the time of interview), from Pinehouse Lake, Saskatchewan. Pinehouse is a village of about a thousand Cree-Metis residents, situated on the west shore of Pinehouse Lake, one of the many lakes the Churchill River passes through on its long journey to Hudson Bay. Located on the upper Churchill River in northwest-central Saskatchewan, the village sits in the boreal forest, just a few miles south of the Canadian Shield. Much of this discussion derives from research carried out in the village during the summer of 1990 by participant observation and interviews conducted by the author. Further interviews with Pinehouse women in Saskatoon took place in 1994.

The author was privileged to meet some fascinating women who shared a multiplicity of experiences ranging from the traditional, mobile way of life at the beginning of this century to contemporary city-dwelling life. Their lives cannot be described as separate from the history of their people, and any description of the changes they have undergone must be couched in a history of the community as a whole.

A brief history of the region, here with an emphasis on the economy, must begin with at least a mention of the pre-contact history and the occupation of the upper Churchill River, probably by Dene peoples, for thousands of years prior to the advent of the fur trade with Europeans. Most fur-trade scholars and historians believe that the Cree moved into the region after 1690 as a result of the fur trade.[9] Regardless of when the Cree arrived, the economy of the Churchill River region in post-contact times has been dominated by the fur trade and by the Cree-Metis in the region.

---

8   For a discussion of the recent social relations of Metis women in northern Saskatchewan villages in the areas of wage labour, volunteer work, and welfare dependency, see Irene A. Poelzer, "Metis Women and the Economy of Northern Saskatchewan," in J. Vorst et al., eds., *Race, Class, Gender*, 196-216.

9   See, for example: David G. Mandelbaum, *The Plains Cree* (1940; Regina: Canadian Plains Research Center, 1979); and Arthur J. Ray, *Indians in the Fur Trade: Their Role as Hunters, Trappers and Middlemen in the Lands Southwest of Hudson Bay, 1660-1870* (Toronto: University of Toronto Press, 1974).

The influence of the fur trade along the Churchill River is well documented by the anthropologists Robert W. Jarvenpa and H. J. Brumbach.[10] The fur trade is a major part of the heritage of all the peoples of this area. The people of Pinehouse are no exception. Indeed, they are largely descended from a "Metis-Cree working class" which developed within the fur-trade economy in the area.[11]

The upper Churchill River Cree were involved in the trade in the early 1700s and were recorded as regular visitors at York Factory by 1714.[12] Toward the end of the eighteenth century, they witnessed the growing competition and proliferation of fur-trade posts established in the vicinity by independent traders, the North-West Company, and eventually the Hudson's Bay Company (HBC). Competition was fierce until 1821 when the two major companies merged. Then, the Aboriginal peoples found themselves under HBC monopoly conditions that dictated prices and conservation measures.[13] The competitive period resulted in chronic and widespread resource depletion which caused hardships for trappers resulting in their increased dependence on fur-trade posts. Trapping under these conditions continued as the Aboriginal peoples adapted to a new commercial climate.

For a period of time during the last century, wage employment at the fur-trade posts was an important part of the economy of the Metis in the region. Gradually, however, as fur-trade employment decreased, the Metis population in the north increased and relied even more heavily on domestic harvesting of resources and the harvesting of furs for commercial purposes.[14] As a commercial venture, fishing in Pinehouse Lake began approximately at the turn of the twentieth century and became more important as the fur market declined in the 1940s.[15]

The community of Pinehouse itself is of relatively recent development and is largely the result of the establishment of a Roman Catholic Church at the village site. Fur-trade posts existed from time to time at various locations on the lake and may have been focal points of summer tent communities. It was not until the establishment of the church and the school in 1944 and 1948 respectively, however, that the families scattered around the lake and elsewhere coalesced and settled at the present village site in significant numbers.[16]

Since the end of World War II, the north has seen a period of unprecedented rapid expansion. Pinehouse shared in this expansion with the infusion of government

---

10   See: Robert W. Jarvenpa, *The Trappers of Patuanak: Toward a Spatial Ecology of Modern Hunters,* Canadian Ethnology Service Paper No. 67, National Museum of Man Series (Ottawa: National Museums of Canada, 1980) and Robert W. Jarvenpa and H. J. Brumbach, "Socio-Spatial Organization and Decision-Making Processes: Observations from the Chipewyan," *American Anthropologist* 90 (1988): 598-618, for examples of the extensive ethnohistorical and archaeological work these authors carried out at Patuanak, a Chipewyan community on the Churchill River neighbouring Pinehouse.

11   Robert W. Jarvenpa and H. J. Brumbach, "Occupational Status, Ethnicity and Ecology: Metis Cree Adaptations in a Canadian Trading Frontier," *Human Ecology* 13, no. 3 (1985): 310.

12   Ray, *Indians in the Fur Trade,* 53.

13   Ibid., 199-204.

14   Jarvenpa and Brumbach, "Occupational Status," 325.

15   Robert W. Jarvenpa, "Intergroup Behavior and Imagery: The Case of Chipewyan and Cree," *Ethnology* 21, no. 4 (1982): 286.

16   See James B. Waldram, "Relocation, Consolidation, and Settlement Pattern in the Canadian Subarctic," *Human Ecology* 15, no. 2 (1987): 117-31 for a discussion of the coalescence and increasing sedentization of subarctic Cree communities.

services and controls which began in the 1940s. The government initiated and extended to the north social assistance, health care and education, as well as conservation and wildlife management programs, including trapping zones and licensing.[17] Such programs had a tremendous impact on the northern people, but actually did little to enhance their quality of life.[18]

By the early 1960s, little had changed and a study for the provincial Department of Natural Resources in 1963 indicated that a social and economic crisis loomed in the north as a result of rapid population growth without corresponding economic growth.[19] It found that, of necessity, the northern peoples were heavily dependent upon hunting, trapping and fishing, with trapping as the main industry and fishing second.[20] Both yielded low returns, however.

Wage employment in the 1960s was scarce and of a seasonal nature, based on the resource industries including the forest industries, guiding, fish plants, power, and the Department of Natural Resources.[21] Underemployment and heavy and increasing dependence upon welfare programs, including family allowance, old age pensions, and social assistance, were rife. According to the Department of Natural Resources study, these conditions threatened the traditional bush economic system:

> For many trappers and fishermen, the day has already arrived when productive activity makes little economic sense — and sometimes, none at all. Earnings of $200 to $300 for a winter's work are well below what a family of four or five could get on Social Aid. If men are not already asking it, the question is bound to come: Why trap?[22]

The 1960s and 1970s saw increasing contact with the outside world and the trend toward greater reliance on government transfer payments and wage labour, with less reliance on the bush harvest. Of the commercial bush activities, fishing took on greater importance than trapping, as dictated by external market trends. In more recent years, however, government regulation and the imposition of quotas on commercial fishing have affected the extent to which Pinehouse could benefit from its fish resources. Another bush commodity which has increased in importance is wild rice. Recently, the market has offered good prices and yields have been excellent. Trapping, the mainstay of the Aboriginal people's economy for generations, has declined almost into oblivion.

Such drastic changes over the past few decades have had a corresponding impact on the social organization of the people. Change was the underlying theme of all the interviews the author conducted with Pinehouse residents. Although technological change was not the focus of this research, it is not surprising that, for a former highly mobile population, most remarks focussed on changes in transportation. An eighty-year-old woman who had travelled first with her father while he worked for the HBC, and then with her first and second husbands, both trappers, remarked in 1990:

---

17   Helen Buckley, J.E.M. Kew and John B. Hawley, *The Indians and Metis of Northern Saskatchewan: A Report of Economic and Social Development* (Saskatoon: Centre for Community Studies, 1963), 32.

18   J.E.M. Kew, "Metis-Indian Housing in Northern Saskatchewan," *Research Review* (Saskatoon: Centre for Community Studies, 1963), 16.

19   Buckley et al., *The Indians and Metis of Northern Saskatchewan*, 1.

20   Ibid., 18.

21   Ibid., 19.

22   Ibid., 25.

the most important thing that I saw was that motor pulling five boats at one
time. And they didn't have to paddle.

Another woman, sixty-nine at the time of the interview, recalled the story her husband
had told of the first airplane the people saw. According to her, it was a two-seater
biplane which flew into the community where they were camped:

> I guess they all went running out 'cause they heard this thing in the sky.
> They didn't know what it was. Some people were kind of scared. "Jesus
> Christ is coming!" one person said.

Motorboats, airplanes, snowmobiles, automobiles, winter and then all-weather
roads revolutionized the transportation of an already very mobile people and
enhanced their economic activities. Doubtless these changes had corresponding
social ramifications, but the larger, external powers of government and the economy
also changed social relations.

In order to examine the changes in social relations of production, it is necessary
first to explain the state of affairs during the fur trade. The mode of production
termed here the "bush" or "traditional" has elsewhere been described as a "fur trade
mode of production" or a duo-sector economy in which the fur trade altered the
pre-contact mode of production to one which, in addition to producing goods for
domestic use, began to also produce commodities for exchange.[23] This combination
of the two modes of production dramatically altered community social relations.

Various anthropologists have reconstructed the pre-contact mode for most of the
Aboriginal peoples of this continent.[24] Based on some of these, P. Ballantyne and
others described the former economy of the Cree of the Churchill River basin and
the social relations of production as follows:

> With the family as the basis of production, it is marriage and procreation
> that creates groups constituted to produce a livelihood, and each family
> contains within it the division of labour of the society as a whole.
> Characteristically, the division of labour is along lines of age (young/old)
> and sex (male/female). Work and production specialization is rare or
> non-existent. The domestic group generates its own productive technology
> from the extraction of raw materials to the completion of the finished
> article. ... Production and exchange of goods and services are oriented to
> providing a sufficient livelihood for the members of the domestic group.
> Surplus is characteristically absent.[25]

The social relations of production and the way in which production is organized in
the capitalist mode of production is fundamentally different, and opposed to, those

---

23   See: P. Ballantyne et al., *Aski-Puko — The Land Alone: A Report on the Expected Effects of the Proposed
     Hydro-Electric Installation at Wintego Rapids on the Cree of the Peter Ballantyne and Lac la Ronge Bands*
     (Federation of Saskatchewan Indians, n.p., 1976); Patricia A. McCormack, "Becoming Trappers: The
     Transformation to a Fur Trade Mode of Production," in Thomas C. Buckley, ed., *Rendezvous: Selected
     Papers of the Fourth North American Fur Trade Conference, 1981* (St. Paul, MN: North American Fur Trade
     Conference, 1984), 155-73; and Adrian Tanner, *Bringing Home Animals: Religious Ideology and Mode of
     Production of the Mistassini Cree Hunters* (St. John's: Memorial University Press, 1979).

24   For a survey of literature on the Subarctic, see Edward S. Rogers, "History of Ethnological Research
     in the Subarctic Shield and Mackenzie Borderlands," in June Helm, ed., *Subarctic*, vol. 6, *Handbook of
     North American Indians*, Wm. C. Sturtevant, gen. ed. (Washington: Smithsonian Institution, 1981),
     19-29.

25   Ballantyne et al., *Aski-Puko*, 4.

of the pre-contact mode of production. A main feature of the social relations of capitalism is the nonegalitarian class divisions which arise and the unequal access to the means of production which accompanies this class division. Far from the pre-contact mode based on household production, modern capitalist production, "in its most advanced manifestation, [evolved from the fur trade of a hundred years ago] is performed by large and highly structured social organizations, which we call corporations."[26]

During the fur trade, the two modes came into contact and the resulting changes led to the increasing vulnerability and dependence of the traditional mode, while the capitalist mode, in its present form, has retained dominance. The impact of nascent capitalism, manifest in the fur trade on pre-contact northern Aboriginal women, has been described elsewhere.[27] Suffice it to say here that the patriarchal ideology of Europe, brought by fur traders and supported by missionaries, eroded the power and autonomy of Aboriginal women, especially in those social relations most directly involved with the fur trade and with Europeans. Many former social relations continued to exist since the new or altered fur trade mode of production allowed a continued bush involvement of the family. Over time, the new mode has been handed down to several generations with little modification to basic aspects until this century.

While there are other differences between the now traditional or bush mode and what probably existed in the pre-contact period, the bush mode involved women in production in much the same way as the pre-contact economy might have. Some aspects of the bush mode early in this century are evident in the oral histories collected at Pinehouse.[28] A group of usually two to four nuclear families, related through either the men or women, lived and trapped together wherever they chose, according to Pinehouse sources. However, recognized family-owned trapping territories, upon which later registered traplines would emerge, probably already existed. There was a seasonal mobility based on trapping and fishing, with a division of labour based on age and gender.

The men, accompanied by their sons aged ten to twelve and over, hunted food for domestic use and trapped furs for the market. They constructed and maintained all of their tools manufactured from wood or local materials, and they purchased traps, guns, ammunition, twine for nets and other important articles from the fur-trade posts.

Women were responsible for the home and the camp, the young children, and the food production, which entailed, among other things, drying meat and smoking fish. While the men hunted large game and trapped at a distance from the home, the women usually snared and trapped small animals close to home. Occasionally, a woman would trap intensively along with the men, but that was unusual. Women's

---

26   Peter J. Usher, "Sustenance or Recreation? The Future of Native Wildlife Harvesting in Northern Canada," in Milton M.R. Freeman, ed., *Renewable Resources and the Economy of the North* (Ottawa: Association of Canadian Universities for Northern Studies, 1981), 58.

27   See, for example: Karen Anderson, "Commodity Exchange and Subordination: Montagnais-Naskapi and Huron Women, 1600-1650," *Signs* 2, no. 1 (Autumn 1985): 48-62; and Bourgeault, "Race, Class and Gender."

28   For further discussion, see Miriam McNab, "Persistence and Change in a Northern Saskatchewan Trapping Community" (MA thesis, University of Saskatchewan, 1992).

work generally entailed skinning animals, preparing furs for the market, processing hides (moose and deer-hide tanning), and manufacturing clothing. They also netted snowshoes and fishnets. Clearly, women's jobs were directly related to the men's — when the men killed and brought animals home, the women's job of processing and distributing the produce began.

Two of the women interviewed in Pinehouse had lived this lifestyle. They were aged ninety-two and eighty in 1990. Neither of them had ever attended school, rather they had grown up and lived the "bush" life with their parents and husbands, sometimes even trapping and hunting for themselves. They had given birth to and/or raised children on the trapline.

The ninety-two-year old may well have been considered an anomaly among women during her life. Her family was the first to settle in the present location of the village of Pinehouse; she was eight years old. At seventeen, she was forced to marry a man from a more southerly Cree reserve whose family then lived at a lake to the west of Pinehouse on the Churchill River. Through an interpreter, she told her story:

> He used to walk from there to come visit Pinehouse. This one time he went through the ice (laughter). He nearly drowned. [We] built their house there [in Sandy Lake]. He kept visiting me and this priest that used to be in this community … kept pushing us to get married. I didn't even know the man. I hardly even talked to him. When he used to talk to me I used to turn away from him. Because in those days, we used to be so modest, not like today.

In response to the question, "Did he force you to get married, or did you love him enough to want to get married?" the elderly woman responded:

> No. They tried so hard. Finally they forced me to marry him, the priest, my mom and dad, and the other older people in the community. Finally he ended up living with us.

Although married, this woman did not settle with her husband immediately. Instead she continued spending months alone in the bush, even in winter, hunting for herself and trapping. She described hunting several species of small game and fowl, and other women mentioned that she had also killed moose. According to her, the main reason for going off on her own was because she did not want to be married. She was forced into the marriage but preferred to be alone. Through the interpreter, she stated:

> A long time ago it didn't matter if you loved somebody; it's who your parents or the older people thought was right for you, that's who you married. So it was to be just fixed marriages; I guess you'd call it.

This woman, who married in the second decade of the twentieth century, eventually spent many years with her husband. At the time of the field research, she was a widow who lived in the village year-round. Due to illness, she had never had any children of her own; however, she did raise at least one adopted daughter. Over the years she had lived an unusual life for a woman. At one time she was a commercial fisher-woman, hiring men to fish for her with her own equipment. She was also the only woman to appear on the trappers' membership list. While in earlier years she often did her own trapping, in later years, she usually purchased a license since she frequently bought furs from others, which she in turn sold.

This particular woman is well known for her midwifery skills and in 1992 she was awarded the Saskatchewan Order of Merit for, among her other achievements, having delivered 502 babies in her lifetime. By the time I met her, she had quit midwifery on account of her failing eyesight and weakness. She was the oldest member of the community, highly regarded by many people, and her bank of oral history was extensive.

Such was the case also for the next oldest member of the community, an eighty-year-old woman. Like the other, this woman spoke only Cree and was a willing and valuable informant. Since she was raising a grandchild, she was mostly confined to the village during the school year; up until this time she had spent most of her life in the bush. One of twelve children, she was born on the Churchill River at Dipper Lake where her Metis father worked as a guide for the HBC trader. She too had trapped a little as a younger woman and had travelled extensively. Her first husband used to travel to Cree Lake to trap. She accompanied him as they travelled by canoe and by dogsled until he died of a heart attack. Her second husband was from the south end of Pinehouse Lake. Together they had four children.

Her second husband is twelve years younger than she and still spends a considerable amount of time at his cabin on his trapline, although he returns quite often to the village because his wife is there. In the summer months, however, she spends much of her time at the cabin, as is the case for many families with school-age children. Every summer, families make a point of spending a week or a month or two out on the land, fishing and living. This is clearly a reversal of the former state of affairs when summer fishing drew people to settle together in tent communities, the forerunners of permanent settlements.

All over the north, over the past seventy years, settled communities arose in response to various factors. Access to the fur trading posts, churches, clinics and schools was a powerful incentive for settling in the villages, and beginning in the 1940s, government-assistance programs such as family allowance and social assistance or "welfare" were significant factors. They represented regular monthly or bi-monthly payments which, in order to be received, required the presence of the recipient in the village, near the post office, to collect the cheques and cash them. As women were often the recipients of these payments, women were increasingly in the village more often or for longer periods. In addition to this logistical factor, the availability of the reliable transfer income reduced the reliance of the family on the income derived from trapping and the bush harvest. As a result, trappers and their families needed to spend less time in the bush seeking furs and could spend more time in the village.[29]

The above incentives, combined with compulsory attendance of children at school, began to erode the traditional lifestyle and social relations of production. During the 1940s, attendance at school became compulsory and the payment of family allowances was made conditional upon the children's school attendance.[30] Regardless of this, during the 1940s, only about half of the Metis children in northern Saskatchewan were actually attending school. Others at Pinehouse attended a Catholic mission residential school at Île-à-la-Crosse during this period. Having the school-age children in residence for many months over the year allowed the rest of the family to continue to live on the trapline and did not necessitate the removal of a productive adult family member. In more recent years, the residential school at Beauval served the same purpose.

---

29 J.W. VanStone, "Changing Patterns of Indian Trapping in the Canadian Subarctic," *Arctic* 16 (1963): 163.

30 Buckley et al., *The Indians and Metis of Northern Saskatchewan*, 32.

In 1948, a school opened in Pinehouse. This put increasing pressure on the family to live in the village. In many cases children would stay with a grandparent, aunt, or older married sibling while attending school. Parents with younger children continued their traditional round of activities. Not wishing to be absent from their children for too long, however, the parents would find themselves spending more and more time in the village if they had accommodation. The housing programs of the 1960s enabled more people to live in the village and often the mothers would stay home with the children while the fathers carried on with trapping and bush activities.

Like Aboriginal people elsewhere, the people of Pinehouse also have the custom of grandparents adopting and raising one or more of their grandchildren. A great deal of open adoption also took place. In the same way that one's children would confine one to the village, so too would one's grandchildren. This study's interviews reveal that the responsibility fell sometimes on the grandmother to remain in the village to keep her grandchildren in school.

The necessity of women staying in the village to keep children in school also kept men in the village more than would otherwise have been the case. Men who did not wish to be absent from their wives and children for very long might trap less or trap closer to town, returning to the village more often than before and staying for longer periods.

The effects of compulsory Canadian education on the children are important and will have a significant impact on the future, particularly because that education interrupts traditional education and socialization. In the village, with the men away, the women are primarily responsible for the socialization of children, but increasingly, the children are subject to external socialization influences from teachers and peers. In more recent times, the television offers a very strong influence and today, satellite television channels from the United States, as well as rented movies on video tape, are very popular. Child rearing, especially the transmission of traditional socio-economic activities, has been significantly undermined by external forces.

The effects on the women of their confinement in the village have not been comprehensively documented; however, it would appear that women are more subject than men to acculturative influences from the outside world. These influences come directly through the schools and their children, through the people from elsewhere living in the village, or through village members who travel between the village and other larger centres. One of the most remarked upon changes for women was the loss of traditional skills, in particular the skinning and tanning of hides. Women removed from the bush had no need to perform these functions since men took over those traditional female tasks connected with the production of furs for the market. The ability to skin a muskrat or a beaver well and prepare the hide is now seen as a trait of an admirable trapper. There were, however, men who brought their animals to the village to be skinned by older women. These men would pay for the service in cash or sometimes with the meat from the skinned animal.[31] Informants remarked that only the older women still maintained the skills and one would not see young women tanning hides because they did not know how to do it. The younger women did not need the skills and therefore they did not learn them.

Another effect of sedentization is evident in the health of the people. Several

---

31   Of the animals trapped for furs, only beaver, muskrat and lynx are eaten.

trappers maintained that the lifestyle of the bush was healthier for the people. Not only is the food superior to that available in the store, but the active lifestyle helped to maintain good health over a longer lifespan. Virtually all the people of Pinehouse aged thirty-five years and older preferred the country food. Further, virtually all the elderly people observed in the village had amazingly youthful physical movement. For example, the eighty-year-old woman rose as easily from sitting on the floor to make tea at the stove as a thirty-year-old would. It is clear that these elderly women benefited from the active lifestyle they lived in the bush.

Another impact of village sedentization is that the women in the village find more opportunities for employment and training. For example, for the past three years one Pinehouse woman, aged fifty years old in 1994, managed her family's rice harvesting while her husband was away labouring in Churchill, Manitoba. She drove the mechanical harvester, dealt with the rice buyers and handled the whole business, which netted over $10,000 in a single season. Generally, wives of trappers obtained jobs in the village as janitors or clerks at the store, village office, Royal Canadian Mounted Police detachment, Northern Resources office, or the medical clinic. They have also proven effective at acquiring full-time work, while their husbands found part-time work in construction, guiding, firefighting, or the bush industries. A young woman, aged thirty-two, commented on this:

> [In her grandmother's time] women mostly stayed at home and do everything. But now it's way different. I think the men stay at home more than the women. [However, the men in Pinehouse] don't mind, because we have lots of women in the workforce now, mostly women probably in Pinehouse, working, than men.

Significantly, women, more than men, are moving away from Pinehouse, lured to the larger centres where there are more opportunities for education and employment. The young woman continued:

> There's not lots in Pinehouse. You can't choose what you want to be. You have to go out of town [to a larger city] if you want a career in life.

This woman knows of what she speaks, having recently moved to Saskatoon to take a ten-month course in administration from a career college in the city. She followed her sister-in-law, also from Pinehouse, who is taking the same course. Further, she has two aunts who have lived in Saskatoon for approximately twenty years. Several women were mentioned who have recently moved to southern cities from Pinehouse, or who plan to move in the fall, for such training opportunities as social work, nursing, administration, and teacher training. A forty-seven-year old Pinehouse woman explains the trend of women leaving the village to move to the cities:

> I think they want to go for education; to educate themselves, do something for themselves. I see a lot of that. And there's a lot of ladies I talk to in Pinehouse that are saying, they say, "ah, I wish I could have done something for myself, get an education." I hear a lot about that, when I go and visit. Like, they'll ask me, how do I do it? Yet, they're much older now and they have so many kids; they're trapped. But the young people, they really want to get out, but they just don't know how. ... Most people are on welfare. But if there's a job, like they go looking for jobs, if they can find one. But there's not very much of that in Pinehouse; not very much of anything. That's why people want to get out of there, like young people especially. And there's also young married couples that have moved to here and Prince Albert to get their education.

Another woman, aged twenty-three, attends university in Saskatoon with her husband. Their two-year-old son needs regular specialized medical attention unavailable in the north. According to her:

> He's "Special Needs" and he needs a lot of doctors' attention. They do all kinds of tests on him. It's better that we're living here. When we were living in La Ronge I had to come here every Monday for six weeks for him just to get a check up, so that's why we moved here, too, for him. He gets all kinds of therapy.

This woman has an eight-year-old niece who also moved to Saskatoon for regular medical therapy. Another example of superior health care drawing women to Saskatoon is northern women with high-risk pregnancies coming to stay in the city for the period of their confinement. Some stay as long as a month or more and are introduced to the attractions of city life.

It appears, therefore, that women are in the forefront of drastic cultural change, even taking the final step of urbanization before men and seemingly without regret. Overwhelmingly, a sense of optimism accompanies these women into the urban centres, which may have as much to do with their children's opportunities as with their own educational aspirations.

The interviewees pointed to the many advantages, especially for their children, of living in the city. They include: superior health care, the perceived better standard of education and other learning opportunities, as well as recreational facilities such as swimming pools for the children. The women also find the lower cost of living and greater opportunities attractive. One twenty-three-year-old women commented on her return visits to the North:

> I have relatives there to feed me and whatever, and to stay where ever I want, but I take some of my money because … I want to buy groceries and whatever, but its so expensive compared to Saskatoon. With five dollars I can buy lots here and ten bucks probably won't even buy three things over there. Plus the Pampers, they're really expensive.

Boredom also is a factor in relocation:

> I think Pinehouse is boring sometimes, compared to here. You can go out and do something [here]. You can even go out for a walk, no dust, with all that pavement. It seems like once you go there, it's so quiet, it's so boring; there's nothing to do, sort of thing. I don't know, I get really lonesome for Saskatoon. Cause I'm used to it now, eh? … Plus there's lots of things happening, you know all these little things happening, parades, whatever, exhibition. There's theatre to watch, movies to rent, videos and stuff like that, instead of staying home all the time.

Garage sales and bingos also provide diversions for these women, and they were pleased to avoid such unpleasant aspects of the village life as the high prices for food and all bought goods, and the negative effects of small-town drinking and partying.

These women brought to the city their friendly caring attitude characteristic of the bush and the small-trapping village, the ability to make friends easily and the kindness of generously sharing the country food they acquired from the return trips to the north. Their attitude to change is optimistic. Rather than viewing life in the city as a challenge to the retention of their culture and language, some women view the overwhelming dominance of English in the city as an opportunity for young children to immerse themselves in the English language. They intend to preserve their first language, however; perhaps a lesson learned from the experience of southern Aboriginal people.

The First Nations women interviewed for this study noted few disadvantages to city life, beyond some minor adjustment problems. One young woman stated:

> I was afraid of coming to Saskatoon to go to university. It's such a big city here. I thought somebody would grab me from the streets or whatever. Now its really ... I like it. I really like it better here. ... For a while I didn't go anywhere cause I was just scared, and I was scared to drive; it was such a big city and I thought I would never ever drive in Saskatoon. Like it was so hard, I thought.

Another possible disadvantage was couched in positive terms by the thirty-two-year-old woman:

> You learn how to be more independent in the city. Like back when I used to stay in Pinehouse, I [would] usually go and eat over at my mom's, [who] cooked everyday for me and baby[sat] free for me, but over here you can't find anyone like that. You have to cook your own meals and find your own babysitter. You have to be prepared, having your family doctor and having a second babysitter ... So far, [I don't get lonely], busy studying. [I have] no time.

This woman's husband makes the five-hour drive to visit her most weekends and plans to move in the fall when his current job is finished. When asked if she could see herself living in Saskatoon forever, she replied:

> Yeah. That's what I told my landlord. He was laughing at me. I have three weeks off next month. I'll probably go and visit for a while. Go stay in the cabin with my dad and them.

For these women, it appeared that they miss the life on the land rather than the life in the village. When asked, "What do you miss about it?" the thirty-two-year-old replied:

> Just the outdoors, camping, having picnics, and having that wild meat, moose and ducks ... sitting around the campfire, eating whatever you want to eat, like fish, moosemeat.

Another woman stated:

> The only thing I like about it when I go there [to the north] is when I go out on the lake, that's about it. Like, going out on picnics or whatever, out on the boat. Now that I have a baby I wouldn't mind taking him out there, on a boat or something.

And another stated: "I miss the quietness, that's what I miss. ... nothing else." The former lifestyle of their grandmothers' generation has seen considerable change. For many women today that lifestyle is reduced to just the summer visits to the cabins, fishing for the family and procuring the country food whenever possible.

In conclusion, within two generations, Pinehouse women were relegated from full involvement in the trapping lifestyle of their families to a sedentary lifestyle, "trapped" in the village. Today Pinehouse women are escaping to pursue meaningful, productive lives in the cities. Their optimism and active participation in the process of cultural change contrasts with the reflective remorse felt by many southern Aboriginal people who feel the need to return to their roots and sometimes blame their ancestors for their perceived losses. Perhaps those same ancestors felt such optimism for the future of their children. Or perhaps the current northern attitudes are reflective of the changed conditions and policies which no longer directly force drastic cultural change on Aboriginal people. While they believe they can maintain their lands and languages, these northern Cree-Metis women cannot be blamed for improving their lives with the benefits of modern urban living and demonstrating resourceful adaptive strategies of which their ancestors would doubtless be proud.

"LIVING IN DREAMS":
ORAL NARRATIVES OF THREE RECENT IMMIGRANT WOMEN

Jo-Anne Lee

Feminist researchers have enthusiastically adopted oral narratives as a tool of research.[1] In oral history, feminists see a way of recovering and redressing absences and silences about women's experiences.[2] Yet, despite advances in Canadian women's history since the 1970s, many women still remain outside the feminist project of historical reclamation.[3] Women who remain invisible in Canadian historiography include non-English and non-French-speaking immigrants and racialized women, along with other women who live their lives beyond white, middle-class, academic feminist historians' gaze.[4] From this perspective, Saskatchewan women's history has yet to be written.

Although, today, Saskatchewan receives a small proportion (less than 2 percent) of the total immigration to Canada, Saskatchewan was once one of Canada's primary

---

1   Shulamit Reinharz, *Feminist Methods in Social Research* (New York: Oxford University Press, 1992).

2   By oral history I refer to Gluck and Patai's description of a methodology for recording, transcribing, editing and making public the life experiences of individuals through oral, not written records. I use oral narratives to mean the telling of a part or a segment of a person's life experience. My use of the term oral narrative differs from Gluck and Patai's where they use the term to refer to the material collected in an oral history process. Oral narrative should be distinguished from the oral interview which is one of the means of obtaining the material for oral history. Other means of obtaining materials in oral history include testimony, life history and story telling; see Sherna Berger Gluck and Daphne Patai, eds., *Women's Words* (New York: Routledge, Chapman and Hall, 1991), 4. The three stories in this chapter did not come about through an interview process. The stories were self-selected by the three women and recounted in a public performance. In this sense they were closer to the oral tradition of personal story telling. I feel that this means of recovering women's experiences is more empowering than the interview method. It reduces power differentials between "researcher" and "researched," it addresses the silencing of immigrant women by opening a public space in which immigrant women can speak and it can only come about when there is a continuing relationship between the researcher and the narrator. In this case, I had worked with all three women for several years in a community-based immigrant women organization.

3   Bettina Bradbury, "Review Essay, Women and the History of Their Work in Canada: Some Recent Books," *Journal of Canadian Studies* 28, no. 3 (Fall 1993): 159-78; Ruth Roach Pierson and Alison Prentice, "Feminism and the Writing and Teaching of History," *Atlantis* 7, no. 2 (1982): 37-46.

4   Nila Gupta and Makeda Silvera, managing eds., *The Issue is "ism": Women of Colour Speak Out* (Toronto: Sister Vision Press, 1989), originally published as issue 16 of *Fireweed, A Feminist Quarterly* (1983); Franca Iacovetta and Mariana Valverde, "Introduction," in *Gender Conflicts: New Essays in Women's History* (Toronto: University of Toronto Press, 1992), xi - xxvii. The term "racialized women" is derived from Robert Miles's work on racialization; see Robert Miles, *Racism* (London: Routledge, 1989). Following Miles, I use the terms racialized and racialization to name the processes by which women, for example, immigrant, refugee, "visible minority" or non-English-speaking women are separated out for differential and unequal treatment on the basis of signifying characteristics including "racial," religious, ethnic and national origins, linguistic, cultural practices as well as other characteristics. The category, "immigrant women," for example, is a category into which some women are placed through racializing processes. Because the label "immigrant women" is used in popular and scholarly discourse, I use this term as well. However, I also use the term racialized women as a way of challenging the unproblematic acceptance of this constructed category.

immigrant-receiving provinces.[5] Present low levels contrast with the situation at the beginning of the century when population censuses showed that over 50 percent of Saskatchewan's population was foreign-born.[6] Across the prairie region, the intake of immigrants has fluctuated widely from 1901 to the present. For example, in 1911 immigrants constituted more than 50 percent of the prairie region's population.[7] In 1991, this proportion declined to around 13.5 percent of the population.[8] Overall, the immigrant population represents 16 percent (4.3 million) of Canada's population in 1991 and this figure has remained constant since 1951 when 15 percent of the population were immigrants.[9] The flood of immigration to the prairie region at the beginning of the century came mainly from the British Isles and Europe. These countries are no longer the main source of immigration to the prairie region or to Canada. Since the 1960s there has been an increase in immigration from Asia, Africa and Latin America. Almost two-thirds of Canada's total immigration since the 1980s have been from non-European sources.[10]

Women have always been part of these successive waves of immigration. Yet the resounding silence in Canadian history of the experiences of women, particularly non-European immigrant women, is very troublesome.[11] However, the purpose of this essay is not to inquire into the reasons for this absence, but to offer a small corrective to the large gap in the emerging canvas of Canadian women's history.

This essay presents and discusses three stories told by immigrant women of their experiences with migration and settlement in Saskatchewan.[12] Unlike extant histories of Saskatchewan women, this is about three quite "ordinary" women — Saratha, Maria and Mandi. These women are not notables — they are not singular pioneers, suffragettes or political leaders — the usual grist for the historical mill.[13] Yet their stories help to reveal a hidden dimension of the immigrant experience. They expose the complexity of building a day-to-day life in a new country while still living the memory of the old. Told from a woman's perspective, the stories reflect upon the personal and emotional experiences of migration. Two women discuss experiencing the death of a parent in Sri Lanka while living in Saskatoon. They talk about the impact this event had on their identity as mother, daughter, sister and community member. The other story, by a domestic worker from the Phillipines, reflects on the pain and isolation of taking up a new life as a nanny in the suburbs of Saskatoon. These are not stories about forging a new and glorious life in Canada, nor are they about being victims of "isms": racism, sexism, or classism. Although they take place against a backdrop of inequality, the central themes in these three women's stories,

---

5   Augie Fleras and Jean Leonard Elliot, *Multiculturalism in Canada* (Scarborough: Nelson, 1992), 38.

6   Leo Driedger, ed., *Ethnic Canada* (Toronto: Copp Clark Pitman, 1987), 97.

7   *Statistics Canada*, Cat. No. 11-008E.

8   *Statistics Canada*, Cat. No. 93-316.

9   Ibid.

10   Fleras and Elliot, *Multiculturalism in Canada*, 38.

11   Veronica Strong-Boag and Anita Clair Fellman, eds., "Introduction," in *Rethinking Canada* (Toronto: Copp Clark Pitman, 1991); Makeda Silvera, *Silenced* (1985; Toronto: Sister Vision Press, 1989).

12   To protect their identity, I have changed their names and refer to the women by first names only.

13   Gail Cuthbert Brandt, "Postmodern Patchwork: Some Recent Trends in the Writing of Women's History in Canada," *Canadian Historical Review* 72, no. 4. (December 1991): 441-70.

are not about "oppression."[14] As personal narratives, they are stories simply told of making a life in Saskatoon, Saskatchewan, Canada.

These stories contribute in several ways to Canadian women's historiography. As a mere fraction of innumerable immigrant women's stories, these narratives cannot claim to be representative. Nor would it be appropriate to generalize from these statements, any meaningful conclusions about these women's personal life histories. Their contributions to Canadian history lie in documenting aspects of women's experiences that are not yet considered "history." Women's experiences with migration have been left out of the written historical record, even feminist history. If history, according to Veronica Strong-Boag begins from, "an understanding of our own family experiences," then, as Strong-Boag concludes, "history must incorporate the collective experience of past generations of women, men, and children — how they brought and coped with change and how they achieved stability in their lives."[15] If we take Strong-Boag's definition of history to heart, then it is important to include all women's stories and experiences in Canadian historical writing, not only those of white, middle-class women.

However, there are few oral histories written about immigrant women and only recently have the lives of non-Anglo immigrant women in Canada been visible in published form.[16] Some literature is available in the form of anthologies, narratives, life-writing, poetry and semi-autobiographical fiction. This literature fills a void. Nevertheless, it is dangerous to read fictional, or constructed, semi-autobiographical accounts, and take the author's selection, treatment and portrayal of a combination of real and imagined events as "true." Depending upon the effects desired, the author may amplify some events and experiences, and gloss over others. Without a point of historical reference through oral narratives and oral history, it is difficult to assess the overall portrayal as an accurate reflection of historical events and experiences.

Rosemary George, a literary critic, writing in the area of cultural studies, identifies a recognizable immigrant genre in literary fiction in which the politics and experience of "dislocation" are the central narrative.[17] This genre, she suggests, is closely related to postcolonial writing and the literature of exile. George notes, however, that there is a need to distinguish the immigrant genre from these other forms, because the writers of these genres identify with nationalism and national allegory and a critique of colonialism. The immigrant genre, she argues, is characterized by a "detached reading of the experience of 'homelessness'," as well

---

14   This is not to say that these women have not experienced oppression. They chose not to tell stories of their oppression in a public forum. To speak publicly entails a tremendous amount of risk when one lives in the margins, hence we must respect the self-editing of their life stories.

15   Veronica Strong-Boag, "Writing About Women," in John Schultz, ed., *Writing About Canada* (Scarborough: Prentice Hall, 1990), 176.

16   See, for example: Franca Iacovetta, *Such Hardworking People: Women, Men and the Italian Immigrant Experience in Postwar Toronto* (Montreal/Kingston: McGill-Queen's University Press, 1992); Arun Mukherjee, ed., *Sharing Our Experience* (Ottawa: Canadian Advisory Council on the Status of Women, 1993), 1-38; Silvera, *Silenced*; Frances Swyripa, *Wedded to the Cause: Ukrainian-Canadian Women and Ethnic Identity 1891-1991* (Toronto: University of Toronto Press, 1993); and Momoye Sugiman, ed., *Jin Guo: Voices of Chinese Canadian Women* (Toronto: Women's Press and The Women's Book Committee, Chinese Canadian National Council, 1992).

17   Rosemary Marangoly George, "Traveling Light: Of Immigration, Invisible Suitcases, and Gunny Sacks," *Differences: A Journal of Feminist Cultural Studies* 4, no. 2 (1992): 72-97.

as by plots that move across several generations. The metaphors of "baggage" and "luggage," as well as "homelessness," are a dominant motif in this form. She suggests that because the author writes for a particular "Western" readership, the narration of events follows the rhythm of the story line as received through the eyes of invisible Western readers.[18] Authors of immigrant fictions are concerned with the experience of relocation to Western nations and write in global languages with stories that traverse the world. Although literary writing recounts the pains, joys and other emotions involved in the migrant experience, historians and other social scientists must move quickly to analyze the details of the actual life experiences of immigrants, especially immigrant women, to guard against the fictional construction of a partial, impoverished discourse on Third World immigrant women.

Yet, until more data are made available, anthologies, poetry and oral narratives based on women's lives are an important corrective to immigrant histories that have tended to ignore the specific experiences of women, generalizing from the experiences of ethnic male leaders. In addition, ethnic male historians tend to interpret and distort, glorify and romanticize selectively ethnic groups' experiences and histories.[19] Moreover, male historians largely assume and ignore the "private," emotional aspects of the immigrant experience. This neglect of the domestic sphere in ethnic immigrant histories is due, in part, to an unquestioned acceptance of the gendered distinction between private and public and the masculinist privileging of the public realm as historically important.[20] This produces a double negation for immigrant women in written history. The first erasure occurs because male historians see women's lives as centred in the "private" sphere in both paid and unpaid work, and this sphere is not considered historically important. The second erasure occurs as a result of first-wave feminist historians' exclusionary perspectives that have pushed non-Anglo/European immigrant women's experiences to the margins. With a few notable exceptions, non-European immigrant women do not show up either in feminist histories or in ethnic histories.

Before addressing the three immigrant women's stories themselves, I want to draw attention to the issue of oracy in oral history. By oracy, I mean the ability to speak and function in the official or public language(s) of a nation. In Canada, this would be either French (mainly in Quebec) or English. Oracy, the ability to speak, needs to be distinguished from literacy, which is the ability to count, read and write. One can be literate and orate in one's own language but be unable to speak or function in the official national language of public life, a condition most Canadians would perceive as illiteracy. It is a mistake to collapse illiteracy with a lack of oral fluency on the official languages of Canada.

Many Canadians are not fluent speakers of English or French, hence they are not all equally capable, willing or permitted to speak in public. Public invisibility means

---

18   Some examples of immigrant fiction are: Amy Tam, *The Joy Luck Club* (New York: Putnam, 1989); M.G. Vasanji, *The Gunny Sack* (London: Heinemann, 1989); and Samuel Selvon, *The Lonely Londoners* (London: Longman Caribbean Writers, 1956).

19   See, for example, Howard Palmer, ed., *Immigration and the Rise of Multiculturalism* (Toronto: Copp Clark Publishing, 1982). Roberto Perin makes this criticism effectively in Roberto Perin, "Writing About Ethinicity," in John Schultz, ed., *Writing About Canada* (Scarborough: Prentice Hall, 1990), 201-30.

20   Strong-Boag, "Writing About Women," 176-79.

that the narratives of non-English- and non-French-speaking peoples are not easily accessible to unilingual historians. Even where immigrants speak English there are difficulties. Although all three women who narrate their stories in this essay were educated in colonial education systems in their country of origin, their mother tongue is not English. English is their second language and they speak with a "non-standard" English-Canadian accent.

The three women originally told their stories at the Oral History Conference organized by the University of Saskatchewan in October 1993.[21] Many immigrant women whom I approached to participate in the session declined because they lacked confidence in speaking publicly in English. Many felt they did not speak English well enough to communicate effectively, or they were self-conscious about their heavily accented English. The process of selecting who gets "voice" is important because lack of English-language fluency is an important mechanism for limiting non-English-speaking immigrant women's participation in public life. Therefore, the background surrounding the selection of these three women was problematic.

Moreover, the politics of listening was also problematic. Before Saratha, Mandi and Maria began, I "set up" their talk by requesting that the audience pay attention to the politics of "who can speak?" and "who will listen?"[22] This was necessary because even when non-English-speaking women come forward, their contributions are often dismissed. Language is often used as a marker of difference and inferiority. For some people, it is too much work to listen, and too difficult to understand, nonstandard English. If non-English-speaking women remain quiet, many people mistakenly equate their silence with ignorance.[23] In my work with immigrant women, I am told that many English-speaking Canadians take accents or grammatical "mistakes" as signifying passivity and inferior intelligence. Many immigrant women from non-English-speaking countries say that native English speakers demonstrate little tolerance for "broken English," an unwillingness to use simple language and a reluctance to slow down speech so that communication can take place. Such linguistic elitism hinders collaboration with and knowledge of immigrant women's lives in Canada. Exclusionary attitudes and behaviours such as this use language as a mechanism to produce and reproduce inequality in Canadian society. For all these reasons, in doing oral history with non-English-speaking women, historians must pay greater attention to issues of oracy as an outcome of power relations.

Questions of oracy are increasingly important in order to penetrate the history of postcolonial migration. Language practices constitute a critical lens of analysis to understand immigrant women's lives. This issue is much broader and more complex than considerations of research methodology in oral history allow. The question of oracy intersects with broader political and economic considerations. For example, the state's ability to regulate, manage and restrict the availability of English language training programs, leaves many non-English-speaking immigrant women with few opportunities to improve their language skills. Immigration and citizenship laws require knowledge of

---

21   The purpose of the session was to provide a forum where immigrant women's voices could be heard and given legitimacy.

22   Gayatri Chakravorty Spivak with Sneja Gunew, "Questions of Multiculturalism," in Sarah Harasym, ed., *Gayatri C. Spivak, The Post-Colonial Critic* (London: Routledge, Chapman and Hall, 1990), 59-66.

23   Mukherjee, *Sharing Our Experience.*

either of the official languages as a condition of entry into Canada and of citizen-ship.[24] Speaking English gives these narrators many advantages over immigrant women without English language skills. In many other ways as well, language operates as an important signifier of difference by marking people as "insiders" or "outsiders." In Canada, as in other countries, language functions as a screen that separates people out as "different," thereby justifying discriminatory treatments.[25]

Poststructuralist social theory draws attention to another dimension of language. This is the importance of language in the construction of subject identities.[26] In post-structuralist theory, an individual does not hold a single, unified identity, but several conflicting identities. Drawing from Saussurean structural linguistics, semiotics, and psychoanalytic theories, poststructuralism views language as a signifying system that works to shape individual consciousness.[27] Language and the meaning systems underlying language are seen as relationships that are linked to social uses and power relations in social interactions. Consciousness, or knowledge of one's self, is not seen as pregiven and fixed, but shaped through shifting symbolic systems. Poststructuralism sees subjectivities as always in process. Poststructuralists ask questions about subjectivity and identity, the fixity of meanings and the symbolic system, and their relationship to power relations in society. Following Mikhail Bakhtin, a Marxist linguist, poststructuralism recognizes that in every society, there are many dialects and languages, hence many meanings and symbolic systems in circulation.[28] But languages and dialects do not circulate equally; some are privileged and some are subordinated. In this way, the meaning and symbolic systems circulating in any given society are restricted and attempts to fix the meaning system are linked to power relations and politics.

Poststructuralist theory helps in analyzing the significance of language in shaping the identities of non-English-speaking immigrant women. Limited fluency in English provides only a partial familiarity and entry into the meaning and symbolic systems circulating in Canada. Without English language skills, full participation in the ongoing construction of the meaning and symbolic system is limited. Limited participation, when English language skills are not fully developed, truncates the development of immigrant women's public selves as fully constituted citizen-subjects. Only in their own ethnolinguistic sphere can immigrant women participate actively and completely through their native language. Full participation in the public sphere of citizen-subjects is limited to those immigrant women who have English language fluency. Because representations of non-English-speaking women as somehow inferior offers negative feedback to immigrant women, they feel embarrassed about speaking. Their identity is shaped by publicly available categories of representation and the meanings implicated therein. They are rendered silent.

24   Fleras and Elliot, *Multiculturalism in Canada*, 42-43.

25   For a definition and rationale for using the term, racialization, see Robert Miles, *Racism* (London: Routledge, 1989). For research on language as a marker of difference and inferiority, see: Tony Crowly, *The Politics of Discourse: The Standard Language Question in British Cultural Debates* (London: MacMillan Education Ltd, 1989); and Nessa Wofson and Joan Manes, eds., *Language of Inequality* (New York: Mouton, 1985).

26   Chris Weedon, *Feminist Practice and Post-Structuralist Theory* (Oxford: Basil Blackwell, 1987).

27   Ibid., 74-106.

28   Mikhail Bakhtin, *The Dialogic Imagination: Four Essays*, M. Holmquist, ed., C. Emerson and M. Holmquist, trans. (Austin, TX: The University of Texas Press, 1981).

In addition, language is a powerful structuring mechanism that reinforces world economic class structures and postcolonial cultural imperialism. Women who come from ex-British or ex-French colonies and American protectorates, and who are of a certain class background, enter into Canada already privileged in relation to their immigrant sisters from non-Anglo-colonial and non-Franco-colonial nations and from lower-class backgrounds. Clearly, immigrant women are not all the same. Beyond its administrative use, the label, "immigrant women," as well as other terms, such as, "refugee women," "women of colour," and "Third World women" must be read as political categories of struggle and not as monolithic categories that take all non-European, non-white women as homogenous and equivalent.[29]

To conclude, language and oracy are sites of struggle for many non-English-speaking immigrant women. They must struggle to make space for their voices. They must struggle to negotiate meanings made available through many languages. They must struggle against categories of representation that silence and immobilize. They know that the ability to speak one of the official languages is critically and fundamentally important to one's life chances in Canada.[30] For all women who want to speak, who need to be heard, who have important things to say about their lives in Canada, who fear their own mistakes with the language and the reactions of those who would listen, English or French language oracy is not a trivial matter and it would be a mistake to assume language as a given in oral history.

The emotional impact of immigration on these women signals the importance of analyzing their experiences through multiple layers of time, space, place and languages as they affect issues of identity. Historians and other social scientists need to pay attention to how immigrant women's lives are constructed through the experience of migrancy. The category of immigrant women is not reflective of any naturally given essence. For immigrant women, time, space, place and language are constantly negotiated, straddled and lived through.

Saratha's, Maria's and Mandi's stories are best heard through a postmodern framework. The three women address a constantly shifting and unfolding social reality. Time does not simply mark its passage and space is not fixed as they live out their roles as mothers or daughters. As Saratha, one of the narrators, says, "immigrant women in Canada are living in dreams." Immigrant women must constantly struggle to bridge diasporic identities. This theme runs through all three stories.

By identity issues I am not referring to the now familiar mantra of race, class and gender chanted in contemporary feminist writing. I am referring to identities or identity positions in terms of how "selves" are constructed and perceived. These three immigrant women show many ways of constructing and managing "selves" so that they can survive the demands of everyday life. They talk about not being themselves, not living a "true life." They are very conscious of the partiality of their lives. In these stories, women show how a letter, a phone call, a memory, or a special event can instantaneously trigger identities that lie just below the surface. These identities relate to other lives in other countries, in other cultures, and to other social relationships.

---

29   Chandra Mohanty, "Introduction: Cartographies of Struggle: Third World Women and the Politics of Feminism," in Chandra Mohanty, Ann Russo and Lourdes Torres, eds., *Third World Women and the Politics of Feminism* (Bloomington, IN: Indiana University Press, 1991), 7.

30   Monica Boyd, "Immigrant Women in Canada," in Arlene Tigar McLaren, ed., *Gender and Society* (Toronto: Copp Clark Pitman Ltd., 1988), 316-36.

To survive and to find ways of making their lives work in Canada, the women talk about denying or hiding those parts of themselves that interfere with the demands of daily life. The narrators are not without agency, but they must struggle to claim their agency.

The stories suggest that the constitution and retention of "ethnic" identity, from the perspective of women's lives, are related to finding ways to bridge different ways of life. When Saratha talks about finding a balance between cultures, she is really talking about the production of an ethnic identity for herself and her children that enables them to live a "balanced" life. Similarly, Maria's story of connecting with other domestic workers from the Phillipines and then formalizing these contacts by establishing a domestic workers' organization, demonstrates how "ethnic" organizations are not necessarily reflective of a primordial ethnic identity.[31] In this particular case, at least, the creation of a community-based organization is a response to social and personal needs that arise in Canada. Both ethnic subjectivity and ethnic organizational development, for these women at least, come out of day-to-day survival needs rather than a pre-existing "ethnic vitality."

In *Third World Women and the Politics of Feminism*, Chandra Mohanty argues that "historically white feminist movements in the West have rarely engaged questions of immigration and nationality."[32] To reiterate an earlier point, immigration, citizenship and nation formation are increasingly important lenses for gaining an understanding of the lives of women from the Third World. Liberalized immigration laws and increasing global movements of people seeking to escape political, economic, and religious conflicts as well as environmental disasters have brought many women to Canada. Once here, the state inscribes many Third World women into a cultural, political and economic order that is already raced, classed and gendered. All three stories unfold against a backdrop of racist and sexist immigration laws that restrict visas to people from such Third World countries as Sri Lanka and the Phillipines, and relegate women wishing to enter as domestic workers to indentured labour.[33] For example, Saratha refers briefly to her reasons for leaving Sri Lanka and her family's long journey from country to country before finally receiving a visa to immigrate to Canada.

In the following stories I have left the patterns of the spoken words intact and have edited only where necessary for clarity. I have done this deliberately to draw attention to the difficulty some non-English-speaking immigrant women have in speaking and being heard in Saskatchewan. Until more minority women from Third World backgrounds are represented in the academic teaching force, the few minority feminist scholars who are present need to offer interpretations and analyses. Given their absence from academic discourse, however, a dialogue over different interpretations is not yet possible. Readers should not view my brief preliminary and concluding comments as privileging analysis over the testimony of oral narratives, but as a modest attempt to assist readers' understandings of the stories.

---

31   For a discussion on debates in theories of ethnic relations, see Peter S. Li, "Race and Ethnicity," in Peter Li, ed., *Race and Ethnic Relations in Canada* (Toronto: Oxford University Press, 1990), 3-17.

32   Mohanty, "Introduction: Cartographies of Struggle," 23.

33   See Sedef Arat Koc, "Immigration Policies, Migrant Domestic Workers and the Definition of Citizenship in Canada," in Vic Satzewich, ed., *Deconstructing a Nation: Immigration, Multiculturalism and Racism in '90s Canada* (Halifax: Fernwood Publishing and Saskatoon: Social Research Unit, Department of Sociology, University of Saskatchewan, 1992).

It Wasn't Me: Maria's Story

I'm Maria. I came to Canada three years ago, under the Live-in Caregiver Program of the Immigration Department.[34] *It used to be called the Foreign Domestic Workers Program. In that program, all people who came to Canada under that program must live in with the employer for two consecutive years. I will share how I went through my two years' experiences as a live-in caregiver.*

My first week in Canada was so exciting to me. I thought this place was almost halfway to heaven! Everything was new, my bed, the people, the language, the weather, the colour of the skin of the people — it was all so exciting. Every day I saw was new. This incredible feeling went on for several weeks. Until after a time I finally got to know what my work was going to be. During those first three months I got used to the work that I was supposed to do: take care of the kids, send them to school, prepare breakfast, make lunch, pick them up from school, bring them home, then go back to school, then bring them home again and then make supper. After a while, I wasn't even thinking about what I was doing anymore.

My days went on like that for a year. I had this feeling that I was working twenty-five hours a day, eight days a week continuously. It was as though I was only working. My feeling was that I was working continuously. I was living in the basement of a bi-level house. I could always hear the voices of the kids and my employer, even if I was already off work. I remember thinking, "I'm still at the workplace." Going to the bathroom was a big deal for me. It meant going out of my bedroom, seeing my workplace and hearing the kids again because they were in the playroom. It was too much!

I did this for a year but I knew I still had another year to go. And so, after almost two years, I was doing everything in a way that it wasn't me anymore who was doing that stuff. It was somebody else; it wasn't me anymore. Waking up in the morning, and going upstairs, doing all the chores; going downstairs, and doing all the chores — it was a different person. I knew it wasn't me anymore. That person was more like a robot. I thought, "Oh God, I have six more months to go. I don't know if I can go through with it." Six months more. I knew I had no choice because of the two year mandatory live-in condition of the Live-in Caregiver Program.

It was such an experience! Then, things changed. I found another nanny who lived quite far from my place, and we became friends. I started sharing what I was feeling, and all of a sudden she talked about the same things. We shared what we were doing. I thought I was all alone doing such kind of stuff, but she told me that she was feeling the same way. Soon after we met another Philippine nanny. Most of us nannies are Filipina so it wasn't long that we met another group who were all Filipina too. It was incredible because we found we were all feeling the same way. These people, these girls were all feeling the same way as me. It wasn't only me who was going through this process. So, I said, why don't we form a group, and we did. We

---

34   On 27 April 1992 the federal government announced its Live-In Caregiver Program which replaced the Foreign Domestic Program. The new program requires domestic workers to live in the employers home for two years. In Saskatchewan, at the time of writing, provincial labour standards legislation do not protect domestic workers. Employers do not have to provide locks on doors, there is no standard of accommodation and many domestic workers complain of invasion and abuse. A standard rate for room and board is deducted from the monthly pay of domestic workers. Domestic workers who live on farms in Saskatchewan have no access to transportation and are virtual prisoners in homes. They are at the mercy of their employer. The Foreign Domestic Worker Organization that was set up helps to educate women of their rights, puts domestic workers in touch with others and through informal networks, helps domestic workers find other employers when there is an unsatisfactory work arrangement. Women often share the rent of an apartment so they have a place to stay on their days off.

formed the Saskatoon Foreign Domestic Workers Association, and it was through the Saskatoon chapter of Immigrant Women of Saskatchewan that we were able to form such a group.

Through this organization the nannies are able to share what they are feeling. They don't feel all alone now; they have a group that they belong to. They feel they are accepted. I felt there, in our organization, I was accepted as a person, not just as a nanny, and it makes a lot of difference. Now thinking back over my experiences of the last three years, the first two years were just indescribable. Now when I think about that time, I often say to myself, "how did I go through with those two years?"

I survived by not thinking and feeling anymore. All of us did that. There were times, like weekends, when we didn't want to go out and spend our money, so we just stayed at home. For me, on these days I often didn't eat. I went without food because to eat meant going upstairs and seeing my workplace again. For two days on my weekend off, I would stay in my bedroom for forty-eight hours rather than go out. I felt better staying in my room than going upstairs and getting my food. I would rather stay in my room than go into the house. I think all the nannies went through this process, some of them just kept food in their rooms. My friend said that when she went grocery shopping she would buy instant food and keep it in the closet, because seeing the workplace was too much. Imagine spending twenty-four hours a day in the workplace. I often wonder why my employer works for eight hours and immediately comes home. It is because she doesn't want to stay in her workplace. Why am I forced to stay? We all question this two-year live-in requirement that the government has imposed on the nannies.

Now I am in my third year in Canada. I'm still doing the same thing; I'm still taking care of kids. I'm still a nanny, but I have finally found a place of my own. I'm living out, and I feel very happy. I'm finally doing great. I work very hard, but I still have time to socialize; I still have time to go to school and take classes. I completed my Grade 12 science course in the summer and now I am at university. I participate in our social organization. As President, I'm so involved in the organization. Now I think, "Two years, why didn't I do anything? Why was I so useless then?" And now, my life is starting to change; I'm recognizing myself again, my real self. It's been very hard, but I don't know, I feel very happy and my life is starting to work again.

I Belong Somewhere Else: Mandi's Story

My name is Mandi and I am from Sri Lanka. I have been living in Saskatoon for nine years. The reason for us coming to Saskatoon was the ethnic problem that occurred in 1983.[35] Anyhow, the story which I am going to tell you is very emotional for me. It is about the confusion I felt during the past year when I lost my mother.

It was October 17, 1992, at 3:00 a.m. when I was woken by a telephone call. It was a friend of my family's calling from Sri Lanka. He told me that my mother was seriously ill, and asked me whether I could come. I immediately said, "I am coming."

After this call I could not sleep at all, I started crying, my thoughts were running riot. I did not know what to do, I was in a daze. My husband said I could go tomorrow, and he booked the flight the next day. I couldn't even pack my suitcase, so he packed the suitcase for me. I didn't have the energy to do anything at all.

I left Saskatoon at 8:00 a.m. in the morning two days later. It was very difficult for me to leave my kids and my husband, but at the same time, I wanted to be with my mother. It was a

---

35   She is referring to political and ethnic violence between the minority Tamils and majority Sinhalese in Sri Lanka.

very long flight, I had to stay overnight in Hong Kong. The trip from Saskatoon to Hong Kong, with waiting time at the airport took seventeen hours. Sri Lanka is a small island, just below the south of India. It takes about two days to fly from Saskatoon to Sri Lanka. My mother lives in a city called Kandy, and it is the second largest city in Sri Lanka.

While I was in Hong Kong, I called my husband to find out what was happening. He said, "You must have lots of strength." I suspected something. Why should he say that to me? What he didn't tell me was that my mother had already passed away. Of course, he didn't want to upset me. He received the news from Kuala Lumpur that my mother had expired while I was on transit in Hong Kong. So I continued on my journey thinking and hoping that my mother would be waiting for me. I wanted to talk with her, I had so many things to tell her. I finally arrived in Colombo at midnight on the 21st of October. My sister-in-law came to meet me, but she didn't tell me anything. I was afraid to ask her. I still believed my mother was waiting for me. I hadn't changed my traveler's cheques. I told my sister-in-law that I would change them in Kandy the next day. She said, "It is better for you to change now, because you might not go to the bank tomorrow." I said, "Why?" She said, "Your mom passed away this morning."

You know, I was like a stone, I couldn't even cry, my emotions were all inside, I couldn't cry at all. I arrived in Kandy, that is where my mom lived with my sister. And when I saw my sister, I broke down and cried. She told me that my mother had asked about me, and that she knew that I was coming. I was sad, but at the same time I was comforted by the thought that at least she knew that I was coming. [sobs] I'm sorry, but it's really emotional. [pause] Anyhow, the funeral was over, everybody was upset and sad. My sister, brother and I met again after ten years' absence. We gave each other tremendous support. Our relationship as brother and sisters and as children was the only thing we could hang on to. I didn't even think about my family in Saskatoon at all. I did not think about my husband and I did not think about my children. It was very strange.

I had to leave my sisters to come back to Saskatoon. I was not sure when or if I would ever see them again. To tell you the truth, I did not want to leave at all. We cried a lot, and, it was [sobs] … We had a lot of things to say to each other. Anyhow, finally, we said good-bye and I arrived in Saskatoon on the 23rd of November. I was naturally glad to see my husband and children, but how do I tell you … about the emptiness that I felt. I left some of me in Sri Lanka.

After I arrived back in Saskatoon, in the days following, I often got angry with my kids. I didn't want to go out, I didn't want to dress up, I felt really isolated and depressed. There was some rejection which I felt, and I thought, I have my family here. But I couldn't get from them what I could get from my family in Sri Lanka. Even though I have a husband and children who were here, I felt I did not belong to them, I felt I belonged somewhere else. I was still blaming myself that I should have been with my mother when she was alive.

It was Christmas time. The children were looking forward to that. But, I told them that we would not be celebrating Christmas, because I'm not in the mood to do anything. Of course, they understood. It got very cold. I got in the car and I started driving my kids to their dancing lessons and swimming lessons. While I was driving my children, all the time, most of the time, my thoughts are with my mother. I thought about the good times and the bad times we shared, and my eyes used to fill with tears. My daughter would ask me, "Mommy, why are you crying?" She knew, of course. And, after a while, she would say, "I know why you're crying, you're thinking about your mother. I feel very sad when you cry." So I felt very bad about that, but then I explained to her why, I loved my mom. And she would say to me, "Of course mommy, I know that."

Suddenly, in the night I will wake up, and I will cry. But it was still really hard for me this past year. I still cry at times thinking of her. I don't think that I, anybody can stop, you know, crying, if they lose their mother or father. Anyway, I just want to stress here, I was fortunate that I was able to go to my mother's funeral, but I know that there are many immigrant women in Canada, who for various reasons just cannot go back to their countries. It can be political reasons, it can be financial reasons. So many things they undergo, but most of the Canadians, some of them, they don't understand this. For instance, I have a friend who's also in the same situation, she's from Sri Lanka too, she can't even go to her father's funeral. So these are some of the difficulties most immigrant women are facing today in Canada.

Living in Dreams: Saratha's Story

My name is Saratha. I was a minority Tamil-speaking citizen in Sri Lanka. I left Sri Lanka because of the political situation due to communal violence between the minority Tamils and the majority Sinhalese. Also because of my husband's job, we moved around to different countries. We wanted to go somewhere where we could settle down and stay permanently. But we couldn't do it all these years because of the immigration policies in the countries where my husband found work. Finally we decided to come to Canada when we were successful in getting a visa and I think this is going to be the place where we will settle down. When we moved around from country to country, we went through a lot of anxiety about getting a visa.

Even though I have lived in many different countries, when I came here, I spent the first year trying to adjust to the Western culture. I come from a family that has strong cultural beliefs. To bring up my children, I have to balance between my culture and Western culture. It has always been a concern of mine to find this balance. I don't want my children to only follow the Western culture. At the same time, I don't want to force them to follow our Eastern culture. I don't want them to hate our culture especially when we don't have the same environment here. This is a struggle for me.

I allow my children to participate in whatever they want but when they come back home, we have our own discipline. I sit and talk to them sometimes. When I receive my mother's letters, they read them too so they know what to expect. I try to keep our language up but the children cannot speak — they understand, but they cannot speak Tamil. It's a concern because when they meet the older people who come to visit, they find it difficult to speak to them because the older people can't speak English. I am concerned about my children losing their identity.

If my parents were here, I would be able to listen to the oral traditions from my parents and I would try to keep up traditional beliefs. I'm finding it very difficult to teach my children because they have been brought up in this Western culture. They are finding it difficult to believe whether the stories I tell them are true or if Mommy is making them up.

Last year my father passed away. I want to tell you about what I went through. Because of the ongoing conflict, I didn't hear this news for one week. There was no telephone communication with the northern part of Sri Lanka where my father lived. Even my mother was not able to communicate with my father because while she was away visiting another village, the army partitioned the area and she could not return to our family home. Communication is still very difficult.

It was shocking news for me but I couldn't cry. My dad was not sick for very long, I knew about his illness for less than a month so I never expected him to die. My father believed in the traditional way of cremation and afterwards, giving money and gifts to the poor. As a daughter it would have been my duty to take care of this. So I was really feeling sorry that not only could I not attend the funeral, I couldn't comfort my father in his last days and I could not console my mother. I went through a lot of emotional struggle. Even now, Jaffna, my family's town, is completely cut off. I still can't talk to my mother by phone.

Last Tuesday, I went to the grocery store where I met an old man. He looked like my father. I couldn't believe my eyes! I thought he was my father, he looked lean, fair and pale but when I looked closely, I saw he was a white Canadian. But I thought he looked just like my father. I honestly didn't know whether I was dreaming or if this vision was real. As I drove back home,

I remembered thinking that most immigrant women, like myself, are living in dreams. Their day-to-day living is not a true life.

What I mean is that most immigrant women who come to Canada are concerned first with finances. They take that as a challenge, they look for jobs, they get frustrated and they don't think about traditions and things like that. But all of a sudden something happens back home then they are immediately in the other world, thinking about their family and their traditions. You don't have much support in Canada. So you go through a lot of suffering on your own. They pretend that they are living an everyday life, but it is not true. In the back of their minds there is a lot of emotional longing. Something happens and it all comes back.

For me, when I received the news of my father's death I was not the mother of my family here, I became instantly the daughter of my father back home, the sister of my brother, the niece of my aunt. Still I am thinking about it. I still cry and try to console myself.

Fortunately, financially we are okay. But emotionally, I am in a struggle. If I think about my home [in Sri Lanka], I regret that I left all my belongings, all my relatives and all my traditions back there and came here to live here. When I'm busy with my day to day life, I don't think about my longing for home. But when we have a special occasion like New Year or the Festival of Light, which is like Christmas for us, I always remember my relatives and think about going back home. This thought is always in the back of my mind. But just daily living is so demanding that I don't have time to think about it. But anything could start me thinking and remembering and dreaming.

In Immigrant Women of Saskatchewan, I come across other immigrant women going through the same struggles as me. Some of their stories are different than mine, but even though each one is facing different emotional struggles, when I share with them, I feel better. I think when we unite together as a women's organization, we can make a difference in this Western world. By making a difference I mean motivating ourselves to practice our traditions more and not to give up. It also means finding a way to make a balance between Western and Eastern cultures in our lives and our children's lives.

Discussion of Oral Narratives

The stories of Saratha, Maria and Mandi prompt a re-examination of assumptions, theories and analytical concepts of family life. They challenge traditional under-standings of female family roles of mother and homemaker, sister and daughter by exposing the significance of factors that are outside the experiences of white European women from which feminist researchers have reconceptualized the Canadian family.[36] They are a reminder of the historically specific contexts that shape different women's experiences in Canada.

Listening to the stories of racialized, immigrant women also helps to broaden our understanding of gender inequality. Attention to their lives brings into sharper focus structures of inequality that heretofore have been obscured. Chandra Mohanty, a feminist social scientist, argues that the experiences of Third World women in Western nations cannot be understood outside of categories of immigration, citizenship and nationality laws.[37] A world economic and political system that has

---

36   See especially: Nancy Mandell and Ann Duffy, *Reconstructing the Canadian Family: Feminist Perspectives* (Toronto: Butterworths, Canada, 1988); and Emily M. Nett, *Canadian Families Past and Present*, 2nd. ed. (Toronto: Butterworths, 1993).

historically restricted the movements of people from the developing south to the north, while not restricting the corresponding movements of peoples from the developed north to most other locations, creates distinct contexts through which immigrant women from the Third World live their lives. Failure to recognize the specificity of women's experiences with migration and resettlement and generalizing from European, Western experiences reproduces the faulty universalizing tendency of orthodox feminist theory[38] and the narrow vision of white male historians.[39]

However, male, eurocentric biases coupled with the inability of many non-English-speaking women immigrants to write in English, have resulted in the loss of early non-Anglo/European immigrant women's experience from the written historical record. These records do not exist; therefore, recovering the experiences of past generations of non-Anglo/European women necessitates the use of alternative methodologies. Listening carefully to the oral narratives of more recent women immigrants may open the possibility of reconnecting to personal experiences of migrancy, uprootedness and dislocation. In this way historians and other social scientists may reclaim the rich details of women's experiences of relocation, dislocation and migrancy in Canada.

Maria's story reveals how her life was severely constrained under the terms of a program intended to extract her labour at the lowest price guaranteed by a mandated live-in requirement.[40] The premise underlining this level of social control is that certain groups of people are not seen to be equal to other persons. Sedef Arat Koc, who has written on the situation of domestic workers, argues that although women's citizenship is usually reduced to their familial status as mothers and dependents, a very different approach is taken to migrant women of colour.[41] She writes, "while emphasizing domesticity and motherhood as the ideal roles for white women, dominant ideologies and institutions have had no problems accepting women of colour as workers first and foremost."[42] Moreover, in their capacity as domestic workers, migrant women of colour are denied the rights and protections given to other workers, male or female.[43]

Maria's story is testimony to the lived reality of women whose lives in Canada are formed around sexist and racist immigration and labour laws. It is not only the individual conditions of employment that need to be analyzed. In terms of physical comfort, many employers try to provide decent accomodations. In terms of personal relationships between employer and nanny, many are quite satisfying. In Maria's case, for instance, she had often commented to me that she liked her employer and

---

37   Chandra Mohanty, "Introduction: Cartographies of Struggle," 1-50.

38   For excellent overviews of contemporary debates in feminist theory, see Michelle Barret and Ann Phillips, eds., *Destabilizing Theory* (Stanford, CA: Stanford University Press, 1992) and Linda Nicholson, ed., *Feminism/Postmodernism* (New York: Routledge, 1990).

39   Strong-Boag, "Writing About Women," 176.

40   See the monthly newsletter, *Domestics: Cross-Cultural News*, of INTERCEDE, a Toronto organization for domestic workers. For more information on the effects of the Live-In Caregiver Program and actions that the foreign domestic workers are taking to voice their opposition to the inequality in the legislation write to: INTERCEDE, 489 College St. Suite 402, Toronto, Ontario M6G 1A5.

41   Sedef Arat Koc, "Immigration Policies," 236.

42   Ibid.

43   Ibid.

thought she was "very nice." The critical point of Maria's story, which she herself identifies, is the terms of the government's Live-In Caregiver Program. The assumptions written into this program have material effects on her life and on the lives of many other women like her.

Survival, to Maria, meant living out the terms of the category "live-in caregiver" by denying her humanity as a person. In her words, she became a machine, a robot. She saw herself becoming nonhuman as she fulfilled the terms of the government's live-in caregiver/foreign domestic worker program. The kind of racism and sexism that Maria endured is not an individual act of irrational prejudice, but the effect of a systemic racism and sexism that is built into immigration and citizenship laws that reflect the state's perception of Canada as a white, patriarchal nation.[44]

Mandi's story reveals another dimension of the subjective experience of migration for women. It is possible to understand Mandi's experience of being a mother, daughter and homemaker through the reality of a diasporic family. National, geographic, political and cultural forces mediate her identities. Her identities as mother and daughter are in conflict and do not comprise a coherent, complementary totality, as often portrayed in Western literature on mothering and gender roles. Mandi's story shows how she consciously struggles with her identities as wife, mother, daughter and sister as they are lived across time, spaces, places and languages. The poignancy of her story ought to trigger memories of other similar experiences of dislocation among women.

In Saratha's story there are similar tensions. Ethnic violence and war emphasize these tensions. They limit the extent to which her identity as daughter can be realized. The past that she thought she had left behind continually inserts itself into her present life. She finds herself caught between two poles of time and place. Saratha talks about the difficulty of mothering between two cultures. She finds that she must manage the boundaries between two cultures as part of the role of mothering. Yet little recognition is given to mothering as a process of managing, maintaining and producing ethnic identities and ethnic processes. The concept and history of mothering as developed in Western discourse have overlooked the interethnic, intercultural aspect of mothering that is part of immigrant and ethnic minority women's experiences. If history is the collective experiences of women, men and children coping with change and building stable lives, then greater attention needs to be paid to this aspect of immigrant women's lives.

All three women mentioned their participation in an immigrant women's organization, the Immigrant Women of Saskatchewan. I met Maria, Mandi and Saratha through the Saskatoon Chapter of this organization. It is a multilingual, multiethnic member-run organization for all women who are racialized. Not all the members are immigrants, but all are perceived as "immigrants" regardless of their citizenship status. This organization provides a haven for racialized and immigrant women. Although not without conflicts, the organization takes up issues raised by its members in ways that women can see that their private troubles are really public issues. This is what Saratha refers to when she says, "I think when we unite together as a women's organization we can make a difference in this Western world." But she does not mean making a difference in a romanticized sense. She clarifies "making a

---

44   Ibid.

difference" as "motivating ourselves to practice our traditions and to not give up." In other words, making a difference to Saratha means not giving up her other identities by resisting their submersion by the dominant Anglo-Western culture. For Saratha, at least, the organization is a place where immigrant women can share experiences and gain strength, "not to give up."

But little is known about the roles and functions of non-Anglo/European women's organizations and how they work to mediate racialized and immigrant women's experiences with migration and resettlement. Even less is known about their historical formation and their internal dynamics. Although considerable attention has been paid to white women's organizations on the Prairies, such as farm women's organizations, the Imperial Order Daughters of the Empire (IODE), the Women's Christian Temperance Union (WCTU), the Voice of Women (VOW) and nationally, the National Action Committee (NAC), little attention has been paid to non-Anglo women's groups and their role in shaping the history of Third World immigrant women's lives. Without such knowledge, the stereotypical accounts of immigrant women as being passive victims, dependent and incapable of organizing to effect positive change will continue without challenge.[45]

These stories run the gamut of emotions: pain, sorrow, happiness, hope, longing and anger. They are testimony to what has been missing in Canadian women's history and they are eloquent evidence for the need to rethink our basic categories of analysis of women's roles as mother, daughter, wife and worker. They point to a need to broaden the project of reclaiming women's history to include the social organization and the lives of immigrant women and to analyze the structural and historical contexts that shape non-European immigrant women's lives in Canada. I hope these narratives have helped to amplify the voices of immigrant women from Third World countries as speaking historical subjects.

---

45   An account of the internal dynamics of an immigrant women's organization is found in: J. Lee, "Organizing with Immigrant Women: A Critique of Community Development in Adult Education," *Canadian Association for the Study of Adult Education (CASAE) Journal* 7, no. 2 (1993): 19-42.

CONTRIBUTORS

DAVE DE BROU, an associate professor of history and a member of the Women and Gender Studies Advisory committee at the University of Saskatchewan, teaches an honours seminar course in Canadian women's history. He coedited *Documenting Canada: A History of Modern Canada in Documents* (1992).

JULIE DORSCH, who grew up on a farm in Saskatchewan, graduated from the University of Saskatchewan in 1992 with a double honours degree in history and political studies. She has resided in Toronto since 1992 when she became a legislative intern in the Legislative Assembly of Ontario. She currently works for a lobby organization.

LESLEY ERICKSON, born in Regina, completed her B.A. (Honours) degree in history at the University of Regina. Her Honours paper examined the lives of first-generation German Catholic women at St. Peter's Catholic Colony, Saskatchewan. Now living in Calgary, Alberta, she plans to pursue further research at the University of Calgary in the areas of ethnicity, religion and gender in western Canada.

ANNA FELDMAN, as a mature student, obtained an A.R.C.T., and, from Carleton University, a B.Mus. and an M.A. in Canadian Studies (with distinction). She received the Norman Pollock Award in Canadian Jewish Studies in 1983. Anna collects oral histories of Saskatchewan's Jewish settlers. The audiocassettes done before 1986 reside in the Feldman Collection, Canadian Centre for Folk Culture Studies, Canadian Museum of Civilization. Those done later make up the Anna Feldman Collection, Congregation Agudas Israel, Saskatoon. She was also a researcher for *A Coat of Many Colours: Two Centuries of Jewish Life in Canada*, the joint presentation of Canadian Friends of Beth Hatefusoth and the Canadian Museum of Civilization.

THERESA HEALY was born in Eire and raised as an Irish Roman Catholic in working-class Britain. After leaving school at fourteen, she did not continue her education until enrolling at the University of Saskatchewan at the age of twenty-eight, where she completed a double honours undergraduate degree and an M.A. Her two daughters are now grown and independent so she is currently pursuing her doctorate in history at Simon Fraser University, where she teaches in the Women's Studies department. She has always maintained a politically active lifestyle and attempts to integrate feminism, academics and community in the various forms of her work.

MATHILDE JUTRAS was born and grew up in Quebec. She holds a B.Ed. and certificate in journalism from Laval University. After completing her B.Ed., she moved to Saskatchewan and taught French immersion for several years. She then undertook a career in journalism and worked for the Francophone paper, *L'Eau Vive*. She is preparing a book about the history of Francophone women in Saskatchewan.

JO-ANNE LEE is completing her doctorate in sociology at the University of Saskatchewan. Her doctoral research is in the area of multiculturalism, minority languages and the state. She is past president of Immigrant Women of Saskatchewan (Saskatoon Chapter). Jo-Anne has worked and published in the areas of community development and adult education.

MIRIAM MCNAB is a Treaty woman from the Gordon First Nation in southern Saskatchewan. She has earned a B.A. and an M.A. in cultural anthropology from the University of Saskatchewan. She has taught in the Department of Native Studies at the University of Saskatchewan and the Department of Indian Studies at the

Saskatchewan Indian Federated College, University of Regina (in Saskatoon) since 1985. She is a wife and a mother of two, and part-time stepmother of four more.

AILEEN C. MOFFATT is a doctoral candidate at the University of Manitoba and a visiting research associate at the College of William and Mary in Virginia. She is currently completing an analysis of Saskatchewan rural women's social identities.

NADINE SMALL received her M.A. in history from the University of Saskatchewan upon completion of her thesis, "'Stand By the Union Jack': The Imperial Order Daughters of the Empire in the Prairie Provinces During the Great War, 1914-1918." She has been an archivist at the Saskatoon Office of the Saskatchewan Archives Board since 1990.

INDEX

Aboriginal peoples: and Aboriginal cultures, 132; anthropologists studying (Ballentyne, P., 136; Brumbach, H.J., 134; Jarvenpa, Robert W., 134); building Jewish houses in Lipton, 64; Churchill River Cree, 133-34, 136; Cree-Metis, 133; Dene peoples, 131, 133; and difficulty in conforming to idealized family models, 97; and French-speaking women, 44; and impact of fur trade, 132-34, 136-37; and intrusion of capitalist mode of production, 133, 136-37; and the intrusion of the state, 133; Inuit, 131; Metis communities, 131; mixed bloods, 131n; northern Metis, 9; southerly Cree reserve, 138; and the Subarctic, 136n; Subarctic Cree, 134n; use of the term, 132n. *See also* Aboriginal women, Saskatchewan

Aboriginal women, Saskatchewan: and Euro-Canadian thirst for Aboriginal land, 6; Cree women 131n; Cree-Metis women, 143; eastern Indian women, 132; Metis women, 132, 133, 143; Plains Indian women, 132. *See also* Aboriginal women's history; Pinehouse Lake Aboriginal women

Aboriginal women's history: and Aboriginal women's voice, 132; lack of publishing in, 25; scholars of, 132; women-centred perspectives in, 132. *See also* Aboriginal women's history, scholars of

Aboriginal women's history, scholars of: Ahenakew, Freda, 132; Albers, Patricia, 132; Anderson, Karen, 132; Bourgeault, Ron, 132; Brown, Jennifer S.H., 132; Buffalohead, Priscilla, 132; Crnkovich, Mary, 132; Cruikshank, Julie, 132; Jaimes, M. Annette, 132; Leacock, Eleanor, 132; McNab, Miriam, 8-9; Medicine, Beatrice, 132; Monture-Okanee, Patricia, 132; Poelzer, Dolores and Irene, 132; Stevenson, Winona, 132; Van Kirk, Sylvia, 132; Waldram, James B., 134n; Wolfart, H.C., 132

Alberta 42, 44, 83: Lethbridge, 81n; Okotoks, 83; Vermillion, 71

Asia, 145: Malayasia, Kuala Lumpur, 154; Phillipines, 145, 151; Sri Lanka, 145, 151, 153-55 (Colombo, 154; Jaffna, 155; Kandy, 154)

Belgium, 41-42, 45-46, 83, 85: Ploegsteert, 45

British Columbia, 77: Victoria, 78

Canada, regions of: the East, eastern Canada, 42, 44n, 48, 50-52, 54, 57-58, 73, 98, 121; Maritimes, 77; the North, 132, 134-35, 137, 139, 142; North-West, Canadian, 62, 63n; Prairies, 12, 14, 21-22, 41, 43, 46, 52-54, 56-57, 59, 60, 77, 77n, 78-80, 79n, 82-83, 86, 91, 160; Subarctic, 136n; the West, western Canada, western provinces, 42, 44n, 44-46, 52, 54-55, 57-58, 77n, 76-79, 90-91

Canadian women's history, writing: age (generational differences), impact of, 1; and androcentric historical profession, 2, 4; challenge from within,

2, 5-6; changing historical importance, 5; class, impact of, 1-3, 1n, 2n, 3n, 5-6, 6n; debate over common woman's experience (commonality), vi, 1, 2, 4; ethnicity, impact of, 1, 2n, 4-6, 6n; first generation of scholars, 2, 6, 148; new generation of scholars, 1, 4-6, 9; parallels with working-class history, 2, 2n, 3; primacy of gender, 1-3, 1n, 2n, 5-6, 6n; race, impact of, 1, 1n, 2n, 4-6, 6n; sexual preference, impact of, 1, 4-5; social history, impact of, 2, 4, 5, 14; three-stage historiographical model, 3-5 (celebration, 3, 3n, 4; exploitation, 3-4, 3n; active agency, 3n, 3-5); and women's voices, multiplicity of, 1-2, 1n, 2n, 5-6

Eastern-European countries, 62, 72

Europe, 43n, 44, 50, 52, 61, 73, 137, 145. *See also* Belgium; eastern-European countries; France

Farm women, Saskatchewan: and agriculture, 117, 123, 126, 130; and child care, 116, 123-25; and commonality of experience, 108; and farm work, 116, 118, 119, 124, 125; and financial independence, 118, 126, 127; and friendship, female, 129; and household maintenance 119-22; and invisibility of their work, 117; and oral history, 116, 117, 119-21, 123-24, 126, 128-30 (Armitage, Susan, 117, 117n, 119, 119n, 122, 128; Portelli, Alessandro, 120n; Thompson, Paul, 120, 120n, 121); and oral history methodology, 119n (Riley, Barbara, 119n); as "ordinary" women, 116; partnership with husbands, 123, 126-28; protesting exclusion, 128; recognition of contribution by husband, 126; as rural women, 116, 118, 123, 129, 130; and sexism, 128-29; and sexual relations, discussion of, 129; sources available for, 117; and sustenance, 122-23, 129; and technology, 116, 120-22, 122n (electrification, 120-21, 120n; washing machines, 121)); and uniqueness of experience, 116; and valorization, 117n; and women's culture, 130; and work before marriage, 118-19; and work, outside, 123-24; and work off farm, 126-27; and World War II, 118-19

First Nations peoples. *See* Aboriginal peoples

France, 41-43, 47-48, 50-52, 54, 58, 85, 87: Crespin, 42; La Rivière Noire, 51; La Seine, 51; Marquette, 52; Mont Saint-Michel, 51; Nantes, 50; Paris, 51; Portneuf, 51

French-speaking Saskatchewan women: adaption of, 52, 56, 58; Belgium, from, 41-42, 45-46; Canadianizing, 44; Catholic clergy's view, 42, 44n, 44-46 (Bolo, Monsignor, 56; Roy, Monsignor Camille, 53); and Catholicism, 41-42, 44, 44n 46-47, 53 (views of Duperreault, Marie-Anne, 46, 46n, 50, 55, 56); France, from, 41-43, 47-48, 50-52, 54, 58, (Crespin, 42; La Seine, 51; La Rivière Noire, 51; Marquette, 52; Mont Saint-Michel, 51; Nantes, 50; Paris, 51; Portneuf, 51); and child rearing, 42, 45, 48-50, 54-57; and differences between European and Canadian French, 47-49; as educators, 45, 46n, 52; and French-language newspapers (*L'Eau vive*,